"十四五"航空运输类空中乘务专业系列教材

中国民航大学"十四五"规划教材

Cabin Service English

客舱服务英语

（第2版）

主 编／林 虹

主 审／刘丽娟

人民交通出版社股份有限公司

北京

内 容 提 要

本书以培养学生英语实际应用能力和职业素养为出发点，融合国内外多家航空公司的服务标准及服务程序，按照空中乘务员的工作流程编写而成。全书共 18 个单元，通过空中乘务员飞行期间各个阶段的服务和机上紧急情况与非正常航班等特殊情况的处理，强化客舱服务英语的训练，帮助学生全方位地了解空中乘务员的工作。本书内容翔实，所有对话、单词都配有英籍专家音频，尽力为学生设定不同情景来提高英语口语表达能力，同时提供大量与空中乘务专业相关的民航知识，加强学生职业素质的培养。在练习题目设计时，考虑到将学生的被动学习转变为主动学习，从学习规律出发、从激发学习兴趣出发、从拓展职业知识面出发，突出职业特色。

本书可供高等院校空中乘务专业的教学选用，亦可供行业相关培训、岗前培训使用。

图书在版编目（CIP）数据

客舱服务英语 / 林虹主编 .—2 版 .—北京：人民交通出版社股份有限公司，2022.1

ISBN 978-7-114-17831-3

Ⅰ.①客… Ⅱ.①林… Ⅲ.①民用航空—商业服务—英语—教材 Ⅳ.①F56

中国版本图书馆 CIP 数据核字（2021）第 276980 号

Kecang Fuwu Yingyu

书　　名：	客舱服务英语（第 2 版）
著 作 者：	林　虹
责任编辑：	吴燕伶　王景景
责任校对：	赵媛媛
责任印制：	张　凯
出版发行：	人民交通出版社股份有限公司
地　　址：	（100011）北京市朝阳区安定门外外馆斜街 3 号
网　　址：	http://www.ccpcl.com.cn
销售电话：	（010）85285857
总 经 销：	人民交通出版社股份有限公司发行部
经　　销：	各地新华书店
印　　刷：	北京市密东印刷有限公司
开　　本：	787×1092　1/16
印　　张：	17.75
字　　数：	547 千
版　　次：	2015 年 2 月　第 1 版 2022 年 1 月　第 2 版
印　　次：	2025 年 1 月　第 2 版　第 3 次印刷　累计第 9 次印刷
书　　号：	ISBN 978-7-114-17831-3
定　　价：	59.00 元

（有印刷、装订质量问题的图书由本公司负责调换）

第 2 版前言

Preface

随着国家民航业的快速发展,我国民航运输规模连续多年位居世界第二,我国已成为世界民航大国,并不断向民航强国迈进。要实现民航强国战略,满足民航运输业的发展需求,急需将高素质、懂管理、技能强的特殊类专业人才充实到生产一线岗位,其中具备较好的英语应用能力是一个很重要的方面。《客舱服务英语》教材就是在这种背景之下编写而成的。

作为中国民用航空局直属唯一一所综合性大学,中国民航大学从 1999 年开办空中乘务专业,拥有 20 多年的办学文化积淀,拥有一支具有丰厚知识底蕴的高水平的民航专业师资团队和规范的专业设置,建立了符合行业需求的人才培养体系。因此,出版空中乘务专业特色教材,对满足教学需求、加快发展民航业高端应用型人才培养将起到保障作用。

本教材以实际应用能力的提高和职业素质的培养为目标,结合学生今后实际工作需要,力求培养学生满足未来岗位所需的客舱服务英语的应用能力。它是针对高等院校空中乘务专业的专业英语课程编写的,以"实际、实用、实践、实效"为编写原则。内容选取上围绕乘务员的工作流程,融合国内与国外多家航空公司服务标准及服务流程,从航前准备开始,包括登机、起飞、飞行期间的餐饮供应、机上娱乐和降落等一系列流程及机上急救、紧急情况和非正常航班等特殊情况,强化客舱服务英语训练。教材还提供与客舱服务相关的词汇、服务用语,设定不同的情境,有针对性地培养学生口头表达能力,帮助学生全方位地了解乘务员的工作,熟悉专业术语,加强专业素质的培养,为今后的工作打下良好的基础。此外,该教材还包括:客舱广播词的训练,知名航空公司、国际民航组织、世界著名城市和景点的介绍及乘务英语中级考试的学习内容。

《客舱服务英语》自 2015 年出版以来,已经 6 次印刷。为了更加突出该教材的实用性,确保教材的实效性,对该教材进行修订。在原教材的基础上,增加了以下内容:

(1) 在 Part A 部分增加了该单元重点客舱术语的讲解与辨析。
(2) 在 Part B 练习部分增加了该单元重点服务用语的汉译英练习。
(3) 在 Part C 练习部分增加了用正确语调朗读句子和短语汉译英 2 个练习。
(4) 重新调整或更新了部分 Part D/E 的拓展知识内容或顺序。
(5) 在 Part C 广播词部分增加了部分最新的广播词。
(6) 对教材的生词部分重新进行梳理。
(7) 删除了第 1 版教材中的真人照片,补充了部分图片。

本教材编写团队由中国民航大学乘务学院和外语学院骨干教师组成,由林虹担任主编,由中国国际航空股份有限公司客舱服务部刘丽娟副总经理担任主审,这样既能保证教材内容突出乘务专业特点,同时又能很好地把握学生学习英语的规律,使该教材更具系统性、完整性和适用性。第1版教材由于佳、吴清然、史艳云、康玉晶、白辉参加编写,第2版教材由赵松子、郑欣欣、李想、王芮琪参加编写。本教材还特别强调了乘务专业英语技能的传授和训练。**为便于教学,本教材配有音频 MP3 文件和课件,选用此教材的教师可来电或来函索要(E-mail:1061108993@qq.com　电话:010-85285995),或加 QQ 群(483017226)下载。**本教材的编写得到了人民交通出版社股份有限公司的高度重视及大力帮助,在此表示衷心的感谢!

　　由于编者业务水平有限,难免存在诸多不当和疏漏之处,敬请广大读者和乘务及英语教学方面的业内专家批评指正。

编　者

2020 年 10 月

目 录
Contents

Unit 1　Greetings and Introductions 1
- Part A　Useful Words and Expressions 2
- Part B　Dialogues 4
- Part C　Public Announcements 7
- Part D　Work-task 10
- Part E　Supplementary Reading 12

Unit 2　Directing Passengers 14
- Part A　Useful Words and Expressions 15
- Part B　Dialogues 16
- Part C　Public Announcements 20
- Part D　Work-task 23
- Part E　Supplementary Reading 26

Unit 3　Boarding and Cabin Check 29
- Part A　Useful Words and Expressions 30
- Part B　Dialogues 31
- Part C　Public Announcements 35
- Part D　Work-task 38
- Part E　Supplementary Reading 40

Unit 4　Take off 42
- Part A　Useful Words and Expressions 43
- Part B　Dialogues 44
- Part C　Public Announcements 48
- Part D　Work-task 51
- Part E　Supplementary Reading 53

Unit 5   Passenger Comfort 55

    Part A   Useful Words and Expressions 56
    Part B   Dialogues 58
    Part C   Public Announcements 62
    Part D   Work-task 64
    Part E   Supplementary Reading 67

Unit 6   Beverage Service 70

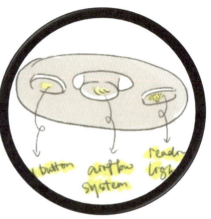

    Part A   Useful Words and Expressions 71
    Part B   Dialogues 72
    Part C   Public Announcements 76
    Part D   Work-task 78
    Part E   Supplementary Reading 80

Unit 7   Food Service I 82

    Part A   Useful Words and Expressions 83
    Part B   Dialogues 84
    Part C   Public Announcements 89
    Part D   Work-task 91
    Part E   Supplementary Reading 93

Unit 8   Food Service II 95

    Part A   Useful Words and Expressions 96
    Part B   Dialogues 97
    Part C   Public Announcements 101
    Part D   Work-task 103
    Part E   Supplementary Reading 106

Unit 9   In-flight Entertainment 108

    Part A   Useful Words and Expressions 109
    Part B   Dialogues 111
    Part C   Public Announcements 115
    Part D   Work-task 117
    Part E   Supplementary Reading 120

Unit 10   Duty-free Sale 123

    Part A   Useful Words and Expressions 124

Part B	Dialogues	126
Part C	Public Announcements	131
Part D	Work-task	133
Part E	Supplementary Reading	135

Unit 11   Delays 138

Part A	Useful Words and Expressions	139
Part B	Dialogues	140
Part C	Public Announcements	144
Part D	Work-task	147
Part E	Supplementary Reading	150

Unit 12   Turbulence 152

Part A	Useful Words and Expressions	153
Part B	Dialogues	155
Part C	Public Announcements	159
Part D	Work-task	161
Part E	Supplementary Reading	163

Unit 13   Weather and Time 166

Part A	Useful Words and Expressions	167
Part B	Dialogues	169
Part C	Public Announcements	173
Part D	Work-task	176
Part E	Supplementary Reading	179

Unit 14   Dealing with Health Issues 181

Part A	Useful Words and Expressions	182
Part B	Dialogues	183
Part C	Public Announcements	188
Part D	Work-task	190
Part E	Supplementary Reading	193

Unit 15   Safety & Emergency I 196

Part A	Useful Words and Expressions	197
Part B	Dialogues	199
Part C	Public Announcements	202

Part D　Work-task 205
Part E　Supplementary Reading　......209

Unit 16　Safety & Emergency II 211

Part A　Useful Words and Expressions　......212
Part B　Dialogues　......214
Part C　Public Announcements　......217
Part D　Work-task 221
Part E　Supplementary Reading　......225

Unit 17　Before Landing 227

Part A　Useful Words and Expressions　......228
Part B　Dialogues　......230
Part C　Public Announcements　......234
Part D　Work-task 236
Part E　Supplementary Reading　......241

Unit 18　Disembarkation 243

Part A　Useful Words and Expressions　......244
Part B　Dialogues　......246
Part C　Public Announcements　......249
Part D　Work-task 252
Part E　Supplementary Reading　......254

Words and Expressions List　......256

Cabin Service English

Greetings and Introductions

- Part A Useful Words and Expressions
- Part B Dialogues
- Part C Public Announcements
- Part D Work-task
- Part E Supplementary Reading

Students will be able to:
memorize the words and expressions about Greetings and Introductions in the cabin;
make up the dialogues about Greetings and Introductions in the cabin;
obtain and improve public announcements skills about Boarding and Greetings;
know about general responsibilities of a cabin attendant;
introduce Air China.

Suggested Hours: *4 class hours*

Part A
Useful Words and Expressions

◉ **Please list as many greetings and ways of addressing to the passengers at the gate as you can.**

- Mr.
- Mrs.
- Ms.
- Miss
- Sir
- Madam
- boarding card/pass
- window seat
- aisle seat
- middle seat
- bulkhead seat
- Good morning.
- Good afternoon.
- Good evening.
- Good day.
- Welcome.
- Thank you.
- You are welcome.
- Good morning, Madam. Welcome aboard.
- Good afternoon. Welcome to the flight, Madam.
- Good evening. It's nice to see you again.
- It's a pleasure to see you.
- It's a pleasure to have you on board.
- May I assist you, Sir?
- May I see/have a look at your boarding card, please?
- May I show you to your seat? This way, please.
- How may I assist you?
- Would you like me to show/assist you to your seat?
- Your seat is 20A. It's a window seat on the right/left.
- My name is … and I'll be preparing/heating your meal today.
- My name is … and I'll be happy to serve you on board today.
- My name is … and I am very happy to be at your service.

Unit 1   Greetings and Introductions

- Good afternoon, Miss Young. I'm Cathy, your purser on today's flight.
- Enjoy your flight.
- Hope you enjoy your flight. / Wish you a pleasant journey.
- If there is anything I can do for you, please (don't hesitate to) let me know.

Culture Tips

➢ Use formal language that meets airlines standards.
➢ Offer your assistance to passengers using the language:
—May I …
—Would you like me to …
➢ Avoid using the following casual language for greeting and welcoming passengers on board:
—Hi
—Kid
—Lady
—Mister
—Big brother
—Big sister
—Uncle
—Auntie
—Do you want help?
—Do you need help?
—You want me to help?
—Maybe I can help you.

Cabin Term

boarding card/boarding pass/boarding check   登机牌

释义：登机牌是机场为乘坐航班的旅客提供的登机凭证，旅客必须在提供有效机票和个人身份证件后才能获得，也有人称之为登机证或登机卡。20世纪80年代之前，我国使用的登机牌印制十分简单，多为手工填写和加盖橡皮戳记。随着计算机技术的广泛应用，现在所有机场或航空公司都采用计算机打印。

⦿ **Match phrases or sentences in column B to the situations in column A.**

Column A	Column B
1. A passenger is reading newspaper.	a. We have comedy, action movie and features movies onboard today.

	continue
Column A	Column B
2. A passenger wants some music.	b. We have amenity kit for children.
3. A passenger can't hear anything through his headsets.	c. We have local newspaper and in-flight magazine.
4. A passenger asks a cabin attendant about movies provided on board.	d. We have light music on channel.
5. A passenger wants to read something.	e. May I turn on the reading light for you?
6. A passenger is worrying about her son on the boring long flight.	f. I will get a pair of new headsets for you.

◉ **Make up a dialogue about greeting passengers and introducing yourself on board.**

Part B
Dialogues

(CA=Cabin Attendant, PAX=Passenger)

   CA: Good morning, Madam! Welcome aboard. May I have a look at your boarding card, please?
PAX: Here you are.
   CA: Your seat is 37A. Please go straight ahead and turn left.
PAX: Thank you very much.
   CA: I am very happy to be at your service. Wish you a pleasant flight.

   CA: Welcome aboard, Sir. How are you today?
PAX: Fine, thank you. I'm not sure where my seat is.
   CA: May I see your boarding card, please?
PAX: Yes, sure, here it is.
   CA: Thank you. Your seat is 46D. It's an aisle seat on the left. This way, please.
PAX: Thank you very much.

   CA: Good afternoon. How may I best assist you?
PAX: I can't find my seat.
   CA: Please show me your boarding card. It's a middle seat. I'll show you to your seat.

PAX: Oh, that's very kind of you. Thank you very much.
  CA: No problem at all. Please follow me.
  CA: This is your seat, Madam. Please enjoy the flight.
PAX: Thank you.

4

  CA: It's a pleasure to have you on board, Madam. How are you today?
PAX: Fine, thanks. Where is my seat? I can't find it.
  CA: No problem. May I see your boarding card, please?
PAX: Alright. Here you are.
  CA: Thank you, Ms Jones. Would you like me to show you to your seat? This way, please.
PAX: Oh, thanks for your help.

5

  CA: Good evening, Madam! I'm Jill, your purser on today's flight. I'm in charge of the cabin. If there is anything I can do for you, please don't hesitate to let me know.
PAX: Very nice to meet you, Jill. When will the plane take off?
  CA: It will take off when we get clearance from ATC.
PAX: Thank you very much.

6

  CA: Good day, Mr. Young. My name is Anna, I'll be serving you and preparing your meal with my colleague Monica today. If there is anything you need, please let me know.
PAX: Thank you. Can I have a copy of newspaper?
  CA: Yes, sure. We have *China Daily* and *South China Morning Post*. Which would you prefer?
PAX: *China Daily* please.

New Words and Expressions

aboard	[ə'bɔːd]	v. 登机
service	['sɜːvɪs]	n. 服务
aisle	[aɪl]	n. 过道
purser	['pɜːsə(r)]	n. 乘务长
in charge of	[ɪn][tʃɑːdʒ][əv]	主管,掌管
hesitate	['hezɪteɪt]	v. 犹豫
clearance	['klɪərəns]	n. 许可
ATC (Air Traffic Control)		空中交通管制
serve	[sɜːv]	v. 服务
colleague	['kɒliːg]	n. 同事

◉ **Role play the cabin attendant's responses.**

CA: _____.
PAX: Good morning.
CA: _____.
PAX: Yes, sure.
CA: _____.
PAX: Thank you.
CA: _____.

CA: _____.
PAX: Thank you. I'm not sure where my seat is.
CA: _____.
PAX: Yes, here you are.

CA: _____.
PAX: Oh, that's very kind of you. Thank you.
CA: _____.
PAX: Thank you very much.

◉ **Discuss the following questions.**

1. How would you greet passengers when they board the plane?
2. How does a cabin attendant make a self-introduction to passengers?

◉ **Make up dialogues based on the following situations.**

1. Jill is a cabin attendant. She is standing at the gate of the cabin to greet passengers who are boarding the aircraft.
2. A passenger is looking for his seat with the boarding card in his hand. A cabin attendant comes towards him and helps him.
3. Shirley is a purser of the flight, and she is introducing her colleagues Carol and Jenny to the passengers.

◉ **Translate following sentences into English.**

1.早上好,女士。欢迎登机。
2.晚上好。很高兴再次见到您。
3.很高兴您能乘坐本次航班。
4.先生有什么我能帮您的吗？
5.请问可以看一下您的登机牌吗？
6.需要我帮您做点什么吗？
7.需要我带您去您的座位吗？

8. 您的座位是20A。就是右边/左边靠窗的座位。
9. 我的名字是凯西。很高兴能在航班上为您服务。今天我将为您准备餐食。
10. 杨小姐下午好。我是凯西，本次航班的乘务长。

Part C
Public Announcements

Boarding

Good morning (afternoon/evening), ladies and gentlemen,

Welcome aboard _____. Please ask the cabin attendants if you cannot find your seat. The seat numbers are shown on/ above the overhead locker.

Please make sure your hand baggage is stored on the overhead locker or under the seat in front of you. Please keep the aisle and the exits clear of all baggage.

Please take your assigned seats as quickly as possible and keep the aisle clear for others to be seated.

Thank you for your cooperation.

Greetings I

Good morning (afternoon/evening), ladies and gentlemen,

Welcome aboard _____ Airlines.

I am _____, the purser for this flight. During the flight, all of my colleagues will be happy to be of service to you. Thank you.

Ladies and gentlemen, we will be taking off in a few minutes, please be seated and fasten your seat-belt. (Please stow your foot rest.) Your seatback and table should be returned to the upright position.

All _____(airline) flights are non-smoking to comply with government regulations. Please refrain from smoking during the flight.

Thank you for your cooperation, and we wish you a pleasant journey!

Greetings II

Good morning (afternoon/evening), ladies and gentlemen,

I am _____, your chief purser. On behalf of _____ Airlines, we extend the most sincere greetings to you and members of our _____ Club. It's a pleasure to see you again.

Our team is looking forward to making a safe and pleasant journey.

Thank you!

Welcome

Ladies and gentlemen,

Welcome aboard _____, a Star Alliance/Sky Team/Oneworld member's flight.

Captain _____, purser _____ and our team will cherish every chance of service to make your journey with us, a safe and pleasant one!

We hope you enjoy the flight.

Thank you!

Charter Flight

Ladies and gentlemen,

On behalf of the captain, we would like to welcome you on board of your charter flight bound for Sanya. The air distance from Tianjin to Sanya is 2,800 kilometers and it will take three hours and forty minutes.

At this time, would you please make sure that your seat-belt is fastened. In accordance with government regulations, all flights are non-smoking. Please refrain from smoking during this flight.

We are glad to have you on board. If there is anything we can do for you, please feel free to tell us. We hope you will have a pleasant flight.

Thank you.

New Words and Expressions

seat number	[siːt]['nʌmbə]	座位号
overhead locker	['əʊvəhed]['lɒkə(r)]	头顶行李箱
hand baggage	[hænd]['bæɡɪdʒ]	手提行李
keep clear of	[kiːp][klɪə(r)][əv]	避开, 不接触
exit	['eksɪt]	n. 出口
assigned seats	[ə'saɪnd][siːt]	指定座位
cooperation	[kəʊˌɒpə'reɪʃn]	n. 合作
seat-belt	[siːt'belt]	安全带
stow	[stəʊ]	v. 收起, 收藏
upright	['ʌpraɪt]	adj. 正直的, 垂直的

comply with	[kəm'plaɪ][wɪð]	遵守,遵从
regulation	[regjʊ'leɪʃən]	n. 条例,章则
refrain from	[rɪ'freɪn][frəm]	限制,抑制
chief purser	[tʃi:f]['pɜ:sə(r)]	主任乘务长
on behalf of	[ɒn][bɪ'haf][əv]	代表
Star Alliance	[stɑ:(r)][ə'laɪəns]	星空联盟
Sky Team	[skaɪ][ti:m]	天合联盟
Oneworld	[wʌnwɜ:ld]	寰宇一家
captain	['kæptɪn]	v. 机长
cherish	['tʃerɪʃ]	v. 珍爱,珍惜
charter flight	[tʃa:tə(r)][flaɪt]	包机
in accordance with	[ɪn][ə'kɔ:dəns][wɪð]	依照;与……一致

Speaking Practice

◉ **Practice making public announcements about greeting with these alternatives.**
- Air China / Phoenix
- China Eastern Airlines / Eastern Miles
- China Southern Airlines / Sky Pearl
- Cathay Pacific / Asia Miles
- Air France / Flying Blue

◉ **Please read following sentences in the right tone(′ for stress, ↗ for rising tone, ↘ for falling tone).**

1. Good ′ morning (afternoon/evening), ladies ↘ and gentlemen. ↘
2. Welcome ↗ aboard. ↘
3. Please ↗ ask the cabin ↗ attendants ↘ ′ if you cannot ↗ find your seat. ↘
4. Please ↗ ′ make sure ↘ your hand baggage is stored ↗ on the overhead ↗ locker ↘ or under ↗ the seat ↘ in front of you ↘.
5. Thank ↗ you for your ↗ cooperation. ↘

◉ **Translate the following expressions into English.**
- 就座
- 尽快
- 保持通道畅通
- 系紧安全带
- 收起小桌板
- 调直座椅背
- 收起脚踏板
- 禁止吸烟
- 包机
- 飞行距离

Part D
Work-task

📋 **Try to discuss:**
1. Why do you want to be a cabin attendant?
2. Are there any differences between cabin attendant and train attendant?

Flight Attendants

Flight attendants or cabin crew (also known as stewards/stewardesses, air hosts/hostesses, cabin attendants) are members of an aircrew employed by airlines primarily to ensure the safety and comfort of passengers aboard commercial flights, on select business jet aircraft and on some military aircraft.❶

The role of a flight attendant derives from that of similar positions on passenger ships or passenger trains, but it has more direct involvement with passengers because of the confined quarters on aircraft.❷ Additionally, the job of a flight attendant revolves around safety to a much greater extent than those of similar staff on other forms of transportation.❸ Flight attendants on board a flight collectively form a cabin crew, as distinguished from pilots and engineers in the cockpit.

The first female flight attendant was a 25-year-old registered nurse, named Ellen Church. Hired by United Airlines in 1930, she also first envisioned nurses on aircraft. Other airlines followed suit, hiring nurses to serve as flight attendants, then called "stewardesses" or "air hostesses", on most of their flights. Female flight attendants rapidly replaced male ones, and by 1936, they had all but taken over the role. They were selected not only for their knowledge but also for their characteristics.

The primary role of a flight attendant is to ensure passenger safety. In addition to this, flight attendants are often tasked with customer service duties such as serving meals and drinks, as a secondary responsibility.

The number of flight attendants required on flights are mandated by international safety regulations. The majority of flight attendants for most airlines are female, though a substantial number of males have entered the industry since the 1970s.❹

(资料来源：http://en.wikipedia.org/wiki/Flight_attendant)

📝 Notes

❶Flight attendants or cabin crew (also known as stewards/stewardesses, air hosts/hostesses, cabin attendants) are members of an aircrew employed by airlines primarily to ensure the safety and comfort of passengers aboard commercial flights, on select business jet aircraft and on some military aircraft.

句子大意：空中乘务员（以下简称"空乘"）是航空公司的机组成员，其职责主要是为了确保商业航班、商用喷气式飞机和某些军用飞机上旅客的安全和舒适。

❷ The role of a flight attendant derives from that of similar positions on passenger ships or passenger trains, but it has more direct involvement with passengers because of the confined quarters on aircraft.

句子大意：空乘的角色起源于客船或客车上提供相似服务的岗位，但由于飞机的空间限制，空乘与旅客之间的联系要更紧密。

其中，"...**that** of similar positions..."中**that**是指示代词（复数形式是those），此处为了避免重复，代替前述名词role。

例如，The price of rice is higher than that of flour. 大米的价格高于面粉（价格）。

❸ Additionally, the job of a flight attendant revolves around safety to a much greater extent than those of similar staff on other forms of transportation.

句子大意：此外，与其他交通工具上的服务人员相比，空乘的工作更注重安全。

其中，"revolves around"意为围绕转动，以……为中心；"... those of similar staff..."中**those**的用法见注释2。

❹ The majority of flight attendants for most airlines are female, though a substantial number of males have entered the industry since the 1970s.

句子大意：虽然自20世纪70年代以来，已有相当数量的男性加入了空乘行业，但大多数航空公司的空乘仍以女性为主。

其中，"a substantial number of"意为"大量的"。

New Words and Expressions

cabin crew	[ˈkæbɪn][kruː]	乘务组；航班空服人员
steward	[ˈstjuːəd]	n. 乘务员（男）；管家（男）
stewardess	[ˈstjuːədɪs]	n. 乘务员（女）；管家（女）
host	[həʊst]	n. 乘务员（男）；主人（男）
hostess	[ˈhəʊstɪs]	n. 乘务员（女）；主人（女）
aircrew	[ˈɛəkruː]	n. 全体机组人员
airline	[ˈɛəlaɪn]	n. 航空公司；航线
primarily	[ˈpraɪmərəli]	adv. 首先；主要地，根本上
commercial flight	[kəˈmɜːʃəl][flaɪt]	商业航班
business jet aircraft	[ˈbɪznəs][dʒet][ˈɛəkrɑːft]	商用喷气飞机
military aircraft	[ˈmɪlətri][ˈɛəkrɑːft]	军用飞机
derive	[dɪˈraɪv]	v. 源于；得自
passenger ship	[ˈpæsɪndʒə(r)][ʃɪp]	客船，客轮
passenger train	[ˈpæsɪndʒə(r)][treɪn]	客运列车；客车
involvement	[ɪnˈvɒlvmənt]	n. 牵连；包含
confined	[kənˈfaɪnd]	adj. 狭窄的；有限制的
quarters	[ˈkwɔːtəz]	n. 住处；四分之一（quarter的复数）
revolve	[rɪˈvɒlv]	v. 使……旋转；使……循环

collectively	[kə'lektɪvlɪ]	adv.	共同地，全体地
cockpit	['kɒkpɪt]	n.	驾驶舱
registered nurse	['redʒɪstəd][nɜːs]		注册护士
United Airlines	[juˈnaɪtɪd]['eɪlaɪns]		美国联合航空公司
envision	[ɪn'vɪʃən]	v.	想象；预想
follow suit	['fɒləʊ][suːt]		跟着做；学样
replace	[rɪ'pleɪs]	v.	取代，代替
secondary	['sekəndərɪ]	adj.	第二的；中等的；次要的
mandate	['mændeɪt]	n.	授权；命令；委托管理

Part E
Supplementary Reading

Try to discuss:
1. Suppose you are a cabin attendant from Air China, how would you introduce your company to your passenger?
2. Which airline is your ideal company?

Air China

Air China Limited ("Air China") and its predecessor, the former Air China, were founded in 1988. Air China is China's exclusive national flag carrier for civil aviation, a member of the Star Alliance, the world's largest airline alliance. In addition to leading ahead of its domestic competitors in passenger and freight air transport and related services, it also provides special flight services for the country's state leaders on official visits to other countries.

Air China's logo consists of an artistic phoenix pattern, the Chinese name of the airline written in calligraphy by former national leader Mr. Deng Xiaoping, and "AIR CHINA" written in English. The phoenix logo is also an artistic transfiguration of the word "VIP". The color is the traditional Chinese red which implies auspiciousness, completion, peace and happiness, and expresses Air China's sincere passion to serve society and endlessly pursue safety. Air China holds its vision and orientation as "a well-established global airline", the connotation of which is to realize four strategic objectives: leading competitiveness in the world market, continuously enhanced development potential, excellent and distinguished travel experiences for passengers, and steadily increasing profits. Its enterprise spirit emphasizes "serving the world with a warm heart and guiding the future by innovation". Its enterprise mission is to "meet the requirements of customers and create mutual value". Its enterprise sense of worth is to "deliver a high level of service and earn universal approval from the public". Its service philosophy is "Credibility, Convenience, Comfort and Choice".

As of December 31, 2019, Air China (including its holding company) owns a total of 699 aircrafts of various types, mainly by Boeing and Airbus, with an average lifespan of 6.96 years. The company's passenger routes have expanded to 770, including 137 international, 27 regional and 606 domestic routes. The company flies to 43 countries (regions) and 187 cities, including 65 international, 3 regional, and 119 domestic cities. Through its collaboration with other Star Alliance member airlines, the company's route network has further extended to 1,317 destinations in 195 countries.

Air China's frequent flyer program, Phoenix Miles, has the longest history of any frequent flyer program in China. Through the integration of its various memberships under Air China holding companies and joint-stock companies, all are unified as "Phoenix Miles". By the end of 2019, the Phoenix Miles program had more than 6,359 million members.In 2019, Air China was named by World Brand Lab as one of the "World's 500 Most Influential Brands" for the 13th consecutive year, and was the only chinese civil aviation company on the list.

(资料来源:http://www.airchina.com.cn/en/about_us/company.shtml)

参考译文

中国国际航空公司

中国国际航空股份有限公司简称"国航",英文名称为"Air China Limited",简称"Air China",其前身为中国国际航空公司,成立于1988年。国航是中国唯一挂载国旗飞行的民用航空公司以及世界最大的航空联盟——星空联盟成员。国航除了在航空客运、货运及相关服务诸方面均处于国内领先地位,它还承担着中国国家领导人出国访问的专机任务。

国航的企业标识由一只艺术化的凤凰和中国前国家领导人邓小平书写的"中国国际航空公司"以及英文"AIR CHINA"构成。国航标志是凤凰,同时又是英文"VIP"(尊贵客人)的艺术变形,颜色为中国传统的大红,具有吉祥、圆满、祥和、幸福的寓意,寄寓着国航人服务社会的真挚情怀和对安全事业的永恒追求。国航的愿景和定位是"具有国际知名度的航空公司",其内涵是实现"竞争实力世界前列、发展能力持续增强、客户体验美好独特、相关利益稳步提升"的四大战略目标;企业精神强调"爱心服务世界、创新导航未来";企业使命是"满足顾客需求,创造共有价值";企业价值观是"服务至高境界、公众普遍认同";服务理念是"放心、顺心、舒心、动心"。

截至2019年12月31日,国航(含控股公司)共拥有以波音、空中客车为主的各型飞机699架,平均机龄6.96年;经营客运航线已达770条,其中国际航线137条,地区航线27条,国内航线606条,通航国家(地区)43个,通航城市187个,其中国际65个,地区3个,国内119个;通过与星空联盟成员等航空公司的合作,将服务进一步拓展到195个国家的1317个目的地。

国航拥有中国历史最长的常旅客计划——"国航知音",又通过整合控股,将参股公司多品牌常旅客会员统一纳入"凤凰知音"品牌。截至2019年底,凤凰知音会员已达到6359万人。2019年,国航连续第13年被评为"世界品牌500强",是中国民航唯一一家进入"世界品牌500强"的企业。

Unit 2

Directing Passengers

- Part A Useful Words and Expressions
- Part B Dialogues
- Part C Public Announcements
- Part D Work-task
- Part E Supplementary Reading

Students will be able to:

memorize the words and expressions about how to direct passengers in the cabin;

make up the dialogues about directing passengers in the cabin;

obtain and improve public announcements skills about directing passengers;

know about what to do in the briefing;

introduce China Southern Airlines.

Suggested Hours: *4 class hours*

Unit 2 Directing Passengers

Part A
Useful Words and Expressions

◉ **Please list as many ways to direct the passengers at the gate as you can.**

_____
_____

- aisle
- the other aisle/next aisle
- on the right/left
- in the middle
- galley
- emergency exit
- at the back/front of the cabin
- in the rear of the cabin
- toilet/lavatory
- Go straight on/ahead.
- Turn left/right.
- Your seat is at the middle/back/front.
- Just take the aisle to the 19th row.
- It's straight ahead and on your right/left.
- May I show you to your seat? This way, please.
- Your seat is on the next aisle. Would you please go that way?
- The seat numbers are indicated/shown on the overhead compartments.
- May I trouble you a minute, Madam? Would you be kind enough to change to another seat?
- I'm afraid we can't manage the upgrade procedures on the flight.
- May I see your boarding pass? I'm afraid you may have the wrong seat.
- Could you take the seat according to your seat number?
- Could you please step aside and allow the other passengers to go through?
- May I assist you with your belongings?
- May I get you some drinks or magazines?
- Have a pleasant flight.

Culture Tips

➢ Use formal language to help passengers take their seats as soon as they get on board.
➢ Avoid using the following casual language for directing passengers on board:
—Please don't sit here.
—You can't sit here.

15

> To show respect and welcome, cabin attendant should use her palm-hand to indicate the position rather than with single finger.

Cabin Term

overhead locker/ overhead compartment/ overhead bin 头顶行李箱
释义：头顶行李箱是飞机上旅客存放随身行李的空间，位于座位上方，所以用overhead修饰，表示特指。Locker/compartment/bin 都是空间、隔间、柜子的意思，可通用。

◉ Match phrases or sentences in column B to the situations in column A.

Column A	Column B
1. Change seat.	a. Could you please step aside and allow the other passengers to go through?
2. Upgrade.	b. May I see your boarding pass, please?
3. A passenger is looking for seat.	c. Would you mind changing to another seat for the passenger over there?
4. A passenger takes the wrong seat.	d. Please check your overhead locker.
5. A passenger is blocking the way in the aisle.	e. According to airline's regulations, we can't provide upgrade service on board.
	f. May I see your boarding pass? I'm afraid you may have the wrong seat.

◉ Make up a dialogue about changing seat for a passenger who wants to sit together with his wife.

Part B
Dialogues

(CA=Cabin Attendant, PAX=Passenger)

1

CA: Good morning. What can I do for you, Madam?
PAX1: Good morning. I'm looking for my seat. Could you guide me to my seat?

Unit 2   Directing Passengers

CA: May I see your boarding pass, please?
PAX1: Here you are.
CA: Your seat number is 19F. It's a window seat in the rear of the cabin. This way, please. I'll show you the seat. Just take the aisle to the 19th row. As you can see, all the seat numbers are shown on the overhead locker.
PAX1: Thank you very much.
(*A passenger is standing in the aisle blocking the way.*)
CA: Excuse me, Sir. Could you please step aside and allow the other passengers to go through?
PAX2: Oh, I'm sorry. I didn't notice that!

2

PAX1: Excuse me.
CA: Yes? How may I assist you?
PAX1: Could you help me with my seat?
CA: May I see your boarding pass?
PAX1: Here you are.
CA: 15A. Thank you. Follow me, please.
(*They find that the seat has been occupied by another passenger.*)
CA: Excuse me, Madam. May I see your boarding pass? I'm afraid you may have the wrong seat.
PAX2: Okay, it's somewhere in my purse. Here you are.
CA: Thank you, Madam. (*The cabin attendant is checking the boarding pass.*) Your seat number is 5A, which is in the forward cabin. The seat numbers are shown along the edge of the overhead compartment. This is 15A.
PAX2: Oh, sorry. I thought it was mine. I'll move then.
CA: That's all right. May I assist you with your belongings?
PAX2: No, thanks, I can do it myself.
CA: (*To PAX1*) Sorry to keep you waiting, Sir. That's alright now.

3

PAX1: Excuse me, Miss. Would you mind asking you a question?
CA: Go ahead, please.
PAX1: Well, the man over there is my friend. I wonder if I could sit next to him, because we have just watched the European Football Championship. The match was really breathtaking and we are so excited. Can you help me change seat with the lady in the window seat?
CA: I'll ask her if she would mind changing.

17

(*To the lady*)

CA: May I trouble you a minute, Madam? The man over there would like to sit together with his friend beside you. Would you be kind enough to change to another seat?

PAX2: Ok, no problem.

CA: Thank you, Miss.

(*To PAX1*)

CA: Sir, you can sit with your friend now.

PAX1: Thanks a lot.

CA: You are welcome.

4

PAX: Excuse me, Miss. Shall I upgrade to the first class? The legroom in the economy class is so narrow that I can't stretch my legs.

CA: I'm sorry to hear that, Sir. According to our airline's regulations, we can't provide upgrade service on board. May I get you some drinks or magazines?

PAX: OK, I see. Water will be fine.

CA: Thank you for understanding. I'll be back soon.

5

(*A passenger doesn't take his assigned seat.*)

CA: Excuse me, Sir. I'm afraid you are in the wrong seat. Could you take the seat according to your seat number?

PAX: But I'm feeling a little dizzy now. I wish I could take a seat where I can stretch my legs.

CA: Sir, I share your feelings. But according to the airline's regulations, passengers should be seated in the assigned seat in order to ensure proper weight and balance for the aircraft when it takes off. After take-off, you can take any empty seat you like.

PAX: I see.

6

CA: Excuse me, Sir. May I see your boarding pass, please?

PAX: Here you are. By the way, I'm pretty sure I have taken my assigned seat.

CA: Yes, Sir. You are right. Here is another problem. We have double booked. Would you mind taking another seat? This passenger wishes to sit with his mother, whose seat is next to you.

PAX: Oh, I see. No problem.

CA: Thank you for your cooperation.

New Words and Expressions

| occupied | ['ɒkjʊpaɪd] | *adj.* 已占用的,无空闲的 |

Unit 2　Directing Passengers

check	[tʃek]	v. 检查
forward cabin	['fɔːwəd]['kæbɪn]	前舱
edge	[edʒ]	n. 边缘
overhead compartment	['əʊvəhed][kəm'pɑːtmənt]	头顶行李箱
belongings	[bɪ'lɒŋɪŋz]	n. 行李，随身物品
European Football Championship	[ˌjʊərə'piːən]['fʊtˌbɔːl] ['tʃæmpɪənʃɪp]	欧洲足球锦标赛
breathtaking	['breθˌteɪkɪŋ]	adj. 令人激动的
legroom	['legruːm]	n.（飞机的）伸腿空间
economy class	[ɪ'kɒnəmɪ][klɑːs]	经济舱
stretch	[stretʃ]	v. 伸展
upgrade	[ʌp'greɪd]	升舱
dizzy	['dɪzɪ]	adj. 使人头晕的
weight	[weɪt]	n. 重量
balance	['bæləns]	n. 平衡
take-off	['teɪkɒf]	n. 起飞

● **Role play the cabin attendant's responses.**

PAX1: Excuse me, could you help me with my seat?
CA: _____.
PAX1: Here you are.
CA: _____.
PAX1: But it has been occupied by another passenger. Could you help me get it back?
CA: _____.
CA: (to PAX 2) _____.
PAX2: Here you are.
CA: _____.
PAX2: Oh, sorry. I'll move, then.

PAX: Excuse me, may I change my seat?
CA: _____.
   (After checking with the passenger…)
CA: _____.
PAX: Oh, that's very kind of you. Thank you.

● **Discuss the following questions.**

1. A passenger's seat number is 4A. How can you help him find his seat?

2. When passengers are boarding, one of them is blocking the way in the cabin, what would you say to him?
3. Will passengers be able to change seats freely during the flight?
4. When a passenger wants to upgrade, what would you say to him?
5. Obviously "double seating" mistake causes inconvenience to passengers. How do you handle such a non-standard situation?
6. Passengers may ask for a seat change during boarding, what would you say to him?

◉ **Make up dialogues based on the following situations.**
1. Jane is a cabin attendant. She is trying to talk to a passenger standing at the gate of the cabin so that the other passengers can't get on the cabin.
2. A passenger is expecting to change his seat with a man sitting next to a window. A cabin attendant comes towards him and helps him.

◉ **Translate the following sentences into English.**
1. 您的座位在客舱中部/后舱/前舱。
2. 您的座位号为20D。请跟我来。
3. 您的座位就在前方右侧/左侧。
4. 我带您去您的座位吧？请走这边。
5. 您的座位在过道对面。请您走那边。
6. 座位号标识于头顶行李箱上。
7. 劳驾您换个座位好吗？
8. 抱歉，飞行中我们不能办理升舱手续。
9. 可以看一下您的登机牌么？恐怕您坐错座位了。
10. 为方便其他旅客通过，您可以让一下吗？

Part C
Public Announcements

Unit 2　Directing Passengers

Special Flight-Greeting

Ladies and gentlemen,

Good morning/afternoon/evening, Your Excellency (Prime Minister/Minister/President/Premier/King/Queen/Ambassador) and Distinguished Guests, Welcome to _____. We are honored to be at your service.

(Our flying time is ____ hour (s) ____ minutes.) Distinguished Guests, our aircraft will be taking off shortly, please make sure you fasten your seat-belt. Thank you for choosing _____ airlines. We wish you a pleasant trip.

Thank you for your cooperation.

Temporarily Adjusting Seats

Ladies and gentlemen,

In order to keep the aircraft in a better balance, the occupation of seats will be adjusted temporarily.

Please follow the direction of the flight attendants.

You may take your booked seats after take-off.

Thank you for your cooperation.

Athlete Group (Greetings)

Ladies and gentlemen,

Good morning (afternoon / evening).

On behalf of _____, we would like to welcome (Group) _____ on board. The air distance from _____ to _____ is _____ kilometers and it will take _____ hours and _____ minutes.

The _____ (Games) will soon be held in _____ and we would like to take this opportunity to wish our athletes great success in the Games.

We hope you will have a nice stay in _____ and enjoy your flight.

Thank you.

Upgrade Announcement

Ladies and gentleman,

Thank you for flying with _____.

We are pleased to inform you that we have some First Class (and Business Class) seats available on our flight today. If you need any of this service, please contact our flight attendant.

Chinese New Year (Greetings)

Ladies and gentlemen,

Good morning (afternoon/evening).

This is your (chief) purser speaking. It is the Spring Festival, Chinese Lunar New Year. On behalf of _____, the entire crew here extends sincere greetings to you. We wish you good health, a happy and prosperous New Year!

Thank you!

New Words and Expressions

minister	[ˈmɪnɪstə(r)]	n.	部长，大臣
premier	[ˈpremɪə(r)]	n.	首相
ambassador	[æmˈbæsədə(r)]	n.	代表，大使
distinguished	[dɪˈstɪŋgwɪʃt]	adj.	高贵的，著名的
occupation	[ˌɒkjʊˈpeɪʃən]	n.	占有；职业
adjust	[əˈdʒʌst]	v.	调整，校准
temporarily	[ˈtempərərɪlɪ]	adv.	临时地
booked	[bʊkt]	adj.	预订的；登记了的
athlete	[ˈæθliːt]	n.	运动员
kilometer	[ˈkɪlɒmiːtə]	n.	公里
opportunity	[ˌɒpəˈtjuːnɪtɪ]	n.	机会
first class	[fɜːst][klɑːs]		头等舱
business class	[ˈbɪznəs][klɑːs]		商务舱
available	[əˈveɪləbl]	adj.	可获得的；有空的
contact	[kənˈtækt]	v.	联系，接触
lunar	[ˈluːnə]	adj.	阴历的；月亮的
extend	[ɪkˈstend]	v.	延伸；伸出；给予
prosperous	[ˈprɒspərəs]	adj.	繁荣的；兴旺的

Speaking Practice

- Practice making announcements about *athlete groups* with these alternatives.
  - China Men's National Football Team
  - China National Basketball Team
  - Tianjin Women's Volleyball Team
  - China National Table-tennis Team
  - Beijing Guoan Football Team

- Practice your own dialogue on *upgrade service* between cabin attendants and passengers with the following sentences.
  - I'm sorry but I'm having trouble with my seat.
  - Where can I get the upgrade service?

- May I see your board pass please?
- In order to keep the aircraft in a better balance, please keep seated temporarily.
- If you need any of this service, please contact our flight attendant.

Read following sentences in the right tone(′ for stress, ↗ for rising tone, ↘ for falling tone).

1. On behalf ↗ of ↘ _____, we would like ↗ to ′ welcome _____(Group) on board ↘.
2. The air distance from _____ ↗ to _____ ↘ is _____ kilometers and it will take ↗ _____ hours ↗ and _____ minutes ↘.
3. The _____ (Games) will soon ↗ be held in _____ ↘ and we would like to take this opportunity ↗/↘ to wish our athletes ′ great success in the Games ↘.
4. We ′ hope you will have a ′ nice ↗ stay ↘ in _____ and enjoy ↗ your flight ↘.
5. If you need any of this ↗ service, please contact our flight ↗ attendant ↘.

Translate the following expressions into English.
- 航班号
- 代表
- 头等舱
- 经济舱
- 联系乘务员
- 运动队伍
- 趁此机会
- 座位安排
- 预订座位
- 起飞后

Part D
Work-task

Try to discuss:
1. What is briefing? What is it for?
2. What would cabin attendants usually do in briefing?

Briefing

A safe flight starts with good planning, and good planning for a flight starts with briefings. Briefing is a very important part of any flight preparation. The aim of briefings is to establish a clear plan of action and to ensure there is a common understanding between all crewmembers.

Briefings are identified as being an important ingredient to effective crew resource management to ensure open communication between the flight crew, the cabin crew and the passengers.❶ An effective briefing is a valuable tool to help manage errors and improve outcomes.

Briefing should provide a clear picture of the flight ahead, and build a common understanding amongst the crew of the expectations of the flight. A successful briefing should be short, interesting and detailed, and should include teamwork, communication, planning and predicting possible unplanned events.

How to make an effective pre-flight briefing? The briefing is addressed to all cabin crewmembers, and is done by the purser. The expectations, tone and the standards for the flight are set during this briefing.

The purser must keep the main objectives of the briefing in mind, as well as important information specific to the flight.

A good tip to conduct an effective briefing is to use the "A, B, C rule":

A for Appropriate: The briefing should be relevant and appropriate to the flight. It should highlight the specific details of the flight. A briefing should be prepared for each individual flight, otherwise it may become routine and repetitive.❷ The purser should:

—Plan and prepare the briefing;

—Select the relevant information before the briefing.

B for Brief: A briefing should be as the word suggests, "brief". The purser should keep the briefing short to ensure that the attention of all cabin crewmembers is focused on the most important points.❸

C for Clear and Concise: The briefing must be understood by all crewmembers. It should be interactive, and encourage cabin crewmembers to share information and ask questions. The purser should adopt good communication methods to encourage feedback.❹

Cabin crew pre-flight briefings should be performed before each duty period. Sufficient time should be spent on the briefing to ensure that all crewmembers are familiar with their operating position and duties. The time will vary depending on the number of crew, size of aircraft, area of operation, etc. When possible, the preflight briefings should be held in a designated briefing room. If this is not possible, the briefing may be performed onboard the aircraft, before passenger boarding begins.❺ In some cases, there may also be other briefings during the flight, for example during unusual, abnormal or emergency situations.

(资料来源：http://www.airbus.com/fileadmin/media_gallery/files/safety_library_items/AirbusSafetyLib_-FLT_OPS-CAB_OPS-SEQ01.pdf)

Notes

❶Briefings are identified as being an important ingredient to effective crew resource management to ensure open communication between the flight crew, the cabin crew and the passengers.

句子大意：航前准备会作为机组资源有效管理的一个重要组成部分,在确保飞行机组、客舱机组和旅客之间有效沟通方面,起到很重要的作用。

❷A briefing should be prepared for each individual flight otherwise it may become routine and repetitive.

句子大意：每趟航班的航前准备会,都应是针对该特定的航班而举行;否则,(航前准备会)会变成流于形式、机械重复的例行公事。

其中,"otherwise"作为连词,在此意为"要不然,否则",例如：
I think he intends otherwise. 我认为他另有打算。
Turn off the gas when the milk boils, otherwise it will be spilt.
牛奶煮沸后就关上煤气,不然牛奶就会溢出来。

❸The purser should keep the briefing short to ensure that the attention of all cabin crewmembers is focused on the most important points.

句子大意：乘务长(主持航前准备会)应确保会议简短、扼要,保证所有客舱组成员对会议要点没有遗漏。

其中,"is focused on"意为"集中于";常用表达式为：focus attention on something.例如：
Like many men, he is focused on what he can do. 跟许多人一样,他专注于他能做的。

❹It should be interactive, and encourage cabin crewmembers to share information and ask questions. The purser should adopt good communication methods to encourage feedback.

句子大意：(航前准备会)应以互动方式,鼓励乘务员在会上分享信息和提问。乘务长应采用积极有效的交流方法,鼓励参会人员提出反馈信息。

❺When possible, the preflight briefings should be held in a designated briefing room. If this is not possible, the briefing may be performed onboard the aircraft, before passenger boarding begins.

句子大意：如有可能的话,航前准备会应在指定的会议室举行。如条件不允许的话,也可以在旅客登机前,在飞机上举行。

其中,"When possible"完整结构为"when it is possible",意为"如果可能",例如：
When possible, let the government manage the resources.
如果可能,应让政府来管理资源。

New Words and Expressions

briefing	[ˈbriːfɪŋ]	n. 航前准备会
identified	[aɪˈdentɪfaɪd]	v. 鉴定（identify的过去分词）
ingredient	[ɪnˈgriːdɪənt]	n. 原料；要素；组成部分
ensure	[ɪnˈʃʊə]	v. 保证,确保
flight crew	[flaɪt][kruː]	飞行机组
expectation	[ˌekspekˈteɪʃən]	n. 期待；预期；指望
detailed	[ˈdiːteɪld]	adj. 详细的,精细的

communication	[kə,mjuːnɪ'keɪʃən]	n. 通信，交流
predict	[prɪ'dɪkt]	v. 预计
objective	[əb'dʒektɪv]	n. 目的；目标
specific	[spɪ'sɪfɪk]	adj. 特殊的，特定的
appropriate	[ə'prəʊprɪeɪt]	adj. 适当的
relevant	['reləvənt]	adj. 有关的；中肯的
highlight	['haɪlaɪt]	v. 突出；强调
concise	[kən'saɪs]	adj. 简明的，简洁的
interactive	[,ɪntər'æktɪv]	adj. 交互式的；相互作用的
adopt	[ə'dɒpt]	v. 采取；接受
feedback	['fiːdbæk]	n. 反馈；成果
vary	['veri]	v. 改变；使多样化
designated	['dezɪg,neɪtɪd]	adj. 指定的；特指的
abnormal	[æb'nɔːməl]	adj. 反常的，不规则的

Part E
Supplementary Reading

Try to discuss:
1. Suppose you are a cabin attendant from China Southern Airline, how would you introduce your company to your passenger?
2. How much do you know about the "Sky Pearl Club"?

China Southern Airlines

China Southern Airlines was established on 1 July 1988. Since then, it acquired and merged with a number of domestic airlines, becoming one of China's "Big Three" airlines (alongside Air China and China Eastern Airlines). With flight operations based at Guangzhou's award-winning Baiyun International Airport, China Southern Airlines' company logo can be seen around the globe with brilliant red kapok delicately adoring a blue vertical tailfin.Taking "Sunshine China Southern Airlines" as its cultural character, with "Connecting to all parts of the world and creating a better life" as its corporate mission, with "Customer First, Respect for Talents, Pursue for Excellence, Continuous Innovation, and Compassionate Return" as its core values, it vigorously promotes "Diligent and Pragmatic, Tolerance and Innovation" spirit, in order to build a world-class air transport company with Chinese characteristics.

With the most numbered transport aircraft, the most developed route network, and the largest annual passenger volume in China, China Southern Airlines has 18 branches, 23 domestic sales offices, 69 foreign sales offices. In 2018, its passenger traffic reached 140 million, ranking first among Chinese airlines for 40 consecutive years. As of October 2019, it has operated more than

850 passenger and cargo transport aircrafts including Boeing B787, B777, B737 series, Airbus A380, A330, and A320 series, making it one of the first airlines in the world to operate Airbus A380. The fleet size ranks first in Asia and third in the world.

The airline owns and operates its own independent training centers for pilots and flight attendants. China Southern Airlines, with more than 3,300 comprehensively trained and experienced pilots, is the only Chinese carrier that has the independent capability of "building its pilots from the ground up".

The Flight Training Center which is a joint venture with CAE, the world's leading manufacturer of flight simulators, is the Asia's largest flight training center. The Airline enjoys a strong aircraft maintenance capability through its joint-venture company Guangzhou Aircraft Maintenance & Engineering Co., Ltd. (GAMECO for short), which has built Asia's largest aircraft maintenance hangar.

China Southern Airlines is the largest airlines in China measured in terms of fleet size as well as the number of passengers carried, and also the 1st in Asia in terms of fleet size. The Airline currently serves destinations to 841 cities in 162 countries. It has developed an extensive network to Southeast Asia and also has become the Chinese airline with the largest presence in Australia. It is also considering expanding into the South American markets, as well as further expansion into the African market.

In 1995, 2001, 2003, 2004 and 2007, China Southern Airlines was honored the "Golden Roc Cup", which is the most prestigious safe flight operation award in the Chinese aviation industry. On July 16, 2008, China Southern Airlines was presented the Five-Star Flight Safety Award by the CAAC which is the current most prestigious award for safe flight operations in the Chinese aviation industry, becoming the only Chinese carrier maintaining and the longest safety record and occupying a leading position in the international aviation industry. From 2011 to 2018, China Southern Airlines earnestly fulfilled its social responsibilities as a central enterprise, and has been widely recognized by the society, and successively received various honors and awards.

(资料来源：http://en.wikipedia.org/wiki/China_Southern_Airlines)

参考译文

中国南方航空公司

中国南方航空股份有限公司（简称"南航"）成立于1988年7月1日。至那时起，它收购和兼并了多家国内航空公司，成为中国航空的"三巨头"之一（另外两家是中国国际航空公司和中国东方航空公司）。南航总部设于屡获殊荣的广州白云国际机场，其公司航徽是蓝色垂直尾翼上镶红色木棉花。南航以"阳光南航"为文化品格，以"连通世界各地，创造美好生活"为企业使命,以"顾客至上、尊重人才、追求卓越、持续创新、爱心回报"为核心价值观,大力弘扬"勤奋、务实、包容、创新"的南航精神,致力于建设具有中国特色的世界一流航空运输企业。

南航是中国运输飞机最多、航线网络最发达、年客运量最大的航空公司,拥有18家分公司,设有23个国内营业部,69个国外营业部。2018年,南航旅客运输量达1.4亿人次,连续40年居中国各航空公司之首。截至2019年10月,南航运营包括波音B787、B777、B737系列,空客A380、A330、A320系列等型号客货运输飞机超过850架,是全球首批运营空客A380的航空公司。机队规模居亚洲第一、世界第三。

南航拥有自己独立的飞行员和乘务员培训中心。南航飞行实力出众,拥有超过3300名训练有素、经验丰富的飞行员,是目前国内唯一一家拥有独立培养飞行员能力的航空公司,其与全球知名飞行模拟器制造商加拿大航空电子设备公司(CAE)合资建立的飞行训练中心是亚洲规模最大的飞行训练中心。南航拥有雄厚的机务维修能力,旗下合资公司广州飞机维修工程有限公司(GAMECO)建有亚洲最大的飞机维修机库。

南航是中国机队规模、载客人数最大的航空公司,也是亚洲机队规模最大的航空公司。南航目前航线涵盖了841个城市在内的162个国家。该公司已建立了庞大的东南亚航线网络,同时也是中国在澳大利亚规模最大的航空公司。目前正考虑进一步拓展南美和非洲市场。

在1995、2001、2003、2004、2007年度,南航五度夺得中国民航年度安全最高奖——"金鹏杯"。2008年7月16日,南航荣获中国民航局颁发的中国民航业飞行安全最高奖——"飞行安全五星奖",成为国内安全星级最高、安全飞行记录最长的航空公司,在国际上也处于领先地位。2012—2018年,南航认真履行中央企业社会责任,得到各界广泛认可,先后被授予多种荣誉和奖项。

Cabin Service English

Unit 3

Boarding and Cabin Check

* Part A Useful Words and Expressions
* Part B Dialogues
* Part C Public Announcements
* Part D Work-task
* Part E Supplementary Reading

Students will be able to:

memorize the words and expressions about how to arrange baggage in the cabin and how to do the cabin check;

make up the dialogues about arranging baggage and cabin check in the cabin;

obtain and improve public announcements skills about arranging baggage and cabin check;

know about how to do the preparations before take-off;

introduce China Eastern Airlines.

Suggested Hours: *4 class hours*

Part A
Useful Words and Expressions

● **Please list as many expressions related to baggage arrangement in the cabin as you can.**

- luggage
- baggage
- Belongings
- carry-on/hand baggage
- checked baggage
- stow
- valuable
- Would you like me to hang up your overcoat for you?
- If you don't mind, I'll hang the coat in the wardrobe compartment for you.
- Would you mind me putting it somewhere else for you?
- Would you mind stowing your bag in the overhead locker?
- Would you please check if you have any valuables in your pockets?
- Please put your baggage under the seat or into the overhead compartment.
- Please take your passport out of your luggage.
- Your luggage is far too heavy and won't fit into the overhead compartment. If you don't mind, I'll keep it somewhere else.
- According to the airline's regulations, baggage is not allowed to leave here as it will block the aisle.
- I'm afraid you cannot take those fruits with you on this international flight.

Culture Tips

➢ Use formal language to help passengers arrange their luggage as soon as they get on board.
➢ Avoid using the following casual language for arranging luggage on board:
—You are not allowed to leave luggage here.
—Get your bag out of here.
➢ What is cross-check? Take a look at the following sentences:
—Cabin crew, please make a cross-check about the grooming of each crew member.
—Before take-off, cabin attendants would make a cross-check to make sure passengers have fastened their seat-belt and seatback is in full and upright position, tray table is closed and locked. For passengers sitting beside a window, check to see the sunshade is lifted.

Cabin Term

bag/baggage/luggage　行李、包、行李箱

释义：三个词都可以指随身行李或行李箱。一般意义上来讲，baggage和luggage指比bag更大的行李，而其中baggage更为正式，luggage较为口语。

● Match phrases or sentences in column B to the situations in column A.

Column A	Column B
1. Baggage is blocking the aisle.	a. We'll be taking off soon. For your safety, could you please close the overhead bin?
2. Baggage is near emergency exit.	b. Lost baggage can be returned to you.
3. Overhead locker is open.	c. Please follow me and put your baggage in the rear of the cabin.
4. Where to put one's coat?	d. I'll hang it in the wardrobe compartment for you.
5. Baggage of fragile items.	e. If you don't mind, I'll keep it safe somewhere else.
6. Bag is too big to go into the compartment or under the seat.	f. According to regulations, passengers are requested to keep the emergency exit seats clear of all baggage.
	g. Would you mind putting it under the seat in front of you or into the overhead locker?

● Make up a dialogue about helping a passenger arrange his baggage in the cabin.

Part B
Dialogues

(CA=Cabin Attendant, PAX=Passenger)

(*A bag is put on the aisle.*)

CA: Excuse me, Sir. Is this your baggage?

PAX: Yes, it's mine. What's up?

CA: According to the airline's regulations, baggage is not allowed to leave here as it will block the aisle. Would you mind putting it under the seat in front of you or into the overhead locker?

PAX: But the problem is that the overhead locker is full and I don't feel very comfortable with the bag by my feet.

CA: Don't worry. Let me assist you. There is some room in the front cabin. May I ask you to carry the bag and follow me?

PAX: That's really nice of you.

2

CA: Excuse me, Sir.
PAX: Yes?
CA: I'm afraid I have to put your baggage in other places.
PAX: Why? It's not in anyone's way.
CA: No, but it might be. You're sitting next to the emergency exit. According to the airline's regulations, passengers are requested to keep the emergency exit seats clear of all baggage.
PAX: So where could I put it? I'll need it during the flight.
CA: Don't worry. Let me assist you with your baggage and put it into other overhead locker.
PAX: All right. I will try.

3

PAX: Excuse me, Miss. Can I put my baggage in the galley?
CA: I'm afraid you can't. We'll be working in the galley preparing the dinner. Besides, we'll stow litter bags there after dinner. Would you mind putting it somewhere else?
PAX: But my baggage is too big to go into the compartment or under my seat.
CA: Well, if you don't mind, I'll keep it somewhere else.
PAX: Well…er…. but there are some fragile items in it.
CA: I see. They need to be kept with care. Please follow me and put your baggage in the rear of the cabin.
PAX: Thank you.

4

CA: Pardon me for interrupting you, Madam. Your baggage is far too heavy and won't fit into the overhead compartment. It might easily fall down in case of turbulence and hurt someone.
PAX: I see. What can I do with it?
CA: I'm afraid you need to put it under the seat in front of you.
PAX: All right.
CA: Please allow me to assist you with it.
PAX: Thank you.
(*The cabin attendant helps the passenger carry the bag down from the locker. Suddenly, some fruits run out of the bag.*)
CA: Excuse me, Madam. I'm afraid you can't take those fruits with you on this international flight. According to the quarantine requirements of Canadian government, all entry passengers to Canada are not allowed to bring in fruits.

PAX: Oh, dear. What am I supposed to do now?

CA: Don't worry, Madam. You can choose to dispose of them by yourself, or you can give them to us, we'll be happy to be at your service.

PAX: Thanks. That's very nice of you.

CA: It's a pleasure. Wish you a pleasant journey.

5

PAX: Excuse me, Miss. May I trouble you for a moment?

CA: Certainly, what can I do for you, Sir?

PAX: It's too hot for me in the cabin. I'm wondering where I can put my coat.

CA: If you don't mind, I'll hang it in the wardrobe compartment for you.

PAX: Yes, that would be great.

CA: Is there anything valuable in your pockets?

PAX: No, I've got my wallet here.

6

CA: Excuse me, Sir. We will be taking off in a few minutes. For your safety, could you please close the overhead bin?

PAX: I'd like to. But my baggage is so big for the compartment that it can't be stowed into the compartment.

CA: I'm afraid your baggage is too big to be put into the compartment. In case of turbulence, it might fall down and hurt somebody. Would you mind me putting it somewhere else for you?

PAX: Alright, it would be great.

CA: Now we can close the overhead locker. We'll take off soon. We hope you have a pleasant journey.

PAX: Thank you very much.

New Words and Expressions

block	[blɒk]	v.	阻碍
emergency exit	[ɪmɜːdʒənsɪ]['eksɪt]		紧急出口
galley	['gælɪ]	n.	厨房
litter	['lɪtə]	n.	垃圾
fragile item	['frædʒaɪl]['aɪtəm]		易碎品
interrupt	[ˌɪntə'rʌpt]	v.	打扰,妨碍
turbulence	['tɜːbjʊləns]	n.	颠簸;紊流
quarantine	['kwɒrəntiːn]	n.	检疫
dispose	[dɪs'pəʊz]	v.	处理
wardrobe compartment	['wɔːdrəʊb][kəm'pɑːtmənt]	n.	衣橱,衣物存储行李箱
wallet	['wɒlɪt]	n.	钱包

◉ **Role play the cabin attendant's responses.**

> PAX: Excuse me. May I put it in the galley?
> CA: _____.
> PAX: But my baggage is too big to go into the compartment or under the seat.
> CA: _____.
> PAX: There are some fragile items in it.
> CA: _____.
>
> CA: Whose baggage is on aisle?
> PAX: It's mine. The overhead locker is full and there is not enough room under my seat.
> CA: _____.
> PAX: That's really nice of you.

◉ **Discuss the following questions.**

1. What do the cabin attendants discuss at the briefing?
2. What do the cabin attendants do in the cabin before passengers get on board?
3. A passenger's baggage is too big to go in the compartment or under the seat. How do you help him?
4. When a passenger wants to put baggage in the galley, what would you say?
5. A passenger doesn't know where to put his coat. How do you help him?

◉ **Make up dialogues based on the following situations.**

1. Lucy is a cabin attendant. She is trying to talk to a passenger who has left his baggage beside the emergency exit.
2. The purser is in charge of the briefing before flight. They are going to go through the procedures of the briefing.
3. A passenger carries fragile items in his luggage. He asks the cabin attendant where he can put his luggage.

◉ **Translate the following sentences into English.**

1. 我帮您把您的上衣挂起来好吗？
2. 您介意把您的包放在头顶上方的行李舱里吗？
3. 请把您的行李放在座位下面或者头顶上方的行李箱里。
4. 请您检查一下上衣口袋里是否有贵重物品。
5. 您的包太重了，不能放进头顶上的行李舱里。
6. 飞机即将起飞。为了您的安全，请您关闭头顶上方的行李舱好吗？
7. 遗失的行李可以返还给您。
8. 请把您的护照从行李舱里拿出来。
9. 如果您不介意，我会把它存放在其他地方。
10. 根据规定，旅客需要保持紧急出口畅通。

Part C
Public Announcements

Greeting (flight time within 50 minutes)

Ladies and gentlemen,

This is your chief perser on this flight. We are honored to welcome you aboard _____. We are looking forward to greeting you a perfect experience on board. We are expected to arrive at _____ airport at _____, the groud temperature is _____ degrees Celsius, or _____ degrees Fahrenheit.

In accordance to the CAAC regulations and for safety reasons, due to the very short duration of this flight, we will not provide meal and drink service on this flight. We appreciate your understanding. Lavatories cannot be used. We hope you accept our sincere apology. We have prepared mineral water in the seat pocket in front of you.

Please put your seatback upright, secure your tray-table and put down your arm-rest. Please ensure your seat-belt is securely fastened, and your window shades are fully open. In order not to interfere with our flight systems, your mobile phones should be switched off or set to airplane mode. All laptops, tablets and other portable electronic devices should be powered off and stowed properly.

Thank you!

Safety Instruction

Ladies and gentlemen,

May we please have your attention for the safety demonstration? If you have any question after the safety video, please contact the flight attendants.

Thank you!

Announcement Made After Cabin Door Closed

Ladies and gentlemen,

The cabin door is closed. For your safety, please do not use your mobile phones and certain electronic devices on board at any time. Laptop computers may not be used during takeoff and landing. Please ensure that your mobile phone is turned off. This is a non-smoking flight; please do not smoke on board.

Thank you for your cooperation.

Safety Announcement

Ladies and gentlemen,

In preparation for departure, please take your seat. Place your seatback in the upright position. Fasten your seat-belt securely. Fold your tray table and open the window shade. Smoking is prohibited throughout the flight, including the use of electronic cigarettes. All mobile phones including those with a flight mode must be switched off during the flight. Please keep your cash and other valuable items in sight and in a secure place during the flight.

We wish you a pleasant journey.

Electronic Devices Restrictions

Ladies and gentlemen,

Please note certain electronic devices must not be used on board at any time. These devices include cellular phones, AM/FM radios, televisions and remote control equipment including toys.

All other electronic devices including laptop computers and CD players must not be switched on until fifteen minutes after take-off, and must be switched off when the seat-belt signs come on for landing.

Your cooperation will be much appreciated.

New Words and Expressions

portable	['pɔːtəbl]	adj. 便携式的
electronic	[ˌɪlek'trɒnɪk]	adj. 电子的
device	[dɪ'vaɪs]	n. 装置
safety demonstration	['seɪftɪ][ˌdemən'streɪʃən]	安全演示
laptop computer	['læptɒp][kəm'pjuːtə]	笔记本电脑
announcement	[ə'naʊnsmənt]	n. 通知, 通告
preparation	[ˌprepə'reɪʃən]	n. 预备; 准备
departure	[dɪ'pɑːtʃə]	n. 离开; 出发
tray table	[treɪ]['teɪbl]	小桌板
prohibit	[prəʊ'hɪbɪt]	v. 阻止, 禁止
flight mode	[flaɪt][məʊd]	飞行模式

cash	[kæʃ]	n. 现款,现金
valuable item	['væljʊəbl]['aɪtəm]	贵重物品
restriction	[rɪ'strɪkʃən]	n. 限制
cellular phone	['seljʊlə][fəʊm]	手机
remote	[rɪ'məʊt]	adj. 远程的;遥远的
switch on/off	[swɪtʃ][ɒn]/[ɒf]	打开/关闭

Answer the questions:

1. Where do passengers need to put their baggage?
2. Where mustn't passengers put their baggage, why?
3. The use of electronic equipment may interfere with the navigational equipment on board, what should cabin attendants be watchful for?
4. What do cabin attendants say to a passenger who is using a laptop computer?

Read following sentences in the right tone.(′ for stress, ↗ for rising tone, ↘ for falling tone).

1. May we please ↗ have your ′ attention ↘ for the safety demonstration ↗ / ↘.
2. Please ′ note that ↘ certain electronic ↗ devices ↘ must ′ not be used on board ↘ at ′ any ↗ time ↘.
3. These devices include ↗ cellular phones ↗, AM/FM radios ↗, televisions ↗ and remote ↗ control equipment ↘ including ↗ toys ↘.
4. All other electronic devices ↘ including ↗ laptop computers ↗ and CD players ↘ must ′ not be switched on until fifteen minutes after take-off ↘, and must be switched off ↘ when the seat-belt signs ′ come on for landing.
5. Your cooperation ↗ will be much ↗ appreciated ↘.

Translate the following expressions into English and practice making public announcement about *electronic devices restrictions*.

- 提供餐饮服务
- 干扰飞行系统
- 移动电话
- 收音机
- 遥控设备
- 笔记本电脑
- 唱片播放器
- 关闭电子设备

- 打开电子设备
- 起飞15分钟后

Part D
Work-task

📋 **Try to discuss:**
1. What do cabin attendants usually do prior to takeoff?
2. Prior to takeoff, what is the safety check for?

Preparations

Flight attendants have a series of preparations to complete before passengers getting on board. The purpose is to ensure a safe and comfortable flight. To achieve the goal, cabin attendants will check passengers' number in each class and will check the demonstrator life jackets, oxygen mask and galley equipment.❶ They will also check all documents necessary for the flight and put everything into right position.

In more details, prior to each flight, a safety check is conducted to ensure all equipment such as life-vests, torches (flashlights) and firefighting equipment are on board, in the right quantity, and in proper condition.❷ Any unserviceable or missing items must be reported and rectified prior to takeoff. Flight attendants must monitor the cabin for any unusual smells or situations. They assist with the loading of carry-on baggage, checking for weight, size and dangerous goods. They make sure those sitting in emergency exit rows are willing and able to assist in an evacuation and move those who are not willing or able out of the row into another seat.❸ They then must do a safety demonstration or monitor passengers as they watch a safety video. They then must "secure the cabin" ensuring tray tables are stowed, seats are in their upright positions, armrests down and carry-ons stowed correctly and seat-belts are fastened prior to take off.❹

(资料来源：http://en.wikipedia.org/wiki/Flight_attendant)

📝 Notes

❶To achieve the goal, cabin attendants will check passengers' number in each class and will check the demonstrator life jackets, oxygen mask and galley equipment.

句子大意：为了实现(安全舒适的航行)目标，乘务员须核实各舱旅客的数量，检查示范用救生衣、氧气面罩和厨房设施是否正常。

❷In more details, prior to each flight, a safety check is conducted to ensure all equipment such as life-vests, torches (flashlights) and firefighting equipment are on board, in the right quantity, and in proper condition.

句子大意:具体来讲,在起飞前,乘务员须对客舱做安全检查,目的是为了确保所有的客舱设备(如救生衣、手电筒和消防设备)均装载得当,且数量准确,状态良好。

其中,"prior to"意为"在……之前;居先",例如:
Wise people estimate the possible results of their plan prior to any actions.
聪明的人在任何行动之前都会事先评估任何可能的后果。

❸ They make sure those sitting in emergency exit rows are willing and able to assist in an evacuation and move those who are not willing or able out of the row into another seat.

句子大意:确保坐在紧急出口附近的旅客,在紧急撤离时,愿意且有能力为机组提供帮助;同时将该位置上不愿或无法提供帮助的旅客更换到其他位置。

❹ They then must "secure the cabin" ensuring tray tables are stowed, seats are in their upright positions, armrests down and carry-ons stowed correctly and seat-belts are fastened prior to takeoff.

句子大意:乘务员须做"客舱安全检查",确保起飞前客舱内的一切均正常:小桌板已收起,旅客座椅已调成竖直状态,座椅扶手已收下,旅客随身携带的行李均装载妥当,安全带已扣紧。

New Words and Expressions

complete	[kəm'pli:t]	v. 完成
demonstrator life jacket	['demənstreɪtə][laɪf]['dʒækɪt]	示范用救生衣
oxygen mask	['ɒksɪdʒən][mɑ:sk]	氧气面罩
galley equipment	['gælɪ][ɪ'kwɪpmənt]	厨房设施
document	['dɒkjumənt]	n. 文件;文档
position	[pə'zɪʃən]	n. 位置,方位;职位
safety check	['seɪftɪ][tʃek]	安全检查
torch	[tɔ:tʃ]	n. 火炬;手电筒
flashlight	['flæʃˌlaɪt]	n. 手电筒;闪光灯
firefighting equipment	['faɪəfaɪtɪŋ][ɪ'kwɪpmənt]	灭火设施
unserviceable	[ʌn'sɜ:vɪsəb(ə)l]	adj. 无用的
rectify	['rektɪfaɪ]	v. 调整;矫正
monitor	['mɒnɪtə]	v. 监控
dangerous goods	['deɪndʒərəs][gʊdz]	危险品
assist	[ə'sɪst]	v. 帮助
evacuation	[ɪˌvækjʊ'eɪʃən]	n. 疏散;撤离
armrest	['ɑ:mrest]	n. 扶手
carry-ons	['kærɪɒnz]	n. 手提行李,随身行李

Part E
Supplementary Reading

📖 **Try to discuss:**
1. Suppose you are a cabin attendant from the China Eastern Airlines, how would you introduce your company to your passenger?
2. How much do you know about the China Eastern Airlines' logo?

China Eastern Airlines

China Eastern Airlines Group Co., Ltd was founded in April 1995, with its headquarters in Shanghai. It ranks second among the three largest airlines in China in terms of passengers carried, next only to China Southern Airlines. In 2019, with a total asset of more than 350 billion yuan, China Eastern Airlines Group continues to promote industrial transformation and upgrading, and strives to build three pillar industries of full-service, low-cost, and logistics, as well as aviation maintenance, aviation catering, innovative technology platforms, financial platforms, and industrial investment platforms.

China Eastern and its subsidiary Shanghai Airlines became the 14th member of Sky Team on June 21, 2011. With its main hub in Shanghai near the Yangtze River Delta Area, China Eastern Airlines develops a route network with 1,150 destinations in 175 countries around the world. With an annual passenger traffic of more than 130 million people, it ranks among the top ten in the world.

China Eastern Airlines' logo is a white artistic swallow on a circle background comprised of a red semicircle resembling the sun and a dark blue semicircle resembling the seas. The tail of the swallow is also a transfiguration of the word "CE," short for "China Eastern."

China Eastern Airlines's frequent-flyer program is called Eastern Miles, the members of which can enjoy the membership rights of 19 Sky Team airlines and more than 750 airport lounges worldwide. Enrollment is free of charge. Eastern Miles members can earn miles on flights as well as through consumption with China Eastern's credit card. When enough miles are collected, members can be upgraded to VIP. VIP membership of Eastern Miles can be divided into two tiers: Golden Card membership and Silver Card membership. VIP membership can enjoy extra privileged services.

China Eastern Airlines was the first civilian airline listed on the New York Stock Exchange, the Shanghai Stock Exchange, and the Hong Kong Stock Exchange. Committed to creating wonderful travel experiences for global passengers with exquisite, precise, and sophisticated services, in recent years, it has won the highest flight safety award in China's civil aviation—"Flight Safety Diamond Award", and has been awarded the "Most Valuable Chinese Brand" among the top 50 bands by WPP (the global brand communication group) for 8 consecutive years, the "Top 500 Global Brand Values" by Brand Finance (the brand rating agency) for 4 consecutive years, and it has won numerous international and domestic awards in the areas of operational quality, service experience, and social responsibility.

(资料来源：http://www.chinahighlights.com/china-airline/eastern-airlines.htm; http://en.wikipedia.org/wiki/China_Eastern_Airlines)

参考译文

中国东方航空公司

中国东方航空集团有限公司(简称"东航")成立于1995年4月，总部设在上海，它是中国三大航空公司之一，载客量仅次于中国南方航空。截至2019年，东航总资产超过3500亿元，持续推进产业转型升级，着力打造全服务、低成本、物流三大支柱产业和航空维修、航空餐食、创新科技平台、金融平台、产业投资平台五大协同产业融合发展的"3+5"产业结构布局。

东航及其子公司上海航空于2011年6月21日成为天合联盟的第14个成员。东航的枢纽机场位于长江三角洲地区的上海，拥有通达全球175个国家1150个目的地的航线网络，年旅客运输量超过1.3亿人，位列全球前十。

东航的航徽基本构图为圆形，取红、蓝、白三色，以寓意太阳、大海的上下半圆与燕子的组合，表现东航的企业形象。燕子尾部的线条勾勒出东航英文名"China Eastern"的首字母CE两字。

东航常旅客计划名为"东方万里行"，其常旅客可享受天合联盟19家航空公司的会员权益及全球超过750间机场贵宾室。会员注册免费。会员可通过乘坐东航航班和消费东航信用卡两种方式累积里程。里程累积达到门槛后，会员可升级为VIP。"东方万里行"VIP会员可分为两种：金卡会员和银卡会员。VIP会员可享受额外的特权服务。

东航是在纽约证券交易所、上海证券交易所和香港联合交易所上市的第一家民用航空公司。致力于以精致、精准、精细的服务，为全球旅客创造精彩旅行体验，近年来荣获中国民航飞行安全最高奖——"飞行安全钻石奖"，连续8年获评全球品牌传播集团WPP"最具价值中国品牌"前50强，连续4年入选品牌评级机构英国品牌金融咨询公司(Brand Finance)"全球品牌价值500强"，在运营品质、服务体验、社会责任等领域屡获国际、国内殊荣。

Cabin Service English

Unit 4

Take off

- Part A Useful Words and Expressions
- Part B Dialogues
- Part C Public Announcements
- Part D Work-task
- Part E Supplementary Reading

Students will be able to:

memorize the words and expressions about how to inform passengers of obeying the rules in cabin before take-off;

make up the dialogues about informing and persuading passengers in the cabin;

obtain and improve public announcements skills about informing passengers of airline's regulations;

know about 30-second review;

introduce International Air Transport Association (IATA).

Suggested Hours: *4 class hours*

Unit 4 Take off

Part A
Useful Words and Expressions

◉ **Please list as many expressions related to the Dos and Don'ts before take off in the cabin as you can.**

_____

_____

- footrest/armrest/headrest
- window shade/blind
- adjust
- switch on/off
- mobile phone
- electronic devices
- laptop computers
- upright/recline seatback
- lift/lower the window blind/shade
- We are preparing the cabin for take-off.
- We are going to dim the cabin light.
- The use of lavatory has been suspended during take-off.
- Our plane has begun taxiing. Please switch off your mobile phone.
- Sir, for your safety, I have to ask you return your seat to the upright position.
- The plane is taking off. It's dangerous to leave your seat.
- You are kindly requested not to use your cell phone.
- Please fasten your seatbelt and adjust your seatback to the upright position.
- May we remind you that all our plane is non-smoking flight and smoking is not allowed in the lavatories, either.

Culture Tips

➤ Passengers are not allowed to do the following things when the plane is about to take off:

—Walking in the cabin.

—Making phone call.

—Smoking in the cabin.

—Sitting with seat-belt unfastened.

—Using electronic devices or remote-control toys.

—…

➤ When talking with passengers about safety issues, it's strongly recommended that cabin attendants should use the confirmative expressions, such as:

—Would you please …
—I have to ask you to …
—I need to ask you to …
—I must ask you to …

Cabin Term

refrain/forbid/suspended 禁止

释义：三个词都有禁止的意思，但refrain为不及物动词，一般后接from使用，如refrain from smoking；forbid则可用作forbid smoking。而suspended比另外两个词多了暂时之意，用作暂停。同时还可以用is not allowed、be requested not to来表示禁止。

Match phrases or sentences in column B to the situations in column A.

Column A	Column B
1. Fasten seat-belt.	a. The estimated flying time is 3 hours.
2. Seat-belt for baby.	b. Please put out your cigarette at once. Smoking is not allowed.
3. Adjust the seatback.	c. Please turn off your cell phone. It might interfere with airplane systems.
4. Go to lavatory before take-off.	d. The use of it has been suspended during take-off. Please wait until we reach the cruising altitude.
5. Smoking.	e. Just press the button on armrest.
6. Making phone call before take-off.	f. I will get you a supplementary seat-belt for the baby.
	g. Insert the link into the main buckle and fasten it tightly.

Make up a dialogue about persuading a passenger putting his cigarette out in the cabin before take-off.

Part B
Dialogues

(CA=Cabin Attendant, PAX=Passenger)

1

PUR: (*announcement*) Ladies and gentlemen: we will be taking off *immediately*. For your safety, please make sure your seat-belt is securely fastened. Thank you.

PAX: Excuse me, Miss. Could you tell me how to fasten my seat-belt?
CA: Certainly, Madam. To fasten your seat-belt, insert the link into the main buckle and fasten it tight.
PAX: I see. Thank you. By the way, the seat-belt seems too short for both my baby and me.
CA: Never mind. Let me assist you. Please hold your baby outside the seat-belt. I will get you an infant seat-belt.

(*After giving the seat-belt to the passenger*)
CA: Madam, is the infant seat-belt comfortable for the baby?
PAX: Yes. Thanks for your help.

PAX: Excuse me, Miss. May I trouble you?
CA: Yes, please.
PAX: I don't know how to adjust the seatback.
CA: Oh. You can see there is a button here on your armrest. Just press it.
(*The passenger pressed the button and reclined the seatback.*)
PAX: Ah. It's more comfortable now. Thanks very much.
CA: You're welcome. But would you please return it to the upright position? We're taking off soon. The adjustment can be made after take-off.
PAX: All right.

CA: Excuse me, Sir. The plane is about to take off. Please don't walk about in the cabin.
PAX: Could you tell me where the lavatory is?
CA: There are lavatories in the front and rear of the cabin.
PAX: I see. I have found that all the lavatories are being occupied.
CA: Sir, the lavatory is vacant but locked, because the plane is about to take off. The use of it has been suspended during take-off. You must remain in your seat with your seat-belt fastened. You'll have to wait until we reach the cruising altitude.
PAX: All right.

CA: Pardon me for interrupting you, Madam. Please turn off your cell phone. Our plane is about to take off.
PAX: Sorry, but I have an emergency e-mail to check and I'll turn it off just in a minute.
CA: Madam, in order to ensure the normal operation of airplane navigation and communication systems, you are kindly requested not to use your cell phone. It might interfere with these systems.

PAX: All right.
CA: Thank you for your cooperation.

5

CA: Excuse me, Sir. Please put out your cigarette immediately. Smoking is not allowed here.
PAX: Ok. By the way, is there any smoking section on board?
CA: No, there isn't, because the airline's regulations forbid smoking on all flights. After take-off, we can offer you some chewing gum.
PAX: Er…I should have tried some cigarettes before boarding.
CA: By the way, Sir. May we remind you that all our plane is non-smoking flight and smoking is not allowed in the lavatories, either.
PAX: Thanks.

6

PAX: Excuse me, Miss. I feel a little cold. Where can I find a blanket?
CA: Blankets and pillows are stowed in the overhead lockers, and eye shades are placed on your seat.
PAX: Could you please help me take the blanket out? It's not convenient to stand up for me.
CA: No problem. Here you are.
PAX: Thank you very much.
CA: It's my duty to make you feel as comfortable as possible.

New Words and Expressions

immediately	[ɪ'mi:dɪətlɪ]	adv.	立即
insert	[ɪn'sə:t]	v.	插入
link	[lɪŋk]	n.	链环,连接片
infant seat-belt	['ɪnfənt][si:tbelt]		婴儿座椅安全带
seatback	[si:tbæk]		座椅靠背
recline	[rɪ'klaɪn]	v.	使斜倚,使躺下
lavatory	['lævətərɪ]	n.	洗手间
rear	[rɪə]	adj.	后面的
vacant	['veɪkənt]	adj.	空的;空闲的
suspend	[sə'spend]	v.	暂停
cruising altitude	['kru:zɪŋ]['æltɪtju:d]		巡航高度
navigation system	[,nævɪ'geɪʃən]['sɪstəm]		导航系统
communication system	[kə,mju:nɪ'keɪʃən]['sɪstəm]		通信系统
interfere	[,ɪntə'fɪə]	v.	干扰
cigarette	[,sɪgə'ret]	n.	香烟
smoking section	['sməʊkɪŋ]['sekʃən]		吸烟区

forbid	[fə'bɪd]	v. 禁止；不允许
chewing gum	['tʃuːɪŋ][gʌm]	口香糖
eye shade	[aɪ][ʃeɪd]	遮光眼罩

● **Role play the cabin attendant's responses.**

(*A passenger is smoking in the cabin before take-off.*)
CA: _____.
PAX: Ok. By the way, is there any smoking section on board?
CA: _____.
PAX: Ok, I see.

(*A passenger is making phone call before take-off.*)
CA: _____.
PAX: Er… I'm making an emergency call. Just give me some minutes and I'll make a call.
CA: _____.
PAX: All right. I see.
CA: _____.

● **Discuss the following questions.**

1. A passenger with a baby doesn't know how to fasten her seat-belt. What would you say to help her?
2. A passenger reclines his seatback as soon as he gets on board. But he does not know how to return it to the upright position before take-off. How do you help him?
3. The plane is going to take off. But a passenger wants to go to the lavatory. What would you say to him?
4. A passenger is smoking in the cabin. How do you stop him?
5. A passenger is using his mobile phone prior to take-off. How do you stop him?
6. A few passengers are still standing after the cabin door is closed. What should you do?

● **Make up dialogues based on the following situations.**

1. There is a passenger making phone call before take-off. The cabin attendant comes to him and persuades him to switch it off.
2. One passenger asks the cabin attendant to help him return his seat to the upright position before take-off.

● **Translate the following sentences into English.**

1. 我们正在为起飞做客舱准备。
2. 我们将会调暗客舱的灯光。
3. 起飞期间洗手间已暂停使用。
4. 我们的飞机已经开始滑行，请关闭您的手机。

5. 先生，为了您的安全，请您回到您的座位。
6. 请系好您的安全带并把您的座椅靠背调到竖直的位置。
7. 飞机即将起飞，请回到您的座位并系好安全带。
8. 预计飞行时间是3小时。
9. 请立刻熄灭您的香烟，吸烟是不允许的。
10. 请关闭您的手机，它可能会干扰到飞机系统。

Part C
Public Announcements

Before Take-off

Ladies and gentlemen,

　　We will be taking off shortly. Please be seated, fasten your seat-belt, make sure that your tray table is closed and your seatback is in upright position. If you are sitting in a window seat, please help us by opening the sunshade.

　　Thank you for your cooperation.

Welcome Announcement

Ladies and gentlemen,

　　Good morning (afternoon/evening).

　　Captain _____ and his crew would like to welcome you aboard _____ flight _____ to _____ (via _____). The air distance from _____ to _____ is _____ kilometers and the flying time is _____ hour(s) and _____ minutes.

　　We will take off soon. Please make sure that your seat-belt is securely fastened. May we remind you that all our flights are non-smoking to comply with the regulations.

　　On our flight today, there are _____ flight attendants at your service. If there is anything we can do for you, please let us know. We hope you will enjoy your flight.

　　Thank you.

After Take-off

Ladies and gentlemen,

We have left _____ for _____, (with a stop-over in _____). The air distance from _____ to _____ is _____ kilometers and the estimated flying time is _____ hour(s) and _____ minutes.

On our way to _____ we will fly over _____.

This flight has been awarded the title of Model Flight by the Civil Aviation Administration of China. Our crew members will take every effort to provide you with the best quality service.

In accordance with regulations, to ensure a clean and comfortable cabin environment, smoking is not allowed during the flight. During our trip, we will provide you with a lunch at 12:30 Beijing time, along with a choice of beverages.

Please keep your seat-belt fastened in case of sudden turbulence. If there is anything we can do for you, please let us know. We will provide you with customer satisfaction cards on your request.

We wish you a very pleasant flight with _____ (Airlines).

Thank you!

Poor Air Conditioning

Good morning (afternoon/evening), ladies and gentlemen,

We are awaiting clearance from air traffic control. We apologize that the air-conditioning is not functioning properly while the plane is still on the ground. It will be improved after take-off.

Thank you for your understanding and cooperation!

No Smoking

Ladies and gentlemen,

In accordance with government health regulations, all flights in China are non-smoking. The "No Smoking" sign will remain switched on throughout the flight. Passengers are also requested to refrain from smoking in the toilets. May we remind you that it is an offence to tamper with the smoke detectors in the toilets.

Your cooperation will be appreciated.

Thank you.

New Words and Expressions

window seat	['wɪndəʊ][siːt]	临窗座位
sunshade	['sʌnʃeɪd]	n. 遮阳板
remind	[rɪ'maɪnd]	v. 提醒; 使想起

stop-over	['stɒpəʊvə]	n. 中途停留
award	[ə'wɔ:d]	v. 授予；判定
Model Flight	['mɒdəl][flaɪt]	模范航班
Civil Aviation Administration of China	['sɪvl][eɪvɪ'eɪʃən][ədmɪnɪ'streɪʃən][əv]['tʃaɪnə]	中国民用航空局
quality	['kwɒlətɪ]	n. 质量，品质
accordance	[ə'kɔ:dəns]	n. 一致
choice	[tʃɔɪs]	n. 选择；精选品
beverage	['bevərɪdʒ]	n. 饮料
customer satisfaction card	['kʌstəmɒ][ˌsætɪs'fækʃən][kɑ:d]	旅客意见卡
request	[rɪ'kwest]	n. 请求；需要
air traffic control (ATC)	[eə(r)]['træfɪk][kən'trəʊl]	空中交通管制
air-conditioning	[eəkən'dɪʃənɪŋ]	n. 空调
properly	['prɒpəlɪ]	adv. 适当地
improve	[ɪm'pru:v]	v. 改善，增进
refrain	[rɪ'freɪn]	v. 避免；制止
offence	[ə'fens]	n. 违反；攻击
tamper	['tæmpə]	v. 做手脚；违反

Speaking Practice

◉ **Make a *welcome* announcement with the following details.**

1. It's 9 o'clock in the morning.
2. The captain is Chen.
3. It is an Air China flight from Chengdu to Guangzhou.
4. The flight number is CA 1405.
5. Flight time is 2 hours and 30 minutes.
6. The flight is a non-smoking flight.
7. There are 6 flight attendants on the flight.

◉ **Practice making announcement about *After Take-off* with these alternatives.**

1. Tianjin/ Guiyang/Taiyuan /2103/3/55/ Guiyang/ Huanghe River/Tianjin Airlines
2. Shanghai/Seattle/San Francisco/9211/11/30 / Seattle /Pacific/China Eastern Airlines

◉ **Read following sentences in the right tone(′ for stress, ↗ for rising tone, ↘ for falling tone).**

1. Captain Chen ↗ and his crew ↘ would like to ′ welcome you aboard ↗ flight ↗ CA1405 ↗ to Guilin ↘.
2. We will ′ take off ↗ soon ↘.

3. Please make sure ↗ that your seat-belt is ↗ securely ↗ fastened ↘.
4. May we remind you ↗ that all our flights ↘ are ↗ non-smoking to ↗ comply with the regulations ↘.
5. If there is anything ↗ we can do for you, please let us know ↘.

Translate the following expressions into English.
- 飞行时间
- 系好安全带
- 禁烟
- 按照规定
- 为您服务
- 临窗座位
- 打开遮光板
- 饮品选择
- 正常运转
- 空中交通管制

Part D
Work-task

Try to discuss:
1. How much do you know about the 30-second review?
2. Do you know the so-called "OLDABC"?

30-second review

The use of the Silent Review or the 30-second review is an excellent tool that the cabin crew can use to prepare for the unexpected events. The Silent Review helps the cabin crew focus their attention on their duties and responsibilities, and on safety.

The cabin crew should perform the Silent Review during the take-off and landing phases of flight. This review helps the cabin crew prepare themselves, and enables them to react rapidly.

The Silent Review should contain all of the elements needed to review evacuation duties and responsibilities. It may include, but is not limited to, the following subjects:❶

- Bracing for impact.
- Commands.
- Initiating evacuation, if necessary (i.e. Identify under what circumstances the cabin crew

will initiate an evacuation: fire, smoke, life-threatening situations, ditching, no response from the flight crew).❷
- Operating exits.
- Assessing outside conditions.
- Self-protection.
- Locating Able-Bodied Passengers (ABPs).❸

For example, the second subject mentioned above is commands. One typical example of commands is the so-called crowd control commands. It means that the cabin crew must have absolute control of the situation, and provide assertive commands and instructions to passengers. There are documented cases of evacuations during which the passengers did not behave appropriately, and did not comply with the instructions provided by the cabin crew.❹

The following is an example of a Silent Review that uses the first word of each subject to form a word that is easy to remember. This example is called "OLDABC":

- **O**peration of exits.
- **L**ocation of equipment.
- **D**rills (Brace for impact).
- **A**ble-Bodied Passengers and disabled passengers.
- **B**race position.
- **C**ommands.

(资料来源：http://www.airbus.com/fileadmin/media_gallery/files/safety_library_items/Airbus SafetyLib_-FLT_OPS-CAB_OPS-SEQ12.pdf)

Notes

❶ It may include, but is not limited to, the following subjects.

句子大意：它包括(但不仅限于)如下内容。

❷ Initiating evacuation, if necessary (i.e. Identify under what circumstances the cabin crew will initiate an evacuation: fire, smoke, life-threatening situations, ditching, no response from the flight crew).

句子大意：如有必要，启动紧急撤离(例如确认在何种情况下客舱乘务员可启动紧急撤离程序：客舱起火、冒烟、生命受到威胁、水上迫降、飞行机组无回应等)。

❸ Locating Able-Bodied Passengers (ABPs).

句子大意：确定体格健壮旅客的位置。

其中，"Able-Bodied"意为"强壮的，健全的"，与之相反的是"disabled passenger"，意为"残障旅客"。

❹ There are documented cases of evacuations during which the passengers did not behave appropriately, and did not comply with the instructions provided by the cabin crew.

句子大意：据记载，在一些紧急撤离案例中，曾有旅客擅自行动，未遵照乘务员的指令进行撤离。

New Words and Expressions

30-second review	['sekənd][rɪ'vju:]	30秒静默
excellent	['eksələnt]	adj. 优秀；美德
responsibility	[rɪˌspɒnsə'bɪlɪti]	n. 责任，职责
perform	[pə'fɔ:m]	v. 执行；完成
phase	[feɪz]	n. 阶段
contain	[kən'teɪn]	v. 包含；控制
element	['elɪmənt]	n. 元素，要素
brace for impact	[breɪs][fɔ:]['ɪmpækt]	防冲撞姿态
command	[kə'mɑ:nd]	n. 指挥，控制；命令
initiate	[ɪ'nɪʃieɪt]	v. 开始，创始；发起
circumstance	['sɜ:kəmstəns]	n. 环境，情况
ditching	[dɪtʃɪŋ]	n. 水面迫降
assess	[ə'ses]	v. 评定；估价
Able-Bodied Passengers (ABPs)	[ˌeɪbl 'bɒdɪd] ['pæsɪndʒəs]	体格健壮的旅客
assertive	[ə'sɜ:tɪv]	adj. 肯定的；坚定而自信的
documented	['dɒkjʊməntɪd]	adj. 备有证明文件的
instruction	[ɪn'strʌkʃən]	n. 指令，命令
drill	[drɪl]	n. 训练；操练

Part E
Supplementary Reading

Try to discuss:
1. Try to guess the full form of IATA.
2. Could you list more aviation organizations?

IATA

IATA was formed in April 19, 1945 in Havana, Cuba. It is the successor to the International Air Transport Association, which was formed in 1919 at the Hague, Netherlands. At its founding, IATA consisted of 57 airlines from 31 countries. Carrying 82% of the world's air transportation, today, it has 290 members from 120 nations in every part of the world, including the world's leading passenger and cargo airlines.

Much of IATA's early work was technical and it provided input to the newly created International Civil Aviation Organization (ICAO), which was reflected in the annexes of the *Chicago Convention*, the international treaty that still governs the conduct of international air transport today.

IATA's aims:

- To promote safe, regular and economical air transport for the benefit of the peoples of the world, to foster air commerce, and to study the problems connected therewith;
- To provide means for collaboration among the air transport enterprises engaged directly or indirectly in international air transport service;
- To cooperate with the newly created International Civil Aviation Organization (ICAO-the specialized United Nations agency for civil aviation) and other international organizations.
- For over 70 years, it has developed global commercial standards upon which the air transport industry is built. The aim is to assist airlines by simplifying processes and increasing passenger convenience while reducing costs and improving efficiency. Aviation grew rapidly over the following decades and IATA's work duly expanded. It transformed its trade association activities to take account of the new dynamics in aviation, which was seeing increasing demand from the leisure sector.

(资料来源：http://en.wikipedia.org/wiki/International_Air_Transport_Association; http://www.iata.org/about/ Pages/history_2.aspx)

参考译文

国际航空运输协会

国际航空运输协会（International Air Transport Association，简称IATA）于1945年4月19日在古巴哈瓦成立。其前身是1919年在荷兰海牙成立的国际航空业务协会。成立之初的成员是来自31个国家的57家航空公司。如今，成员拓展到120个国家的290家航空公司。国际航空运输协会（IATA）的成员占全球航空运输量的82%，其中包括世界领先的客运和货运航空公司。

国际航空运输协会的早期任务是给国际民用航空组织（简称"国际民航组织"，缩写为ICAO）提供技术支持。国际民航组织是依照《芝加哥公约》规定而成立的。该公约至今在技术领域仍然进行着大量的工作，对国际民航运输进行管理。

国际航空运输协会的宗旨是：

- 保障世界人民的利益，促进安全、准时和经济的航空运输发展，扶持航空商业并研究与之相关的问题；
- 为直接或间接从事国际航空运输服务的各航空运输企业提供协作的途径；
- 为开展与国际民航组织、其他国际组织和地区航空公司协会的合作提供便利。

70多年来，国际航空运输协会已经制定了航空运输业的全球商业标准。目的是通过简化流程和增加旅客便利性，同时降低成本和提高效率来帮助航空公司。在接下来的几十年里，民航业快速发展，国际航空运输协会的工作适时扩大。鉴于人们休闲出行的需求不断增加，国际航空运输协会的工作也在考虑向这一航空新动态做出改变。

Cabin Service English

Unit 5

Passenger Comfort

* Part A Useful Words and Expressions
* Part B Dialogues
* Part C Public Announcements
* Part D Work-task
* Part E Supplementary Reading

Students will be able to:

memorize the words and expressions about Ensuring Passenger Comfort in cabin service;

make up the dialogues about Ensuring Passenger Comfort during the flight;

obtain and improve public announcements skills about Introducing Cabin Devices to Ensure Passenger Comfort;

know about Cabin Service;

introduce International Civil Aviation Organization (ICAO).

Suggested Hours: *4 class hours*

Part A
Useful Words and Expressions

◉ **Please list as many as expressions related to ensure passenger comfort in the cabin.**

_____

_____

- button
- tray table
- recline/lean back
- press
- armrest/foot rest
- pillow
- slippers
- blanket
- air conditioner
- reading light
- ear plugs
- headset
- eye mask/eye shades
- lean back
- set a channel
- crew call button
- amenity kit/overnight kit
- How may I best assist you?
- May I assist you in adjusting the seat?
- The lavatory is at the back/at the front.
- Press this button and lean back.
- Here is the toy for your child.
- It's quite cold .Would you like a cup of hot tea?
- Air travel is the safest means of modern travel.
- Sir, may I lower the window shade for you?
- Would you like an extra pillow and blanket?
- We are pleased to answer any question at any time.
- We will be right here with you anytime you press the call button.
- Would you like to put on slippers? You will be more comfortable with it.

- The reading light switch is on the left armrest.
- The tray table of the first row is in the armrest.
- We have in-flight entertainment of micro-TV and music system.
- Turn the knob of the air flow to whichever direction you like.

Culture Tips

> When talking with passengers about issues rather than safety, it's recommended that cabin attendants should use more gentle and polite expression, such as:

—Would you mind …

—Would you like to…

—May I suggest …

> While daily life English can be causal and informal, cabin English should be formal and in complete form, such as:

—Tea or coffee? (daily life English)

—Would you like some tea or coffee? (cabin English)

—Please take a look at our duty-free items? (daily life English)

—May I show/interest you our duty-free items? (cabin English)

Cabin Term

knob/button   按钮

释义：两种都指按钮，区别是button常指按下去进行开关的按钮，而knob则多指需要旋转操作的按钮。如客舱中出现的呼叫按钮、座椅调整按钮都为button；而阅读灯和空调因需要调节灯光或风力大小，都使用knob。

● **Match phrases or sentences in column B to the situations in column A.**

Column A	Column B
1. Call button	a. If you need anything, please press it.
2. Airflow system	b. You should keep the seat-belt fastened when the plane takes off or lands.
3. Reading light	c. If you press it, your seatback will recline as you like.
4. Seat-reclining button	d. By adjusting the knob, fresh air will flow in or be cut off.
5. Window shade	e. Please check your overhead locker.
6. Seat-belt	f. If you want to read something, you can turn it on.
	g. It's adjustable. But you should keep it open during taking off and landing.

● **Make up a dialogue about introducing the cabin equipment for normal use to passengers.**

Part B
Dialogues

(CA=Cabin Attendant, PAX=Passenger)

PAX: Miss, it's my first time to take your company's flight. Could you tell me what's the difference between your company and the other competing companies?

CA: As passenger requirements have changed, all our aircrafts are designed for today's comfort standards to benefit travelers.

PAX: For example?

CA: We are transforming our fleet by purchasing hundreds of new planes and refreshing existing ones to help passengers travel in comfort. Look forward to new seats, extra leg room, and bigger overhead bins to more easily store your carry-on luggage.

PAX: That's a great job!

CA: Moreover, to bring each passenger a modern and comfortable flight experience, we have made a lot of improvements to upgrade your flight experience in every cabin. Amenity kits and fully lie flat seats are available.

PAX: That's a remarkable achievement.

PAX: Excuse me. This is my first time to take a flight. I'm so nervous.

CA: Take it easy, Sir. There is a saying "Air travel is the safest means of modern travel". Furthermore, this plane is one of the most advanced types of airplane in the world, and the pilots on our flight are the most skilled aviators in our airlines. So don't worry about that.

PAX: Could you show me how to use all these buttons above my head?

CA: This is the passenger service unit system. It includes the call button, reading light and airflow system. This one is the call button. If you need anything, please press it.

PAX: Thank you. I will.

CA: You can find the reading light on the passenger service unit over your head. You can operate it by turning on or off with the button.

PAX: Good. I like to read during flight.

CA: The last one is the airflow system. By adjusting the knob, fresh air will flow in or be cut off.

PAX: I see. Let me try. Thanks.

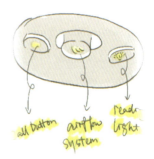

3

CA: Did you press the call button?
PAX: Yes. Everyone has a tray table but I can't find mine. Could you locate my tray table and show me how to set it?
CA: Certainly. As you are in the first row, the tray table is in the armrest. Just open the cover, pull it out and place it in front of you.
PAX: Oh, I see. Thanks.

4

PAX: Excuse me. Could you introduce the cabin equipment for normal use to me? I don't know how to use them, which makes me nervous.
CA: No problem, Sir. This one is the seat-reclining button. If you press it, your seatback will recline as you like, so you can relax and be comfortable. But you should keep it in upright position when we take off, descend and meet turbulence. Now you can try it.
PAX: Great! It's really comfortable.
CA: This is your seat-belt. For the sake of your safety, you should keep your seat-belt fastened when the plane takes off or lands. It's very easy to use it. Insert the link into the main buckle and fasten it tight and low.
PAX: Ok, it's easy.
CA: Your window shade is also adjustable. But you should lift shelter during taking off and landing.
PAX: Yes, I can lower it if I want to sleep.
CA: We have in-flight entertainment of micro-TV and music system. You can adjust the volume and select the language as you like.
PAX: Yes, that's convenient.

5

PAX: Excuse me. Do you have a cot for my baby on board?
CA: Madam, cots are not available on board. But there are some vacant seats. If the cot is needed, an armrest can be removed so your baby can lie there.
PAX: It's very kind of you to do so. Thanks.
CA: You're welcome.

6

PAX: Oh! Would you please help me adjust the air flow? It's blowing right on my head. I feel a bit cold. How can I adjust it?
CA: Don't worry Madam. You just turn the knob to whichever direction you like, or you can also shut it off by turning it tightly to the right. Have you got that?
PAX: Yes. Thank you.

New Words and Expressions

aircraft	[ˈeəkrɑːft]	n.	飞机,航空器
comfort	[ˈkʌmfət]	n.	舒适
benefit	[ˈbenɪfɪt]	v.	有益于,对……有益
transform	[trænsˈfɔːm]	v.	变换,改变
fleet	[fliːt]	n.	舰队
refresh	[rɪˈfreʃ]	v.	更新;使……恢复
amenity	[əˈmiːnəti]	n.	便利设施
kit	[kɪt]	n.	工具箱;成套工具
lie flat seat	[laɪ][flæt][siːt]		平躺座位
remarkable	[rɪˈmɑːkəbl]	adj.	卓越的;非凡的
aviator	[ˈeɪvɪeɪtə]	n.	飞行员
passenger service unit (PSU)	[ˈpæsɪndʒə(r)][ˈsəːvɪs][ˈjuːnɪt]		旅客服务组件
call button	[kɔːl][ˈbʌtən]		呼唤铃
reading light	[ˈriːdɪŋ][ˈlaɪt]		阅读灯
airflow system	[ˈeəfləʊ][ˈsɪstəm]		通风系统
knob	[nɒb]	n.	把手;旋钮
fresh air	[freʃ][eə(r)]		新鲜空气
descend	[dɪˈsend]	v.	下降
window shade	[ˈwɪndəʊ][ʃeɪd]		遮阳板
adjustable	[əˈdʒʌstəbl]	adj.	可调节的
volume	[ˈvɒljuːm]	n.	音量
convenient	[kənˈviːnjənt]	adj.	方便的
cot	[kɒt]	n.	简易床,婴儿床
whichever	[hwɪtʃˈevə]	adj.	无论哪个
direction	[dɪˈrekʃən]	n.	方向
tightly	[ˈtaɪtli]	adv.	紧紧地;坚固地

Role play the cabin attendant's responses.

PAX: Excuse me, could you come here for a moment?
CA: _____.
PAX: The air is blowing right on my head. How can I adjust it?
CA: _____.

> PAX: Yes. Thank you.
>
> PAX: Excuse me. Could you show me how to use seat-reclining button?
>   CA: _____.
> PAX: Let me try it. Er…It's really comfortable. Thank you.
>   CA: _____.
> PAX: Oh, I never notice that, thanks for your reminding.

◉ Discuss the following questions.

1. A passenger with a baby wants to have a cot, but there are no cots on the plane. What would you say to her?
2. Say something about the passenger service unit system.
3. A passenger asks: "The airflow is blowing right on me. How can I adjust it?" what would you say to him?
4. The passenger wants to get more information about safety. What would you explain to them?

◉ Make up dialogues based on the following situations.

1. Jenifer is a cabin attendant. She is trying to comfort a passenger who seems nervous with his first flight.
2. A passenger in the first row is wondering where to get his tray table. A cabin attendant comes towards him and helps him.
3. There is a passenger making phone call before take-off. The cabin attendant comes to him and persuades him to switch it off.

◉ Translate the following sentences into English.

1. 有什么我能帮忙的吗？
2. 在任何时候我们都愿意回答您的任何问题。
3. 卫生间在后面。
4. 按下这个按钮，往后躺。
5. 这是给您孩子的玩具。
6. 阅读灯的开关在左侧扶手上。
7. 现在很冷，您想喝杯热茶吗？
8. 航空旅行是现代旅行最安全的方式。
9. 先生，我可以给您关上遮阳板吗？
10. 您想多要一个枕头和毯子吗？

Part C
Public Announcements

Cabin Installations

Good morning (afternoon/evening), ladies and gentlemen,

Our aircraft for today's flight is a Boeing _____.

Your seatback can be adjusted by pressing the button on your armrest. The reading light, call button and air vents are located above your head.

The lavatory for first class passengers is in the front of the aircraft and those in the rear of the aircraft are for passengers in the main cabin. (Lavatories in the front and rear of the cabin are all available.)

If there is anything that we can do for you, please let us know.

Thank you!

Night Flight

Good evening ladies and gentlemen,

To ensure a good rest for you, we will be dimming the cabin lights. If you wish to read, please turn on the reading light switch on the overhead passenger service unit.

Because your safety is our primary concern, we strongly recommend you keep your seat-belt fastened throughout the flight.

Your cooperation in keeping the cabin quiet will be appreciated. Should you need any assistance, please press your call button.

Thank you!

WIFI

Ladies and gentlemen,

Our in-flight Wi-Fi is now available. To access a wide range of online information and services, activate the Wi-Fi function on your notebook to access a wide range of online information and services. For your safety, please make sure that your mobile phones remain switched off or set to airplane mode for the entire duration of this flight. The operation guide is available in your seat pocket.

We hope our new wireless service enhances your flying experience.

Thank you!

Poor Air Conditioning System

Ladies and gentlemen,

Good morning (afternoon/evening).

As the air conditioning system of this aircraft does not work well on the ground, you may feel a little hot at the moment. We are sorry for this inconvenience. After take-off, the cabin temperature will go down. Your understanding will be much appreciated.

Inaugural Flight

Ladies and gentlemen,

Good morning (afternoon/evening).

Welcome aboard this inaugural flight from _____ to _____. (Via _____)

We are very glad to serve you. The air distance is _____, our flying time is _____ hour(s) and _____ minutes.

At this time, please make sure that your seat-belt is fastened and the flight is refrained from smoking during the whole flight.

We are pleased to serve you onboard. If there is anything we can do for you, please let us know. We wish you a pleasant flight with _____ (Airlines).

Thank you!

New Words and Expressions

installation	[ˌɪnstəˈleɪʃən]	n.	设施；安装
air vent	[eə(r)][vent]		通风系统
locate	[ləʊˈkeɪt]	v.	定位
dim	[dɪm]	v.	使暗淡；使变暗
primary	[ˈpraɪməri]	adj.	主要的；基本的
recommend	[ˌrekəˈmend]	v.	推荐，介绍
appreciate	[əˈpriːʃieɪt]	v.	欣赏；感激
assistance	[əˈsɪstəns]	n.	援助，帮助
access	[ˈækses]	v.	使用
range	[reɪndʒ]	n.	范围，幅度
enhance	[ɪnˈhɑːns]	v.	加强，增加
air conditioning system	[eə(r)][kənˈdɪʃənɪŋ][ˈsɪstəm]		空调系统
inconvenience	[ˌɪnkənˈviːnjəns]	n.	不便；麻烦

temperature	['temprətʃə]	n. 温度,气温
inaugural flight	[ɪ'nɔːgjʊrəl][flaɪt]	首航

Speaking Practice

⦿ **Answer the following questions:**
1. Why do you think the cabin lighting is turned down on a night flight?
2. List as many possible reasons as you can to explain why cabin crew should be careful about hot drinks on board.

⦿ **Read following sentences in the right tone(′ for stress, ↗ for rising tone, ↘ for falling tone).**
1. To ensure ↗ a good ↗ rest for you ↘, we will be dimming ↗ the cabin lights ↘.
2. If you wish ↗ to read ↘, please turn on the reading ↗ light switch ↘ on the ′ overhead ↗ passenger service unit ↘.
3. Because your safety is our primary ↗ concern ↘, we ′ strongly ↗ recommend ↘ you keep your seat-belt ↘ fastened throughout ↗ the flight ↘.
4. Your cooperation in keeping the cabin quiet ↘ ′ will be appreciated ↘.
5. If you need ↗ ′ any assistance ↘, please press your call button ↘.

⦿ **Translate the following expressions into English and practice making public announcement about *cabin installations*.**
- 调暗灯光
- 座椅靠背
- 座椅扶手
- 阅读灯
- 呼唤铃
- 通风系统
- 厕所
- 前舱
- 后舱
- 安全第一
- 系紧安全带

Part D
Work-task

📋 **Try to discuss:**
1. In your understanding, how can the airline provide a 5-star cabin service?

2. Besides servicing foods or drinks to passengers in the air, what else should cabin attendants do on the flight?

Cabin Service

It's without any doubt that one of the goals of each airline's cabin service is to deliver the highest quality of cabin experience to passengers at the most cost-effective price.❶ There are several key areas that an airline needs to focus on if it aims to provide the 5-star cabin service:
- Improving and maintaining a high standard of on-board cabin experience for the passenger.
- Providing a superior level of cabin cleaning and presentation.
- Maximizing seat.
- Working on product improvements.

This approach brings the following benefits:
- Overall cabin image reaches a higher standard—passenger satisfaction levels increased.❷
- Seats achieve higher in service availability—greater airline revenue.
- Seats, seat covers, carpets and galley items gain extended in-service life and reliability—reduction in cost.❸
- Reduction in demand for seats and spares during Heavy Maintenance and reduced risk of cabin-related delays—reduction in cost, avoidance of delays.❹

As for the cabin attendant personally, to provide the best quality cabin service means a lot of patience and carefulness in his/her daily work. Once up in the air, flight attendants will usually serve drinks and/or food to passengers. When not performing customer service duties, flight attendants must periodically conduct cabin checks and listen for any unusual noises or situations. Checks must also be done on the lavatory to ensure the smoke detector hasn't been deactivated and to restock supplies as needed.❺ They must also respond to call lights dealing with special requests.

To provide the 5-star cabin service consists of a lot of key elements, such as spares and logistics management, quality inspection, cost management and reduction, and innovation in service.❻ Such an important and complex set of tasks rightly takes time to bring into being.

(资料来源：http://en.wikipedia.org/wiki/Flight_attendant; http://www.airline-services.com/Cabin-Solutions/5-star-cabin-service.php)

Notes

❶ It's without any doubt that one of the goals of each airline's cabin service is to deliver the highest quality of cabin experience to passengers at the most cost-effective price.

句子大意：毫无疑问，航空公司客舱服务的目标之一就是在最理想的成本支出下，为旅客提供最高质量的客舱体验。

其中，"It's without any doubt that…"意为"毫无疑问"，等同于"There is no doubt that…"，"There is little doubt that…"，"Without doubt"，例如：

There is little/no doubt that he will pass the test. 毫无疑问，他会通过这次测试。

Without (any) doubt, he will come to school tomorrow. 毫无疑问，明天他会去学校。

❷Overall cabin image reaches a higher standard—passenger satisfaction levels increased.

句子大意：客舱整体的体验感觉达到一个更高的标准——旅客满意度得到提升。

❸Seats, seat covers, carpets and galley items gain extended in-service life and reliability—reduction in cost.

句子大意：座椅、座套、地毯以及厨房设施的服役时间得到延长，且可靠性得到提高——成本支出得到削减。

❹Reduction in demand for seats and spares during Heavy Maintenance and reduced risk of cabin-related delays—reduction in cost, avoidance of delays.

句子大意：减少维修高峰期间对座椅和配件的维修需求，减少因客舱设施故障而引起的航班延误的风险——成本支出得到削减，并且避免了航班延误。

❺Checks must also be done on the lavatory to ensure the smoke detector hasn't been deactivated and to restock supplies as needed.

句子大意：(乘务员)须对厕所进行检查，以确保厕所内的烟雾探测器处于正常工作状态，并且及时补充洗刷用品。

❻To provide the 5-star cabin service consists of a lot of key elements, such as spares and logistics management, quality inspection, cost management and reduction, and innovation in service.

句子大意：5星级的客舱服务涉及很多关键环节：配件和后勤管理、质量检查、成本管理和控制以及服务创新等。

New Words and Expressions

deliver	[dɪˈlɪvə]	v. 实现；传送；履行
cost-effective	[ˌkɒstɪˈfektɪv]	adj. 成本效益好的；划算的
maintain	[meɪnˈteɪn]	v. 维持；继续；维修
superior	[sjuːˈpɪrɪə]	adj. 优秀的，出众的
presentation	[ˌprezənˈteɪʃən]	n. 呈现；陈述；介绍
approach	[əˈprəʊtʃ]	n. 方法；途径
overall	[ˈəʊvərɔːl]	adj. 全部的；全体的
image	[ˈɪmɪdʒ]	n. 印象；图像；影像
revenue	[ˈrevənjuː]	n. 收益；税收
carpet	[ˈkɑːpɪt]	n. 地毯
reliability	[rɪˌlaɪəˈbɪlətɪ]	n. 可靠性
spares	[speəz]	n. 备件

reduction	[rɪ'dʌkʃən]	n.	减少；下降
delay	[dɪ'leɪ]	n.	延期；推迟
patience	['peɪʃns]	n.	耐心
periodically	[ˌpɪərɪ'ɒdɪkəlɪ]	adv.	定期地；周期性地
smoke detector	[sməʊk][dɪtektə]		烟雾探测器
deactivate	[diːˈæktɪveɪt]	v.	使无效；使不活动
restock	[ˌriː'stɒk]	v.	补充货源；补足
logistics	[ləʊ'dʒɪstɪks]	n.	后勤
inspection	[ɪn'spekʃən]	n.	视察，检查
innovation	[ˌɪnəʊ'veɪʃən]	n.	创新，革新

Part E
Supplementary Reading

Try to discuss:
1. How would you introduce the International Civil Aviation Organization (ICAO)?
2. What are the main goals of ICAO?

IACO

The International Civil Aviation Organization (ICAO) is a specialized agency of the United Nations established by various countries in 1944 to manage the administrative and governance aspects of the *Convention on International Civil Aviation* (*Chicago Convention*). ICAO is composed of a three-tier framework of General Assembly, Council and Secretariat. The General Assembly is the highest authority and is composed of all member states, which is convened by the Council and is generally held every three years. The Council is a permanent body responsible to the Assembly and is composed of 33 contracting states elected by the Assembly. The council meets three times a year, and the duration of each meeting is approximately two months. The Secretariat is the permanent administrative body of the ICAO, and the Secretary-General is responsible for ensuring the smooth progress of the various tasks of it.

ICAO cooperates with 193 member states and industry groups of the *Convention on International Civil Aviation* to reach consensus on International Civil Aviation standards and recommended practices (SARPs) to support a safe, effective, secure, economically sustainable and environmentally responsible civil aviation industry. ICAO member states use these standards and recommended practices to ensure that their local civil aviation operations and regulations comply with global

norms, which in turn enables more than 100,000 flights per day within the global aviation network to operate safely and reliably in various regions of the world.

The purpose of the ICAO is to develop the principles and technologies of international navigation and to promote the development of international air transport in order to achieve the following goals:

- Ensure the safe and orderly development of international civil aviation worldwide;
- Encourage the design and operation of aircraft for peaceful purposes;
- Encourage the development of routes, airports and navigation facilities for international civil aviation applications;
- Meet the needs of the people of the world for safe, normal, efficient and economical air transportation;
- Prevent economic waste caused by unreasonable competition;
- Ensure that the rights of contracting countries are fully respected, and that every contracting country has a fair opportunity to operate an international airline;
- Avoid differential treatment between contracting countries;
- Promote flight safety in international navigation;
- Promote the development of international civil aviation in all aspects.

In addition to the core work of reaching consensus on international standards, measures and policies among its member states and industry, as well as many other priorities and programs, ICAO also coordinates assistance and capacity-building activities for states to support various aviation development goals; prepares global plans to coordinate multilateral strategic progress in safety and air navigation; monitors and reports on various performance measurement standards of the air transport sector; and audits the civil aviation supervision of various countries in safety and security ability.

(资料来源:https://www.icao.int/Pages/default.aspx)

参考译文

国际民用航空组织

国际民用航空组织(ICAO,以下简称国际民航组织)是各国于1944年创建的一个联合国专门机构,旨在对《国际民用航空公约》(《芝加哥公约》)的行政和治理方面进行管理。国际民航组织由大会、理事会和秘书处三级框架组成。大会是国际民航组织的最高权力机构,由全体成员国组成。大会由理事会召集,一般情况下每三年举行一次。理事会是向大会负责的常设机构,由大会选出的33个缔约国组成。理事会每年召开三次会议,每次会议会期约为两个月。秘书处是国际民航组织的常设行政机构,由秘书长负责保证国际民航组织各项工作的顺利进行。

国际民航组织与《国际民用航空公约》193个成员国和行业集团进行合作,就国际民用航空的标准和建议措施(SARPs)及政策达成协商一致,以支持一个安全、有效、可靠、经济上可持续和对环境负责的民用航空业。国际民航组织成员国使用这些标准和建议措施及政策来确保其本地民用航空运行和规章符合全球规范,这反过来又使得全球航空网络内每天10万多架次航班在世界各个地区安全和可靠地运行。

国际民航组织的宗旨和目的在于发展国际航行的原则和技术,促进国际航空运输的规划和发展,以便实现下列各项目标:
- 确保全世界国际民用航空安全和有秩序地发展;
- 鼓励用来维持和平的航空器的设计和操作技术;
- 鼓励发展国际民用航空应用的航路、机场和航行设施;
- 满足世界人民对安全、正常、有效和经济的航空运输的需要;
- 防止因不合理的竞争而造成经济上的浪费;
- 保证各缔约国的权利充分受到尊重,每一缔约国均有经营国际空运企业的公平的机会;
- 避免各缔约国之间的差别待遇;
- 促进国际航行的飞行安全;
- 普遍促进国际民用航空在各方面的发展。

除了在其成员国和行业之间就国际标准和建议措施及政策达成共识的这一核心工作,以及许多其他优先事项和方案之外,国际民航组织还为针对各国的援助和能力建设活动进行协调,以支持各项航空发展目标;编写全球计划,对安全和空中航行的多边战略性进展进行协调;监测并报告航空运输部门各种绩效衡量标准;审计各国在安全和安保方面的民用航空监督能力。

Unit 6

Beverage Service

✿ Part A Useful Words and Expressions   ✿ Part B Dialogues
✿ Part C Public Announcements   ✿ Part D Work-task
✿ Part E Supplementary Reading

Students will be able to:
memorize the words and expressions about beverage service in the cabin;
make up the dialogues about beverage service in the cabin;
obtain and improve public announcements skills about beverage service;
know about general knowledge of beverage service in the cabin;
introduce the Star Alliance.

Suggested Hours: *4 class hours*

Unit 6　Beverage Service

Part A
Useful Words and Expressions

◉ **Please list as many ways to serve beverages and give suggestions to passengers as possible.**

_____

_____

- soft drink
- alcohol
- refreshments
- black coffee / white coffee
- weak tea / strong tea
- Coke / Sprite / fruit juice / mineral water
- Excuse me, Sir / Miss.
- Sorry to interrupt you, Sir / Madam.
- Is there anything you like?
- We have … options available.
- … might be better.
- Which would you prefer / care for / like?
- Would you like / prefer / care for something else?
- Would you like to have a try / have a taste?
- Would you like to / care to have something to drink?
- Would you like … instead?
- May I make a suggestion that…
- May I offer you … instead?
- How would you like your coffee / your tea / your whiskey?
- Enjoy your drinks!
- Please take care. It's so hot.

Culture Tips

➢ Use formal and courteous language that meets airlines standards.
➢ Offer your assistance and suggestion to passengers using the language:
— How would you like…
— Would you like …
— Which would you prefer…
➢ Avoid using casual and impolite language like:
— Can I give you…
— Do you like…
— Do you want…

— Which do you want?
— This one or that one?

Cabin Term

drinks/beverages 饮料

释义：两个词均泛指所有可饮用的饮料，包括水、狭义的饮料、酒水等。以下列出客舱英语中较为常见的饮料：

tea (with lemon / milk、hot/ice、black/green)
coffee (with sugar / milk、hot/ice)
Coke / Sprite (with ice)
mineral water (with ice)
alcoholic drinks: wine / brandy/whisky / gin / vodka / cognac (straight / on the rocks)

● Match phrases or sentences in column B to the situations in column A.

Column A	Column B
1. How would you like your Whiskey?	a. That would be nice.
2. How would you like your tea?	b. Make it straight, please.
3. How would you like your coffee?	c. Ok, why not.
4. Would you care to have a try?	d. With some milk, please.
5. How about having some hot liquid?	e. Make it strong.
6. What would you like to drink, Sir?	f. Nothing. Thank you.
7. Would you prefer coffee or tea?	g. Either will be ok for me.

● Make up a dialogue about beverage service on board.

Part B
Dialogues

(CA=Cabin Attendant, PAX=Passenger)

1

PAX: Excuse me, Miss. I've got a question.
CA: Yes, what can I do for you?
PAX: This is the very first time I take plane and do I have to pay for any of the drinks on the plane?

Unit 6　Beverage Service

CA: Not necessarily, Madam. All the soft drinks are free to all passengers. However, bar service is offered to first class and business class passengers on a complimentary basis.

PAX: Oh, thank you, I see. What soft drinks do you serve?

CA: We have prepared tea, coffee, Coke, Sprite, fruit juice and mineral water. Which would you prefer?

PAX: It is quite cold outside. I think just a cup of hot tea will do.

2

CA: Excuse me, Miss. We have prepared various tea and refreshments for you to enjoy the leisure onboard. Which would you prefer?

PAX: I have no idea. Would you like to give me some recommendations?

CA: Would you like a cup of coffee? It's about to land and a cup of coffee will give you a lift.

PAX: I can't agree with you more. In that case, please give me a cup of coffee.

CA: Sure. Then how would you like your coffee, black or white?

PAX: Black coffee will be better.

CA: Enjoy your coffee!

3

CA: Excuse me, Sir. Would you care for some hot drinks? Today we have coffee and tea. Which one would you prefer?

PAX: Coffee, please.

CA: With milk and sugar?

PAX: Black coffee, please.

CA: Please take care. It's very hot.

4

PAX: Miss, why haven't I got any drinks? I am so thirsty. When will the drinks be served to me?

CA: I'll be serving right now. What would you like to drink? We have prepared tea, coffee, juice, carbonated drinks, mineral water, and alcoholic drinks like wine, brandy, whisky, gin and vodka, what would you like to have?

PAX: Just a cup of Black Label.

CA: Sorry, Sir. Black Label is not available on board. Would you like something instead?

PAX: Since there is no Black Label on board, I'd rather have a cup of green tea.

CA: Thank you for understanding, Sir. This is your green tea. Please enjoy it!

5

CA: Excuse me, Madam. It seems that the tea is getting cold. Let me make a new one for you.

PAX: Oh, finally you come! I have asked many times to refill my tea. Nobody is answering me. I have been waiting for almost ten minutes!

CA: I am awfully sorry for that, Madam. I'll get you one right away. With lemon or milk?

PAX: I don't feel like tea any more. I am very thirsty now. Do you have mineral water?

CA: Yes, Madam. Let me get you one at once.

6

PAX: I'd like to taste some wine, please. What wine do you serve on board?

CA: We have red wine, white wine, cognac, whisky, gin, vodka, which would you like?

PAX: Let me see…how about whiskey?

CA: Sure, Sir. Then, how would you like your whiskey? Straight or on the rocks?

PAX: On the rocks, please. It's a little bit hot here.

CA: Certainly, a glass of whiskey on the rocks. This is your whiskey on the rocks, Sir. Would you like a cup of water as well?

PAX: That would be perfect! Thank you for your service!

New Words and Expressions

necessarily	[ˌnesə'serəlɪ]	adv.	必然地;必定地
complimentary	[ˌkɒmplɪ'mentrɪ]	adj.	免费的
sprite	[spraɪt]	n.	雪碧;妖精
fruit juice	[fruːt][dʒuːs]	n.	果汁
mineral water	['mɪnərəl]['wɔːtə(r)]	n.	矿泉水
refreshment	[rɪ'freʃmənt]	n.	点心;精力恢复
enjoy the leisure	[en'dʒɒɪ][ðə]['leʒə]		享受休闲时光
give sb a lift	[gɪv][əɪ][lɪft]		提神
black coffee	[blæk]['kɒfɪ]		不加牛奶(或糖)的咖啡
carbonated	['kɑːbəneɪtɪd]	adj.	碳化的,含碳酸的
Black Label	[blæk]['leɪbəl]	n.	酒水名称,黑方威士忌
refill	[riː'fɪl]	v.	再装满
straight or on the rocks	[streɪt][ɔː][ɒn][ðə][rɒks]		直喝还是加冰喝(酒水)

● Role play the cabin attendant's responses.

CA: _____.
PAX: A cup of tea, please.
CA: _____.

Unit 6　Beverage Service

> PAX: With lemon please.
> CA: _____.
> PAX: Thank you very much.
> CA: You're welcome.
>
> PAX: What do you have for drinks?
> CA: _____.
> PAX: Well, you have a wide selection of drinks. Are all the drinks free on board?
> CA: _____.
> PAX: Miss, I am thirsty now. Can I have Coke with some ice?
> CA: _____.

⦿ Discuss the following questions.

1. How would the cabin attendants tell the passengers what drinks are available?
2. A passenger wants a bottle of Black Label that has run out of stock on the flight. what would you say to the passenger?
3. A passenger has asked many times for a cup of tea, but he hasn't got it. When you face such an irritated passenger, what would you say?
4. A passenger was sleeping while you were serving. After he wakes up, he complains he hasn't got a drink. What would you say to the passenger?
5. What do you do with drunk or disorderly passengers?

⦿ Make up dialogues based on the following situations.

1. A cabin attendant is trying to give suggestions to a passenger who feels hot and thirsty and wants to have some drinks.
2. A cabin attendant is talking to a passenger who asks whiskey for the fourth time but it is obvious that he is kind of drunk.
3. Try to talk to a passenger who takes plane for the very first time, and he asked about the beverage service on board.
4. A passenger is very angry because his drink has not been served yet while other passengers have got their drinks already.

⦿ Translate the following sentences into English.

1. 您要什么样的咖啡，黑咖啡还是加奶咖啡？
2. 您要什么样的茶，淡茶还是浓茶？
3. 我们有各种酒水可供选择。
4. 来些点心可能会更好。
5. 您更喜欢哪一个？您还要些其他的吗？
6. 不然换成橙汁可以吗？

7. 我建议您来些茶和点心，享受一下机上休闲时光吧。
8. 给您提供一杯红酒代替可以吗？
9. 您要什么样的威士忌，加冰还是不加冰？
10. 您想喝点什么吗？

Part C
Public Announcements

Beverage Service Announcement

Ladies and gentlemen,

We will be serving you tea, coffee, and other soft drinks. You're welcome to make your choice. Please put down the table in front of you. For the convenience of the passenger behind you, please return your seatback to the upright position.

Thank you!

Drink Service before Meal

Ladies and gentlemen,

Now we are going to serve refreshments and drinks. We shall be serving tea, coffee, Coke, Sprite, orange juice and mineral water in a moment. You are welcome to take your choice.

Thank you!

No Beverage Service Announcement

Ladies and gentlemen,

We are sorry to inform you that we cannot serve you hot drinks on this flight because the water system is out of order. However, we will be able to serve cold drinks.

We apologize for the inconvenience caused.

Thank you for your understanding.

Unit 6 Beverage Service

Sale of Beverages

Ladies and gentlemen,

We will begin our beverage service shortly, followed by lunch (dinner). (Whiskey and brandy at __ US dollars are available for purchase in the main cabin.)

Thank you!

Beverage and Food Service

Ladies and gentlemen,

On this flight, we will serve you soft drinks and a main course (snacks, refreshment, breakfast, light meal, souvenir, and duty-free shop). We wish you a pleasant and comfortable flight.

Thank you!

New Words and Expressions

soft drinks	[sɒft][drɪŋks]	软饮料（不含酒精）
make your choice	[meɪk][jɒr][tʃɒɪs]	做出选择
convenience	[kən'viːnɪəns]	n. 方便,合宜
for the convenience of	[fɔː][ðə][kən'viːnɪəns][əv]	为了……的方便
in a moment	[ɪn][eɪ]['wɔːdtə]	立刻,马上
take your choice	[teɪk][jɔː(r)][tʃɒɪs]	做出选择
hot drink	[hɒt][drɪŋk]	热饮
out of order	[aʊt][əv]['ɔːdə]	故障
cold drink	[kəʊld][drɪŋk]	冷饮
main course	[meɪn][kɔːs]	主食
snack	[snæk]	n. 小吃,点心
light meal	[laɪt][miːl]	便餐
souvenir	[ˌsuːvə'nɪə(r)]	n. 纪念品,礼物

Speaking Practice

● **Practice making announcements about *beverage* with these alternatives.**

- tomato juice/orange juice/coconut milk
- champagne/wine/whiskey/beer
- lemonade/sprite/seven-up
- gin and tonic water/mineral water

⦿ **Read following sentences in the right tone(′ for stress, ↗ for rising tone, ↘ for falling tone).**

1. ′Now we are going ↗ to serve ↘ refreshments ↗ and drinks ↘.
2. We shall be serving ↗ tea ↗, coffee ↗, Coke ↗, sprite ↗, orange juice ↗ and mineral water ↘ in a moment ↘.
3. You are ′ welcome ↗ to take your choice ↘.
4. We ′ apologize for the inconvenience ↗ caused ↘.
5. We wish ↗ you a pleasant ↗ and comfortable flight ↘.

⦿ **Translate the following expressions into English and practice making public announcement about beverage service.**

- 放下小桌板
- 饮品服务
- 欢迎选择饮料
- 谢谢您的理解
- 故障
- 主菜和点心
- 为了他人的方便
- 饮料供应的时间到了
- 冷饮、热饮
- 祝您旅途愉快

Part D
Work-task

📋 **Try to discuss:**
1. What drinks can passengers enjoy on board?
2. Are all the drinks on board free?

Flight Drinks

With the exception of very short-haul flights, the majority of airlines provide food and beverages to passengers.❶ A number of different beverages are served throughout the flight. They range from tea and coffee to alcoholic drinks such as wines, spirits and also soft drinks. Food is not usually cooked on the plane, but can be heated using the ovens in the galley (the kitchen area in an aircraft).

The meals are cooked either by catering companies in different cities or in the airline's own kitchens near the airport. The airline catering companies deliver the food and drink to the aircraft before take-off.

Unit 6　Beverage Service

　　In economy class, the drink trolley is pushed along the aisle stopping at all passengers' seats and drinks are poured there, whereas in business and first class the drinks are ordered by the passengers and prepared in the galley area and served to the passengers on a tray.❷

　　Drink service varies considerably from airline to airline. Some alcoholic drinks are free to all passengers, whereas, other airlines will charge economy class passengers whilst there is no charge for business and first class passengers.❸ Soft drinks, tea and coffee are usually always free.

　　Most CAs are trained in how to set tables, wine and champagne presentation, plating, garnishing or napkin folds as serving techniques.❹ And these skills can be utilized in first class and business class. After passengers have had their meals, the CAs must then collect the meal trays and trash and stow everything away in its proper place.

（资料来源：http://wenku.baidu.com）

Notes

❶With the exception of very short-haul flights, the majority of airlines provide food and beverages to passengers.

句子大意：除非是非常短的短程航班，大多数航空公司都会为旅客提供食物和饮料。

short-haul flights指的是短程航班，而长途飞行则为long-haul flights。

❷In economy class, the drink trolley is pushed along the aisle stopping at all passengers' seats and drinks are poured there, whereas in business and first class the drinks are ordered by the passengers and prepared in the galley area and served to the passengers on a tray.

句子大意：在经济舱，装有饮料的推车会在走廊上穿梭，乘务员将推车停在旅客的座位旁边，为旅客提供饮料。然而在商务舱或者头等舱，饮料往往是由旅客先从菜单上点，然后由乘务员在厨房准备后用托盘向旅客提供。

其中，trolley指手推车，tray指托盘。

❸Some alcoholic drinks are free to all passengers, whereas, other airlines will charge economy class passengers whilst there is no charge for business and first class passengers.

句子大意：某些酒水对所有旅客都是免费的。也有一些航空公司酒水对经济舱的旅客收费，而对商务舱和头等舱的旅客则是免费的。

charge sb.：问某人索取费用。

例如，He always charges me too much for his goods. 他总是向我索取过高的货价。

❹Most CAs are trained in how to set tables, wine and champagne presentation, plating, garnishing or napkin folds as serving techniques.

句子大意：大多数乘务员会参加培训，培训内容包括诸如以下几方面的服务技巧：摆放桌子、酒水以及香槟等，如何放置餐盘、装饰物以及折叠餐巾等。

garnishing指装饰物。napkin folds指餐巾折叠。

79

New Words and Expressions

short-haul	[ˈʃɒtːˈhɔːl]	短途
majority	[məˈdʒɒrətɪ]	n. 多数,大多数
throughout	[θrʊˈaʊt]	prep. 遍及;贯穿
alcoholic	[ˌælkəˈhɒlɪk]	n. 含酒精的饮料,酒精
catering company	[ˈkeɪtərɪŋ][ˈkʌmp(ə)nɪ]	配餐公司
trolley	[ˈtrɒlɪ]	n. 手推车,台车;无轨电车;有轨电车
tray	[treɪ]	n. 盘,托盘,碟
considerably	[kənˈsɪdərəblɪ]	adv. 显著地;十分
CA (cabin attendant)		乘务员
champagne	[ʃæmˈpen]	n. 香槟酒
garnish	[ˈgarnɪʃ]	n. 装饰
napkin	[ˈnæpkɪn]	n. 装饰
trash	[træʃ]	n. 垃圾;废物

Part E
Supplementary Reading

Try to discuss:
1. Have you heard of Star Alliance?
2. Which airline in China joins Star Alliance?

Star Alliance

On May 14, 1997, five airlines from three continents-Scandinavian Airlines, Thai Airways International, Air Canada, Lufthansa, and United Airlines came together to launch Star Alliance, headquartered in Frankfurt am Main, Germany. The five airlines shared the traditional star logo from the beginning with the five points representing the five founding airlines. The alliance also adopted their first slogan "The Airline Network for Earth", with the goal being to have "an alliance that will take passengers to every major city on earth". As the first global airline alliance to "better meet the needs of the frequent international traveler" and is now the world's largest global alliance.

In May 2017, Star Alliance and its members celebrated the alliance's 20th anniversary of "connecting people and cultures". Also, a new strategy of harnessing digital technology to further enhance the journey experience of Star Alliance customers comes into action. Initially, Star Alliance only had a membership of five airlines. Today, the Alliance has expanded to 26 member airlines, who together offer a comprehensive network spanning 195 countries worldwide.

Star Alliance has two premium levels, Silver and Gold, based on a customer's tier status in a member carrier's frequent flyer program. The statuses have no specific requirements of their own, membership is based solely on the frequent flyer programs of individual member airlines. Many member airlines also have an additional premium status beyond Gold which is not recognized across Star Alliance.

Until 2019, Star Alliance is named Best Airline Alliance for the fourth time running and its Los Angeles Lounge receives Best Airline Alliance Lounge for the fifth consecutive year at the Skytrax World Airline Awards.

(资料来源：http://en.wikipedia.org/wiki/Star_Alliance)

参考译文

星 空 联 盟

星空联盟成立于1997年5月14日，总部位于德国法兰克福。星空联盟的企业识别标志是一个由5个三角形图样组合而成的五角星，象征创立联盟的5个初始会员：北欧航空、泰国国际航空、加拿大航空、汉莎航空以及联合航空。之前使用的标语"地球的航空网络"如今已经被"地球联结的方式"所取代。作为全球第一个为了更好地迎合国际常旅客的需要而成立的航空联盟，星空联盟现如今是全球最大的航空联盟。

2017年5月，星空联盟及其成员以"将人与文化融合"为主题庆祝该联盟成立20周年。此外，一项利用数字技术进一步增强星空联盟客户旅程体验的新策略也已付诸实践。最初，星空联盟只有5个航空公司成员。如今，该联盟已扩展到26个航空公司成员，它们共同提供了覆盖全球195个国家的全面网络。

星空联盟有银卡和金卡两个级别。级别的认定基于旅客在联盟中任何一个航空公司常旅客计划的级别水准。卡的等级获得没有什么特殊要求；会员是完全基于个人会员航空公司的飞行常旅客计划。许多成员航空公司也有额外的优惠，但是在星空联盟不通用。

截至2019年，星空联盟连续四次蝉联最佳航空公司联盟，其洛杉矶贵宾室连续第五年获得五星航空公司(Skytrax)世界航空公司大奖的"最佳航空公司联盟贵宾室"称号。

Cabin Service English

Unit 7

Food Service I

* Part A Useful Words and Expressions
* Part B Dialogues
* Part C Public Announcements
* Part D Work-task
* Part E Supplementary Reading

Students will be able to:
memorize the words and expressions about food service in the cabin;
make up the dialogues about food service in the cabin;
obtain and improve public announcements skills about food service;
know about general knowledge of food service in the cabin;
introduce the Oneworld.

Suggested Hours: *4 class hours*

Unit 7　Food Service I

Part A
Useful Words and Expressions

◉ **Please list ways to serve food and give suggestions to passengers on board as many as possible.**

_____
_____

- main dish / main course
- allergic
- appetite
- hors d'oeuvres / starters / appetisers
- Dinner will be served soon.
- Dinner is going to be served at …
- We will serve your dinner soon.
- We will be serving dinner soon.
- We are going to serve dinner in a moment.
- Here is the menu. / May I present you the menu?
- Here is your fish / chicken / steak / beef.
- I strongly recommend Roast Duck. It's specialty here.
- We have chicken with rice and beef with noddles, which one would you prefer?
- May I offer you some drinks to go with your meal?
- Please make/take your choice.
- You're welcome to make your choice.
- May I take your order?
- Are you ready to order?
- What would you like for the main dish/ dessert/ hors d'oeuvres/ dinner?
- What would you like to go with your main dish?
- Would you like to try / taste some beef/ chicken?
- Would you like some beef?
- How would you like your steak, rare, medium or well-done?
- How would you like your salad, with French dressing or Thousand Island dressing?
- Would you like anything else?

Culture Tips

> When passengers express their dissatisfaction or unhappiness, try to show your empathy by using language like:

— I can understand you. / I can totally understand you.

e.g. — My stomach is uncomfortable when taking plane…
　　　— I can totally understand you…would you like to have…

> When passengers ask questions like "May I …" or "can I …", avoid using "Ok", try to say "sure" or "certainly".

e.g. — May I have another cup of tea, please?

— Sure / certainly.

Cabin Term

Hors d'oeuvres / Starters / Appetisers 开胃菜

释义：Hors d'oeuvres源自于法语，一般指招待会、晚餐前吃的开胃小菜。Starter 用来指餐前的第一道分量稍少的菜品。Appetiser 指小份的餐前菜或酒。开胃菜是西餐中第一道菜肴，用来开胃唤起食欲，具有数量少、口感清爽的特点。

● Match phrases or sentences in column B to the situations in column A.

Column A	Column B
1. How would you like your steak?	a. I have no idea what to order.
2. May I take your order?	b. Rare, please.
3. How would you like your cheese?	c. Thank you.
4. Would you like anything else?	d. Sharp, please.
5. Here is your fish.	e. I am stuffed.
6. What would you like for dessert?	f. Just some cake, please.

● Make up a dialogue about food service on board.

Part B
Dialogues

(CA=Cabin Attendant, PAX=Passenger)

PAX: Excuse me, Miss. When will you serve dinner? I am kind of hungry now.

CA: I am afraid that dinner will not be available on short flights. Refreshments and beverages will be provided. We have prepared various tea and refreshments for you to enjoy. May I offer you some refreshments, Sir?

PAX: Oh, you are so thoughtful! Speaking of refreshments, what do you usually have?
CA: We have biscuits, bread and cakes. What would you care to have?
PAX: Er…none of them is to my taste.
CA: Would you like some fruit? I am glad to tell you that we have prepared some fresh fruit this morning, they are sweet and juicy. Would you like to have a try?
PAX: My mouth has already been watering. Fresh fruit is my favorite! Do you have melon?
CA: Yes. Here is your melon, Sir. Hope you enjoy the taste!

2

CA: May I present you the menu for today? There are some options for the main course on this page. You may have a look at the menu first, and I will be coming along to take your order in a short while.
PAX: Ok, let me see…what is generally the main dish on board?
CA: As they are on the menu, roast beef, chicken, fish and steak are always prepared.
PAX: I have no idea what to order. Would you like to give me some suggestions?
CA: Fish is very popular on board. It is cooked with a special flavour.

PAX: What a pity! I am allergic to fish.
CA: I am sorry to hear that. In that case, would you like to try some roast beef? It is also popular on board.
PAX: Roast beef will be fine for me. Then, a serving of roast beef, please!
CA: Certainly. I will be back in a minute with the roast beef.

3

CA: Excuse me, Sir, but could you pass the tray to the passenger by the window?
PAX: All right.
CA: Thank you, Sir. And may I take your order now?
PAX: Yes, I think so. I've read the menu. But I don't have any appetite. Do you have any good recommendations?
CA: Would you like some hors d'oeuvres? They are light and easily digested.
PAX: What kind of hors d'oeuvres do you serve?
CA: We have a wide choice of hors d'oeuvres, such as salmon, pate and some Chinese delicacies.

PAX: Then some Chinese delicacies, please. Also I want to try a serving of chicken. I've heard that chicken in your flight is tasty.
CA: No problem. Chinese delicacies and chicken will be served in a minute.

④

CA: Excuse me, Sir. The meal will start at 11:30. Are you ready to take a look at the menu and later I'll come back to find out what you like.

PAX: Ok, Miss. I also have a question. What's the difference between the meal service of First Class and Economy?

CA: The service in First Class is similar to that in a fine restaurant, with many different courses and wines. In the Economy Class, the procedure and the course are much simpler.

PAX: Ok, I see. What is popular on board today?

CA: We have a selection of Chinese dishes. And I strongly recommend Roast Duck. It's specialty here.

PAX: Wow! That's fantastic; then give me a serving of Roast Duck.

CA: Hope you enjoy the meal.

⑤

CA: Excuse me, Sir. We will serve you dinner soon. May I unfold the tray table for you?

PAX: Yes, please.

CA: For the main dish today, we have chicken with rice and beef with bread. Which one would you prefer?

PAX: Beef please.

CA: Certainly, Sir. May I offer you some drink to go with your meal?

PAX: Would you please give me some recommendations?

CA: According to your preference, I will suggest you the red wine. It goes well with your meal. Would you like to have a taste?

PAX: Yes, please.

⑥

CA: How is the dinner, Sir? Did you enjoy it?

PAX: Fantastic! Chinese dish has never been out of my expectation! I enjoyed it a lot!

CA: I am glad to hear that. Would you like something else, Sir?

PAX: No, thank you. I've had quite enough.

CA: We've got a wide choice of desserts, would you care to have some?

PAX: But I feel like a cup of coffee…black coffee.

CA: Sure. I'll go and get one for you.

PAX: Thank you!

Unit 7 Food Service I

New Words and Expressions

short flights	[fɔːt][flaɪt]		短途航班
thoughtful	[ˈθɔːtfl]	adj.	深思的；体贴的
juicy	[ˈdʒuːsi]	adj.	多汁的
mouth is watering	[maʊθ][ɪz][ˈwɒtərɪŋ]		流口水
menu	[ˈmenjuː]	n.	菜单
flavour	[ˈfleɪvə(r)]	n.	香味，滋味
allergic	[əˈledʒɪk]	adj.	过敏
allergic to	[əˈledʒɪk][tuː]		对……过敏
a serving of	[ə][ˈsɜːvɪŋ][əv]		一份
appetite	[ˈæpɪtaɪt]	n.	胃口
digest	[daɪˈdʒest]	v.	消化
hors d'oeuvres	[ɒˈdəvrəs]	n.	（法）开胃菜
easily digested	[ˈiːzɪli][daɪˈdʒestɪd]		容易消化的
delicacy	[ˈdelɪkəsi]	n.	美味；精美
specialty	[ˈspeʃəlti]	n.	招牌菜

Role play the cabin attendant's responses.

CA: _____.
PAX: Ok, a serving of fish, please.
CA: _____.
PAX: Rare, please.
CA: _____.
PAX: Thank you.
CA: _____.
PAX: I've got enough.
CA: _____.
PAX: That would be better. What drinks do you have?
CA: _____.
PAX: Coffee, please.

PAX: Excuse me, when will the dinner be served?
CA: _____.
PAX: What do you have for main course?
CA: _____.

> PAX: What do you offer beside main dish?
> CA: _____.
> PAX: What's the difference between the meal service of First Class and Economy?
> CA: _____.

◉ Discuss the following questions.

1. Generally, what is main dish on board?
2. A passenger wants some more chicken, but actually there is no more chicken left in the galley. What would you say to him?
3. When passengers are offered meals on board, besides the main dish, what else can they be served?
4. If a cabin attendant wants to pass the tray to the passengers by the window, who are out of her reach, what should she do?
5. What is the difference between the meal service of First and Economy Class?

◉ Make up dialogues based on the following situations.

1. Talk to a passenger who is allergic to sea food and needs your recommendations about what food he can have on board.
2. A passenger prefers another serving of fish since the fish is to his taste. A cabin attendant needs to go to check whether there is more left.
3. Please try to give suggestions to a passenger who reads the menu for a while, but still has no idea in his mind what to order.

◉ Translate the following sentences into English.

1. 我们将很快为您提供晚餐。
2. 这是您的鱼/牛肉/牛排。
3. 请您点餐。/欢迎您点餐。
4. 您要点餐了吗?
5. 主菜/甜点/餐前小菜(冷盘)/晚餐您要点什么?
6. 您的主菜要什么配菜呢?
7. 您想尝尝牛肉/鸡肉吗?
8. 您的牛排要几分熟? 三分熟、五分熟还是全熟?
9. 沙拉您要什么口味,是法式调味酱还是千岛酱?
10. 我对鱼过敏,而且也没什么胃口,您有什么好的建议吗?

Unit 7　Food Service I

Part C
Public Announcements

📢 Meal Service Announcements on Short-haul Flights

Ladies and gentlemen,

　　You may enjoy (breakfast / lunch / supper/ refreshments / dinner / night snack) and various drinks service in about _____ minutes.

　　Thank you!

📢 Meal Announcements on International Long-haul Flights

Ladies and gentlemen,

　　You may enjoy (breakfast / lunch / supper/ refreshments/ dinner/ night snack) and various drinks service in about _____ minutes. Also the second meal will be served _____ hours before landing. (The second meal will be served at _____.)

　　During the meal service, please return your seatback to the upright position for the convenience of the passengers seated behind you.

　　Thank you!

📢 Meal Service Announcement on Long-haul Flights I

Ladies and gentlemen,

　　The meal will be serving soon. We have a selection of main course today. You're welcome to make your choice. Please put down the table in front of you while we are serving you the meal. For the convenience of the passenger behind you, please return your seatback to the upright position during the meal service.

　　Thank you!

📢 Meal Service Announcement on Long-haul Flights II

Good morning (afternoon/evening), ladies and gentlemen,

The meal will be served in a minute. We have prepared a good selection of dishes with both Chinese cuisine and western cuisine for you. We also carry tins of vegetarian food in case that you forgot to remind us of your special diet when booking the flight. You can read the menu carefully and you're welcome to make your choice. We will take your order later.

Please put down the table in front of you. For the convenience of the passenger behind you, please return your seatback to the upright position during the meal service.

Thank you!

New Words and Expressions

a selection of	[ə][sɪˈlekʃən][əv]	一系列的
cuisine	[kwɪˈzɪn]	n. 风味
Chinese cuisine	[ˌtʃaɪˈniːz][kwɪˈziːn]	中国风味
Western cuisine	[ˈwestən][kwɪˈziːn]	西方风味
vegetarian	[ˈvedʒəˈtɛrɪən]	n. 素食主义者,素食餐
vegetarian diet	[ˈvedʒəˈtɛrɪən][ˈdaɪət]	素食餐
special diet	[ˈspeʃəl][ˈdaɪət]	特殊餐饮
book the flight	[bʊk][ðə][flaɪt]	预订机票
take order	[teɪk][ˈɔːdə]	点餐

Speaking Practice

⦿ **Practice making announcements about special meal service with these alternatives.**
- main course
- Muslim food
- vegetarian diet
- special meal
- Chinese cuisine

⦿ **Please read following sentences in the right tone(′ for stress, ↗ for rising tone, ↘ for falling tone).**

1. We have a ′ selection ↗ of main ′ course today. ↘
2. You may ′ enjoy refreshments ↗ and various drinks service ↘ in about ′ 10 minutes.
3. Please put down the table in front of you ↘ while we are serving you the meal. ↘
4. You can read ′ the menu ↗ carefully ↘ and you're welcome ↗ to make your choice. ↘
5. For the ′ convenience ↗ of the passenger behind you, please return your seatback ↘ to the ′ upright position during the meal service.

● **Translate the following expressions into English and practice making public announcement about food service on board.**
- 正餐提供
- 欢迎选择
- 点餐
- 阅读菜单
- 中国风味
- 西方风味
- 素食餐
- 特殊餐食
- 预订机票
- 餐食服务

Part D
Work-task

Try to discuss:
1. What is always served as main dish on board?
2. Are all the meals on board free?

Meal Service

An airline meal or in-flight meal is a meal served to passengers on board by a commercial airliner. These meals are prepared by airline catering services.❶

The first kitchens preparing meals in-flight were established by United Airlines in 1936. These meals vary widely in quality and quantity across different airline companies and classes of travel. They range from a simple beverage in short-haul economy class to a seven-course gourmet meal in long-haul first class.❷

The type of food varies depending upon the Airline Company and class of travel. Meals may be served on one tray or in multiple courses with no tray and with a tablecloth, metal cutlery, and glassware (generally in first and business classes).

The airline dinner typically includes meat (most commonly chicken or beef) or fish, a salad or vegetable, a small bread roll, and a dessert.

Before the September 11 attacks in 2001, first class passengers were often provided with full sets of metal cutlery. Afterward, common household items were evaluated more closely for their potential use as weapons on aircraft, and both first class and coach class passengers

were restricted to plastic utensils. This restriction has since been relaxed in many countries.❸

Before the SARS outbreak in 2003, many airlines offered metal cutlery in all classes. During the outbreak, several airlines used plastic/metal cutlery (plastic on the tip, metal on the handle), and several airlines used all plastic cutlery. This is because the virus transfers from person to person easily. To prevent infection, plastic cutlery was needed. They can be thrown away after use, handling the spread on-board. Those airlines switched back to metal cutlery.

In May 2010, concerns were raised in Australia and New Zealand over their respective flag carriers, Qantas and Air New Zealand, reusing their plastic cutlery for international flights between 10 and 30 times before replacement. Both airlines cited cost-cutting, international quarantine, and environmental reasons for the choice, and said that the plastic cutlery is commercially washed and sterilized before reuse.❹

Other non-food items Condiments (typically salt, pepper, and sugar) are supplied in small sachets. For cleanliness most meals come with a napkin and a moist towelette. First and business class passengers are often provided with hot towels and proper salt and pepper shakers.

(资料来源：http://wenku.baidu.com)

Notes

❶These meals are prepared by airline catering services.

句子大意：飞机餐食由航空公司的饮食厂商供应。

Catering 指饮食，餐饮。例如catering company 指餐饮公司，餐饮企业。

❷They range from a simple beverage in short-haul economy class to a seven-course gourmet meal in long-haul first class.

句子大意：从短途经济舱的简单的饮料供应到长途头等舱的七道美味菜肴，不同等级舱位的飞机餐，在菜式、分量及成本各方面都有区别。

"seven-course"表示七道菜。

❸This restriction has been relaxed in many countries.

句子大意：这种限制在很多国家已经有所松动。

例如，Smocking is strictly prohibited in the public places and this regulation will never be relaxed. 严格禁止在公共场所吸烟，这项规定将不会松动。

❹Qantas and Air New Zealand, reusing their plastic cutlery for international flights between 10 and 30 times before replacement. Both airlines cited cost-cutting, international quarantine, and environmental reasons for the choice, and said that the plastic cutlery is commercially washed and sterilized before reuse.

句子大意：澳大利亚航空公司和新西兰航空公司在其国际航线上重复使用塑料餐具，一般在使用10~30次之后再换新。两家航空公司都以节约成本、国际检疫和环境的原因为理由，而且坚称他们的塑料餐具在重复使用之前经过消毒。

"cite"表示"引用"。

例如，The lawyer cite a previous case to support his argument. 律师引用了以前的案例来支持他的论点。

New Words and Expressions

catering services	[keɪtərɪŋ]['sɜːvɪsɪs]		餐饮服务
gourmet	['gʊəmeɪ]	n.	美食家
tablecloth	['teɪb(ə)lkl ɒθ]	n.	台布,桌布
cutlery	['kʌtlərɪ]	n.	刀叉餐具
glassware	['glɑːsweə]		玻璃器皿 [玻璃]
potential	[pə'tenʃl]	adj.	潜在的;可能的
restrict	[rɪ'strɪkt]	v.	节流;限制
utensil	[juː'tensəl]	n.	器皿,器具
infection	[ɪn'fekʃən]	n.	传染病;传染,传播,感染
switch	[swɪtʃ]	v.	转变,转换
respective	[rɪ'spektɪv]	adj.	各自的,各个的
sterilize	['sterɪlaɪz]	v.	使不育,杀菌
condiment	['kɒndɪmənt]	n.	调味品,佐料
sachet	['sæʃeɪ]	n.	小袋,小香袋
moist	[mɒɪst]	adj.	潮湿的,湿润的
towelette	[ˌtaʊə'let]	n.	湿餐巾纸 [纸]

Part E
Supplementary Reading

> **Try to discuss:**
> 1. What is Oneworld?
> 2. Could you list other aviation alliance?

Oneworld

Oneworld Alliance is one of the world's three largest global airline alliances and was founded in 1999. Its central alliance office is currently based in New York City, New York, in the United States. Its slogan is "An alliance of the world's leading airlines working as one." The alliance's stated objective is to be the first-choice airline alliance for the world's frequent international travelers.

The member airlines of Oneworld completed the procedures for e-ticket interoperability in April 2005, and it is also the world's first airline alliance to implement e-ticket interoperability between member airlines. Its member airlines

and their affiliated airlines also cooperate in many aspects such as flight time, ticketing, code sharing (shared flight number), passenger transfers, frequent flyer programs, airport lounges, and cost reduction.

In February 2009, Oneworld celebrated its 10th anniversary with its ten member airlines—American Airlines, British Airways, Cathay Pacific, Finnair, Iberia Airlines, Japan Airlines, LAN, Malév, Qantas, and Royal Jordanian. In the past decade, membership has doubled from an initial five members to ten members.

Up to now its member airlines include Air Berlin, American Airlines, British Airways, Cathay Pacific, Finnair, Iberia, Japan Airlines, LAN Airlines, Malaysia Airlines, Qantas, Qatar Airways, Royal Jordanian, and S7 Airlines, plus some 30 affiliated airlines. There are 13 member airlines, 3,500 flights, 1,000 airports and 650 VIP lounges for passengers to choose from.

(资料来源：http://en.wikipedia.org/wiki/Oneworld)

参考译文

寰宇一家

寰宇一家成立于1999年，是全球三大航空联盟之一。总部目前在美国纽约市。其口号是"全球主要航空公司精诚合作的联盟。"联盟致力于成为世界旅客的首选。

寰宇一家各成员航空公司已于2005年4月完成电子机票互通安排的程序，亦是全球首个在成员航空公司之间实现电子机票互通安排的航空联盟。其成员航空公司及其附属航空公司亦在航班时间、票务、代码共享(共挂班号、班号共享)、旅客转机、飞行常旅客计划、机场贵宾室以及降低支出等多方面进行合作。

2009年2月，寰宇一家十个成员——美国航空、英国航空、国泰航空、芬兰航空、伊比利亚航空(西班牙国家航空)、日本航空、智利航空、匈牙利航空、澳洲航空和约旦皇家航空公司——共同庆祝联盟成立十周年。在过去的十年里，其成员数从最初的5个发展到当今的10个。

直至今日，寰宇一家有13家成员航空公司，包括柏林航空、美国航空、英国航空、国泰航空、芬兰航空、西班牙国家航空、日本航空、智利国家航空、马来西亚航空、澳洲航空、卡塔尔航空、皇家约旦航空、S7航空，以及约30家附属成员航空公司。13家成员航空公司，3500架次飞机、1000个机场和650个贵宾休息室可供旅客选择。

Cabin Service English

Unit 8

Food Service II

* Part A Useful Words and Expressions
* Part B Dialogues
* Part C Public Announcements
* Part D Work-task
* Part E Supplementary Reading

Students will be able to:
memorize the words and expressions about special food service in the cabin;
make up the dialogues about special food service in the cabin;
obtain and improve public announcements skills about special food service;
know about general knowledge of special food service in the cabin;
introduce Sky Team.

Suggested Hours: *4 class hours*

Part A
Useful Words and Expressions

◉ **Please list as many ways to provide service and corresponding suggestions to those who have special meal requirements as possible.**

_____

_____

- vegetarian
- special diet
- Muslim meal
- diabetes
- congee
- vegetarian meal / fruits and sweets / some hot congee is/ are the best alternative
- Would you like to / prefer to try / taste some congee?
- Would you care for a serving of Hindu meal?
- Would you like some / a serving of...?
- Are you fond of having some…
- Next time you fly, you can order a special meal when you book the ticket.
- Please reserve your special meal when you book the ticket.
- Please remind us of your special meal requirements when you book your flight next time.

Culture Tips

➤ Avoid using casual language like "Wait a minute" or "Wait a moment" when you need to let passengers wait for a moment or when making suggestions. Use formal and courteous language that meets airlines standards:

—I'll be back within a minute.

—I will come back as quickly as I can.

e.g.

—Can I have another serving of chicken, please?

—Sure, I'll be back within a minute. / I will come back as quickly as I can.

Cabin Term

Vegetarian/Vegan　素食主义者

释义：Vegetarian一般指普通的素食主义者,可以吃蛋类、奶类、奶制品以及蜂蜜等。Vegan一般指严格的素食主义者,只食用植物食品,既不食用肉、禽、蛋、海鲜类,也不食用任何来自动物的食品,包括动物脂肪、奶类、奶制品以及蜂蜜等。

Unit 8   Food Service II

◉ **Match phrases or sentences in column B to the situations in column A.**

Column A	Column B
1. Can you prepare some hot milk for my baby?	a. Sorry to hear that.
2. Do you have any Muslim meal today?	b. Sure, Madam.
3. Are you serving meal on the flight?	c. Terribly sorry, it should be reserved beforehand.
4. My son has no appetite today.	d. Food will not be served on short-haul flights.

◉ **Make up a dialogue about special food service on board.**

Part B
Dialogues

(CA=Cabin Attendant, PAX=Passenger)

CA: Excuse me, Sir. It's 6 O'clock now, shall we serve dinner for you?
PAX: Yes. But I don't want to have anything on the menu. I'm a vegetarian. But I didn't know that I should reserve my special diet when booking the ticket. So I want to know if I could request a vegetarian meal now.
CA: Don't worry, Sir. We'll try to meet your need. We always carry tins of vegetarian food in case anyone fails to tell us his special diet when booking the flight.
PAX: Wow…you are so considerate. What do you usually have for a vegetarian?
CA: We have tomato, eggplant, lettuce, mushroom and fruit salad. What would you prefer?
PAX: Fruit salad is always my favorite!
CA: Certainly, Sir. A serving of fruit salad.

PAX: Excuse me, Miss.
CA: Yes, Madam. Is there anything I can help you with?
PAX: Yes. My baby is hungry. Will you please prepare some milk for her?
CA: Of course, Madam. I am glad to. How much would you like to have?
PAX: Two-thirds of this bottle will be enough for her… And make it warm.
CA: I see. I'll go to get it for her … Is it warm enough?

PAX: Oh, yes. It is just fine. Thank you, Miss.

3

PAX: Excuse me, Miss. When will we be served our meals?

CA: The meal service will start 15 minutes after taking off, Sir. May I hand you the menu and wine list. You may have a look at the menu first and I'll take your order soon. (*Minutes later…*)

CA: Excuse me, Sir. May I take your order now? What would you prefer on the menu?

PAX: I can not take all the food on the menu. I am a Jew. Do you have any special meal such as Muslim meal?

CA: I am awfully sorry, Sir. Muslim meals on board need to be reserved when booking the flight. I understand you are feeling frustrated because your Muslim meal is not available on the flight. I fully appreciate how important the special meal is for you. I'm going to check in another cabin and I'll do my best to arrange an alternative vegetarian meal for you.

(*A minute later*)

CA: Sir, spiced vegetable stew with rice, vegetable soup, fruit or a sweet are still available. Which would you care for?

PAX: Vegetable soup, fruit salad and a cup of black tea would be better.

4

PAX: Excuse me, Miss. I have diabetes. But I forgot to make an order when booking the flight. Do you have some special food for me?

CA: Don't worry, Sir. We will try to meet your need. I'll check in the galley for the special meal.

PAX: Thank you so much.

CA: Sir, we have pancake, fish ball with rice, some fresh fruit or vegetables. Which would you prefer?

PAX: A serving of vegetable salad would be better.

5

CA: Excuse me, Madam. Did you press the call button? What can I do for you?

PAX: Yes. But my baby is not used to the food on the plane. Do you have anything else for him?

CA: I am sorry to hear that, Madam. We have soft cake and milk. And we can cook some hot congee if he doesn't mind waiting a few minutes.

PAX: Then please make him some hot congee. It's easy to digest.

CA: I see, Madam. Would you like anything else?

PAX: The fried noodles are really delicious today. I enjoyed

it a lot. Can I have another serving?

CA: Well, let me check in the galley. I will bring it over if there is an extra.

6

PAX: Excuse me, Miss. I am sort of hungry, when will the dinner be served?

CA: I am sorry, Sir. This is a short flight. Dinner will not be served on short flights? Only beverages and refreshments are served.

PAX: Oh, so it is! Then what kind of refreshments do you have?

CA: We have cakes, peanuts and some fresh fruit. What would you care for?

PAX: I am allergic to peanuts and anything with egg in it. So it seems I can only have some fresh fruit.

CA: I can totally understand you, Sir. You can have a cup of hot liquid. We have coffee, milk, and tea.

PAX: Great! A cup of coffee with milk, please. And make it hot.

CA: I see. Would you like to wait for just a minute, I'll go to prepare it.

PAX: Go ahead!

New Words and Expressions

reserve	[rɪˈzɜːv]	v.	预订
vegetarian meal	[vedʒɪˈteərɪən][miːl]		素食餐
considerate	[kənˈsɪdərɪt]	adj.	体贴的；体谅的；考虑周到的
eggplant	[ˈegplænt]	n.	茄子
lettuce	[ˈletɪs]	n.	生菜，莴苣
mushroom	[ˈmʌʃrʊm]	n.	蘑菇，伞菌；
Jew	[dʒuː]	n.	犹太人；犹太教徒；守财奴
Muslim	[ˈmʊzlɪm; ˈmʌz-]	n.	穆斯林；穆罕默德信徒
Muslim meal	[ˈmʊzlɪm;ˈmʌz-][miːl]		穆斯林餐
frustrated	[frʌˈstreɪtɪd]	adj.	沮丧的；不得志的
alternative	[ɔːlˈtɜːnətɪv]	n.	二中择一；供替代的选择
stew	[stjuː]	v.	炖；忧虑
diabetes	[ˌdaɪəˈbiːtɪz]	n.	糖尿病；多尿症
congee	[ˈkɒndʒiː]	n.	粥；告别

● **Role play the cabin attendant's responses.**

PAX: What do you have for a vegetarian?
CA: _____.

PAX: I am a Muslim, what can I have for dinner?
CA: _____.

PAX: I am not used to the food on plane.
CA: _____.

PAX: Can you bring me a cup of hot coffee?
CA: _____.

PAX: I am a vegetarian, do you have vegetarian meal for me?
CA: _____.

PAX: My baby is not used to the food on the plane. Do you have anything else for him?
CA: _____.

PAX: When are passengers served meals on board?
CA: _____.

PAX: I am not satisfied with the food on the menu!
CA: _____.

PAX: The fried noodles are really delicious, can I have one serving more?
CA: _____.

PAX: I am hungry, when will be served dinner?
CA: _____.

Discuss the following questions.

1. A passenger is a vegetarian. He asks: "Do you have a vegetarian meal for me?" What would you say to him?
2. A mother asked a cabin attendant: "My baby is not used to the food on the plane. Do you have anything else for him?" What would you say to her?
3. When are passengers served meals on board?
4. If it is a short flight, what can passengers be served?
5. When a passenger isn't satisfied with the food served on the menu, what would you say to her?

Make up dialogues based on the following situations.

1. A passenger is asking the cabin attendant whether there is anything he can eat on the plane since he has diabetes.

2. Try to serve a passenger who is very hungry but he is allergic to anything with egg in it.
3. Try to serve a passenger who can not eat anything on the menu since he is a vegetarian and forgot to reserve his special diet when booking the flight.
4. A child is upset in his stomach; his mother asks the cabin attendant if there is anything appropriate for her child.
5. Talk to a passenger who asks for meal because he is kind of hungry. However, this is a short-haul flight.

◉ **Translate the following sentences into English.**
1. 机上没有穆斯林餐，素食可能是最好的替代餐。
2. 机上没有糖尿病餐，您要试一下蔬菜沙拉吗？
3. 来一些水果和甜点怎么样？
4. 您要一份印度餐吗？
5. 短程航班只提供饮品和点心。
6. 如果您不介意，我们可以为宝宝煮一份粥。
7. 您喜欢吃水果沙拉吗？
8. 下次您在预订机票时可以点一份特殊餐。
9. 当您预订机票时请您预订一下特殊餐。
10. 下次预订机票时，请提醒我们您的特殊用餐要求。

Part C

Public Announcements

Special Meal Service I

Ladies and gentlemen,
　　May I have your attention, please.
　　Those passengers who requested a special meal, please press your call button to identify yourself.
　　Thank you!

Special Meal Service II

Ladies and gentlemen,

In a few minutes, food and beverages will be served by our flight attendants. We hope you will enjoy them.

If you reserve your special diet, please press your button to remind us. If you forgot to reserve your special diet when booking the ticket, please feel free to tell us so that we can prepare some alternatives for you.

Thank you for your cooperation.

Pre-Meal Service I

Ladies and gentlemen,

We will arrive at _____ airport in about _____ hour(s) and _____ minutes, and now we are going to serve beverages and then breakfast. You are welcome to take your choice.

Thank you!

Pre-meal Announcement II

Ladies and gentlemen,

We will be serving you a meal with tea, coffee and other soft drinks. You're welcome to make your choice. Please put down the table in front of you. For the convenience of the passenger behind you, please return your seatback to the upright position during the meal service.

Thank you!

Pre-Meal Announcement III

Ladies and gentlemen,

In a few moments, the flight attendants will be serving meal (snacks) and beverages. We hope you will enjoy them.

For the convenience of the passenger seated behind you, please return your seatback to the upright position during our meal service. If you need any assistance, please contact flight attendants.

Thank you!

New Words and Expressions

attention	[əˈtenʃən]	n. 注意
special meal	[ˈspeʃ(ə)l][miːl]	特殊餐饮
diet	[ˈdaɪət]	n. 饮食
book the ticket	[bʊk][ðə][ˈtɪkɪt]	预订机票

Unit 8　Food Service II

● **Practice making announcements about special meal service with these alternatives.**

- Vegetarian meal
- Muslim meal
- Kosher meal
- Sugar-free meal

● **Please read following sentences in the right tone(′ for stress, ↗ for rising tone, ↘ for falling tone).**

1. Those passengers who ⎕ requested a special meal ↗ please press your call button ↘ to identify yourself.
2. In a ⎕ few minutes, ↗ food and beverages will be ⎕ served by our flight attendants. ↘
3. You're ⎕ welcome to make your choice. ↘
4. Please put down the ⎕ table in front of you. ↘
5. If you need any ⎕ assistance, ↗ please contact flight attendants. ↘

● **Translate the following expressions into English and practice making public announcement about special food service.**

- 请注意
- 穆斯林餐
- 特殊餐
- 预订机票
- 替代餐
- 做出选择
- 放下前方小桌板
- 联系空乘人员
- 感谢合作
- 按呼唤铃

Part D
Work-task

📋 **Try to discuss:**

1. What is always served as special meal on board?
2. How to order special meal on board?

103

Meal Service—special meal service

The majority of airlines today also cater for passengers who have special dietary requirements, such as vegetarians, vegans, and low cholesterol diets as well as religious groups such as Moslems and Hindus.❶ To request a special meal, a passenger must contact reservations at least 24 hours before the scheduled flight departure.

It is advisable that after checking in, the passenger informs the cabin attendant that he has ordered a special meal.❷ At the briefing the purser will also inform the CA's of such passengers' needs to make some necessary preparation. Usually, a stewardess will approach the passenger who has special dietary needs after take-off to confirm his requirements.❸

These special diets include:

- Cultural diets, such as French, Italian, Chinese, Japanese or Indian style.
- Infant and baby meals. Some airlines also offer children's meals, containing foods that children will enjoy such as baked beans, mini-hamburgers and hot dogs.
- Medical diets, including low/high fiber, low fat/cholesterol, diabetic, peanut free, non-lactose, low salt/sodium, low-purine, low-calorie, low-protein, bland (non-spicy) and gluten-free meals.
- Religious diets, including kosher, halal, and Hindu, Buddhist and Jain vegetarian (sometimes termed Asian vegetarian) meals.
- Vegetarian and vegan meals. Some airlines do not offer a specific meal for vegetarians, instead, they are given a vegan meal.❹

(资料来源:http://wenku.baidu.com)

Notes

❶ The majority of airlines today also cater for passengers who have special dietary requirements, such as vegetarians, vegans, and low cholesterol diets as well as religious groups such as Moslems and Hindus.

句子大意:今天,大多数的航空公司能够为有特殊餐食需求的旅客提供服务。此类旅客包括普通素食主义者、纯素食主义者、低胆固醇餐者以及一些宗教信徒,比如穆斯林和印度教信徒。

vegan指严格的素食主义者,指只食用植物食品,即不食用肉、禽、蛋、海鲜类,也不食用任何来自动物的食品,包括动物脂肪、奶类、奶制品以及蜂蜜等。纯素食者区别于普通的素食者,普通的素食主义可以允许吃蛋类、奶类、奶制品以及蜂蜜等。

❷ It is advisable that after checking in, the passenger informs the cabin attendant that he has ordered a special meal.

句子大意:旅客最好在登机后告知乘务员他们已经定制特殊餐。

It is advisable that...最好……

例如，It is advisable that everyone should have a map. 最好让每个人都有一张地图。

❸ Usually, a stewardess will approach the passenger who has special dietary needs after take-off to confirm his requirements.

句子大意：一般情况下，乘务员在飞机起飞后会走到已经预订过特殊餐食的旅客旁边确定他们的预定。

"approach"指靠近，接近。

❹ Some airlines do not offer a specific meal for vegetarians, instead, they are given a vegan meal.

句子大意：一些航空公司不为素食主义者提供具体的餐食，但会为他们提供纯素食餐。Vegan 与 vegetarian 的区别请见note 1。

New Words and Expressions

cater for	['keɪtə][fɔː]	满足……的需要，迎合
dietary	['daɪə,terɪ]	adj. 饮食的
cholesterol	[kə'lestərɒl]	n 规定的食物；饮食的规定；食谱
		adj. 饮食的，饭食的，规定食物
vegan	['viːgən]	n. 严格的素食主义者
Moslem	['mazləm]	n. 穆斯林，伊斯兰，穆罕默德信徒
		adj. 穆斯林的，伊斯兰的，伊斯兰教的
Hindu	['hɪnduː]	n. 印度人；印度教教徒
reservation	[ˌrezə'veɪʃən]	n.（火车，旅馆，机票的）的预约和预定
fiber	['faɪbə]	n. 纤维；光纤（等于fibre）
diabetic	[daɪə'betɪk]	n. 糖尿病患者
peanut	['pɪnɑt]	n. 花生
peanut free	['piːnʌt][friː]	不含坚果的
lactosen	['læktəuz; -s]	n. [有化] 乳糖
sodium	['səudɪəm]	n. [化学] 钠（11号元素，符号Na）
purine	['pjʊəriːn]	n. [有化] 嘌呤（四氮杂䓬，尿杂环）；咖啡因
calorie	['kælərɪ]	n. 卡路里（热量单位）
protein	['prəutiːn]	n. 蛋白质
gluten	['gluːtən]	n. 面筋；麸质；谷蛋白
kosher	['kəuʃə]	adj.（食物，尤指肉类）卫生合格的，经正式处理的，清净的（依照犹太人的规矩而烹调的）
Buddhist	['budɪst]	n. 佛教徒

Part E
Supplementary Reading

Try to discuss:
1. What does Sky Team mean?
2. Which airline in China joins Sky Team?

Sky Team

On June 22, 2000, representatives of Aeroméxico, Air France, Delta Air Lines, and Korean Air held a meeting in New York to announce the founding of a third airline alliance. These became the four founding carriers of Sky Team. Sky Team was the last of the three major airline alliances to be formed, the first two being Star Alliance and Oneworld. However, in terms of the number of passengers and the number of members, Sky Team has grown and is now the second largest alliance in the world, second only to Star Alliance and ahead of Oneworld.

The establishment of Sky Team provides its customers with 6,402 daily flights to 451 destinations in 98 countries. In November 2012, adhering to the alliance purpose of "Caring more about you", the number of members has grown to 19, covering five continents. Through the

information of flight, seat and price of all airlines in the alliance, it helps passengers book tickets and seats, and sends transit passengers to cities in the other country through the domestic routes of alliance airlines. Sky Team airline members come from major countries in the world, and Chinese members include China Eastern Airlines, China Airlines and Xiamen Airlines. Since January 2020, the original Sky Team alliance member, China Southern Airlines has withdrawn from the Sky Team alliance.

In 2004, the alliance had its biggest expansion when Continental Airlines, KLM, and Northwest Airlines simultaneously joined as full members. In 2010, the alliance celebrated its 10th anniversary with the introduction of a special livery, the joining or upgrading status of four airlines, followed by the announcements of Aerolíneas Argentinas, China Eastern Airlines, China Airlines, and Garuda Indonesia to become full members.

(资料来源：http://en.wikipedia.org/wiki/SkyTeam?oldid=430938088)

参考译文

天 合 联 盟

天合联盟（又译"空中联队"）于2000年6月22日，由墨西哥航空公司、法国航空公司、达美航空公司和大韩航空公司四个初始会员创立。天合联盟是继星空联盟和寰宇一家之后成立的航空联盟。然而，就旅客数量和成员数量而言，如今天合联盟已经超越寰宇一家，成为三大联盟中的老二——仅次于星空联盟。

　　天合联盟的成立将为其客户每日提供6402个航班,前往98个国家的451个目的地。2012年11月,天合联盟成员秉承"竭诚为您服务"的联盟宗旨,会员数已发展到19个,覆盖五大洲。通过联盟内所有航空公司的航班信息、座位信息和价格信息,帮助旅客预订机票和座位,把中转旅客通过联盟航空公司的国内航线送到对方国家的各个城市。天合联盟航空成员来自世界各大国家,中国成员有中国东方航空、台湾中华航空和厦门航空。自2020年1月份起原天合联盟加盟中国南方航空,退出天合联盟。

　　2004年,天合联盟因美国大陆航空公司、美国西北航空公司和荷兰皇家航空公司的加入而迎来了史上最大的扩展。2010年,为庆祝天合联盟成立十周年,阿根廷航空、中国东方航空公司、中华航空公司和印度尼西亚航空公司成为天合联盟正式成员,并且推出了特别的机身涂装。

Unit 9

In-flight Entertainment

✦ Part A Useful Words and Expressions   ✦ Part B Dialogues
✦ Part C Public Announcements   ✦ Part D Work-task
✦ Part E Supplementary Reading

Students will be able to:
  memorize the words and expressions about in-flight entertainment in the cabin;
  make up the dialogues about in-flight entertainment in the cabin;
  obtain and improve public announcements skills about in-flight entertainment;
  know about in-flight entertainment system;
  introduce the city Shanghai.
Suggested Hours: *4 class hours*

Unit 9　In-flight Entertainment

Part A
Useful Words and Expressions

◉ **Please list as many expressions related to in-flight entertainment service as possible.**

_____

_____

- local newspaper
- in-flight magazine
- reading light
- pillow
- blanket
- window shade/blind
- channel
- headset
- Beijing Evening
- Beijing Youth
- Economics Daily
- Global Times
- Life Weekly
- folk songs
- classical music
- light classics
- pop music
- Chinese opera
- Sir/ Madam, may I turn on the reading light for you?
- Here's the newspaper we've prepared for you.
- I'll bring the magazine for you shortly.
- I'll change another headset for you.
- We hope you'll like it.
- Mr. / Mrs. / Ms. ____, Would you need a blanket?
- Mr.____, may I lower the window shade so that the bright sunlight won't disturb you?
- Excuse me, here's the entertainment system guide.
- If you have any questions, please ask me.
- We are pleased to answer any questions at any time.
- Press the call button right here if you need some assistance.
- Here's the entertainment guide. Enjoy your time.
- The movies we have onboard include comedy, action movie and features.
- You can select any channel you like.

109

- May I help you in adjusting the seat to a more comfortable position so that you can have a good rest?

Culture Tips

- Business frequent fliers know how to get the best out of their cross-country flights. They choose airlines by which one has the best reclining seats, in-flight entertainment, and food. But the true traveler knows that the real perk of flying first/ business class is the bag of goodies that comes along with it—amenity kit.
- Amenity kits are generally used in long-haul aircraft on international flights and they are the only things you can legally take off the plane and use afterward.
- Amenity kits can be called as travel kits or overnight kits, composed of below or more components:

—toothbrush

—toothpaste

—eyeshade

—facial tissues

—floss

—socks

—slippers

—shoe polish

—comb

—pen

—earplugs

Cabin Term

Window shade / blind   遮光板

释义：shade具有阴影、遮阳物的含义；blind除了常用的盲人、盲目的含义，还有名词百叶窗的含义。飞机在起飞、降落的过程中，都要将遮光板打开，这是因为飞机在起飞降落的过程中有着一定的危险，打开遮光板能够更好地观察到飞机外面的情况，保障旅客安全，所以要求飞机在起飞、降落的过程中都要打开遮光板。

Match phrases or sentences in column B to the situations in column A.

Column A	Column B
1. A passenger is reading newspaper.	a. We have comedy, action movie and features movies onboard today.
2. A passenger wants some music.	b. We have amenity kit for children.
3. A passenger can't hear anything through his headsets.	c. We have local newspaper and in-flight magazine.

continue

Column A	Column B
4. A passenger asks a cabin attendant about movies provided on board.	d. We have light music on channel.
5. A passenger wants to read something.	e. May I turn on the reading light for you?
6. A passenger is worrying about her son on the boring long flight.	f. I will get a pair of new headsets for you.

◉ **According to the picture given below, have a discussion on in-flight entertainment with your partner.**

Part B
Dialogues

(CA=Cabin Attendant, PAX=Passenger)

1

CA: Would you care for a copy of newspaper, Sir?
PAX: What newspapers do you have?
CA: We have Beijing Daily, Global Times, Life Weekly, and Beijing Youth. Would you care for one of them?
PAX: Don't you have any newspapers in English?
CA: English newspapers are not available on board. We have the Chinese version of some local newspapers and some magazines in English. Would you like to have a copy?

2

PAX: Could you introduce in-flight entertainment for me?
CA: Certainly. You can read some newspapers and in-flight magazines. You can also choose some newly released movies, music videos and songs from our music library. You can even play games.

PAX: That's great. I want to watch some movies. How can I unfold the screen?

CA: You may adjust the angle of the screen on the seatback in front of you. There are several channels to choose from. You can operate it with the touch screen.

PAX: Oh, I see. How can I use the headsets then?

CA: Let me show you. First, put the plugs into your ears. Then put the jack into this hole on your armrest. After that, press this button to select the channel you like.

PAX: Great. I will enjoy it.

CA: Please press the call button right there if you need some assistance.

PAX: Thanks very much.

CA: You're welcome. Enjoy the flight.

PAX: Excuse me, Miss. Can you do me a favor?

CA: Certainly, what can I do for you?

PAX: This is my daughter's first flight. She is a little bit nervous. So I wondered if you could provide something for her to play with.

CA: Certainly. I may get an amenity kit for her.

PAX: What's that?

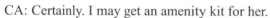

CA: We provide children amenity kits which contain a story-book, crayons and so forth.

PAX: How considerate you are.

CA: Excuse me would you like to read some newspapers or magazines?

PAX: No, thank you. I prefer to have a nap.

CA: Oh, may I lower the window shade for you? The sunlight is so bright that it will disturb your sleeping?

PAX: Thank you so much. By the way, I like to listen to music to help me go to sleep. Do you have music channels?

CA: Yes. Folk songs, classical music, pop music, light classics and Chinese operas will be available in our in-flight entertainment system. You can select any channel you like.

PAX: Light classics are my favorite. Which channel shall I select?

CA: Channel 2 is for light classics. Just press the "up" button on your armrest, please. Hope you enjoy the music.

PAX: I got it. Thank you.

CA: Sir, you just pressed the call button. What can I do for you?

Unit 9　In-flight Entertainment

PAX: I want to read something.
CA: Here's the newspaper we've prepared for you. May I turn on the reading light for you?
PAX: Thank you so much. Can I have a pillow and blanket? I feel somewhat cold and tired.
CA: No problem, I'll bring them for you shortly.

6

PAX: Excuse me, what kind of in-flight entertainment program do you have on board? Say, movies?
CA: Sir. The movies we have onboard include comedy, action movies and features. You may find the entertainment system guide in your seat pocket. The information related to in-flight entertainment can be found there. If you have any questions, please let me know. We are pleased to answer any questions at any time.
PAX: Fine. Thank you.
　　(...minutes later)
CA: Sir, what can I do for you?
PAX: I bet the headset I got is broken. I can hear nothing.
CA: I'm sorry for the inconvenience. I'll change another headset for you. I'll be back in a minute.

New Words and Expressions

care for	[keəfɔː][fɔː]	照顾;喜欢
copy	[ˈkɒpɪ]	n. 一册;一份
daily	[ˈdeɪlɪ]	n. 日报
global	[ˈgləʊbəl]	adj 全球的
version	[ˈvɜːʃən]	n. 版本
entertainment	[ˌentəˈteɪnmənt]	n. 娱乐;消遣;款待
newly	[ˈnjuːlɪ]	adv. 新近,最近
release	[rɪˈliːs]	vt. 发布;发行
angle	[ˈæŋgl]	n. 角
operate	[ˈɒpəreɪt]	v. 操作;运转
touch screen	[tʌtʃ][skriːn]	n. 触摸屏
plug	[plʌg]	n. 塞子;插头
jack	[dʒæk]	n. [信]插孔,插座
channel	[ˈtʃænl]	n. 频道;途径;海峡
crayon	[ˈkreɪən]	n. 蜡笔;有色粉笔
have a nap	[hæv][ə][næp]	休息一下;小睡一会儿
disturb	[dɪˈstɜːb]	v. 扰乱;妨碍

113

| say | [seɪ] | v. 比如说 |
| comedy | [ˈkɒmədɪ] | n. 喜剧；有趣的事情 |

Role play the cabin attendant's responses.

CA: _____.
PAX: Yes, I'd like China Daily in English.
CA: _____.
PAX: I'd like some light music. How can I get access to that?
CA: _____.
PAX: Thank you.
CA: _____.

CA: _____.
PAX: I want to watch some movies. How can I unfold the screen?
CA: _____.
PAX: Can you help me operate my headsets?
CA: _____.
PAX: Oh, that's very kind of you. Thank you.
CA: _____.

Discuss the following questions.

1. A passenger wants to read something. What would you say?
2. How would you introduce the in-flight entertainment to passengers?
3. When passengers don't know how to use the headsets, how would you instruct them?
4. What would you often provide for children on board?
5. The audio/video system is inoperative. What should you say to the passengers?

Make up dialogues based on the following situations.

1. Jill is a cabin attendant. She is introducing in-flight entertainment to a passenger.
2. A passenger has no idea about the programs operating on board. He is asking for help from a cabin attendant.
3. Shirley is a purser of the flight, and she is offering help to a mother to comfort her son.

Please translate following sentences into English.

1. 我们有一些当地的报纸和机上杂志。
2. 我会给您换一个耳机，一会就回来。
3. 我们的机上娱乐系统里有民歌、古典音乐、流行音乐、轻音乐和京剧。
4. 先生/女士，我可以为您打开阅读灯吗？
5. 这是我们为您准备的报纸。

6. 先生，您需要毯子吗？
7. 如果您有任何问题，请告诉我。
8. 我们机上的电影包括喜剧片、动作片和故事片。
9. 您可以选择任何您喜爱的频道。
10. 我可以帮助您把座位调整到一个更舒适的位置吗？这样您就可以好好休息了。

Part C
Public Announcements

Film

Good morning (afternoon/evening), ladies and gentlemen,

Now we will be showing a film. Today's movie is _____ followed by _____.

Please use the headsets in the seat pocket in front of you. Choose channel 1 or 2 to select the language you require for the movie you are watching. You may ask your cabin attendants for assistance.

We hope you enjoy your movie.

In-flight Baduanjin

Good morning (afternoon/evening), ladies and gentlemen,

In order to relieve your fatigue during the journey, we have prepared the in-flight exercises called "BA DUAN JIN", which will be broadcasted at Channel 1 in loop with the entertainment program.

For your safety, please keep your seat-belts fastened when doing the exercises.

We hope that our in-flight exercises will make your journey more comfortable!

Thank you!

In-flight Entertainment

Ladies and gentlemen,

We are pleased to offer you our _____ Airlines Comfort in-flight entertainment program. We hope you will enjoy it.

(When channels are selectable) Please put on your headsets and select the channel which corresponds with the programme that you wish to view. If you have any questions, please call your flight attendant for assistance.

(When channels are not selectable) Headsets will be available from your flight attendants. If you have any questions, please contact flight attendants.

Thank you!

Video System Breakdown

Ladies and gentlemen,

We regret to inform you that the video entertainment system is not available on this flight. Only audio programs are available.

Thank you!

AVOD (Audio-Video-on-Demand)

Ladies and gentlemen,

Our personal in-flight entertainment system will soon be turned on and various video and audio programs will be offered in order to enrich your experience onboard. These include movies, selected television short features and numerous additional channel selections offering a range of music, games, flight information and ____ product information. Details are available in the Inflight Entertainment Guide in the seat pocket in front of you.

We wish you a relaxed and pleasant journey.

Thank you!

New Words and Expressions

fatigue	[fə'ti:g]	n. 疲劳；杂役
broadcast	['brɔ:dkɑ:st]	vt. 广播
in loop with	[ɪn][lu:p][wɪð]	循环
selectable	['sɪlektəbəl]	adj. 可选择的
short feature	[ʃɔ:t] ['fi:tʃə(r)]	n. 纪录短片
numerous	['nju:mərəs]	adj. 很多的

Speaking Practice

◉ Practice making public announcements about film with these alternatives.

- Captain America
- London Has Fallen
- Titanic

- Harry Potter
- Forrest Gump

◉ **Please read following sentences in the right tone(′ for stress, ↗ for rising tone, ↘ for falling tone).**

1. Now ↗ we will be │ showing a film. ↘
2. Please use the │ headsets in the seat pocket ↘ in front of you. ↘
3. Choose channel 1 ↗ or 2 ↘ to select the │ language you require ↘ for the movie you are watching. ↘
4. We hope that our │ in-flight exercises ↗ will make your journey more comfortable! ↘
5. Please put on your │ headsets ↗ and select the channel ↘ which corresponds with the │ programme ↗ that you wish to view. ↘

◉ **Translate the following expressions into English and practice making public announcement about in-flight entertainment.**
- 请使用座椅口袋中的耳机
- 为了缓解您的旅途疲劳
- 古典音乐
- 为您播放机上娱乐节目
- 保证您在旅途中得到良好的休息
- 调暗客舱灯光
- 打开头顶上方的阅读灯光
- 娱乐节目
- 音频节目
- 机上娱乐服指南

Part D
Work-task

> **Try to discuss:**
> 1. Do you have any ideas about in-flight entertainment system?
> 2. Do you think in-flight entertainment program is essential on board?

In-flight Entertainment

In-flight entertainment (IFE) refers to the entertainment available to aircraft passengers during a flight.① Controversy still exists today about the exact date when in-flight entertainment was first introduced on an airplane. Early in-flight entertainment included live singers, musicians,

117

fashion shows, etc. All performances were designed to become media events within themselves, not specifically to entertain passengers.❷ Today, in-flight entertainment is offered as an option on almost all wide body aircraft, while some narrow body aircraft are not equipped with any form of in-flight entertainment at all. This is mainly due to the aircraft storage and weight limits.

In-flight entertainment systems have come a long way from the days where everyone watched the same movie on a screen where the picture was sometimes distorted or blocked by another passenger's head to today's new audio/video-on-demand systems. Most major commercial airlines throughout the world are now flying with fold-up, swing-out, or seatback mounted LCD video screens.❸

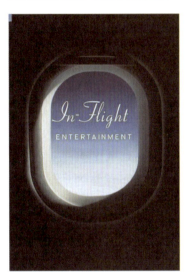

More recently, a new generation of in-flight entertainment, or IFE, systems, such as satellite TV, allows passengers to choose from new Hollywood films or television shows. An abundance of innovative options now exist for passenger use on modern aircraft. They can start, stop, and fast-forward them on individual screens, adding choice and control. In today's leading-edge systems, a passenger can sit in a seat, watch one of dozens or over a hundred movies on demand, select audio programming of choice from hundreds of availabilities, and scan the menu or beverage listing. He can view the duty-free merchandise selections, look at the duty-paid merchandise listings, etc., and be able to press several buttons, "swipe" a credit card through a built-in unit, and order whatever he or she desires.

However, this battle has a double-edged sword: it can offer airlines the potential for more income, but the costs are often huge.❹ Much of what's happening in the areas of in-flight entertainment is being driven by very sophisticated and very expensive technology. Some airlines are trying to recoup entertainment-system costs through on-board advertising or charging for services. Airlines, offers live seat-back TV and pay-per-view movies and a new entertainment system let passengers order meals and drinks through their touch-screens, whenever they want. Leading-edge systems like this can cut costs on a flight and can boost a flight crew's efficiency. An airline can also use these interactive systems to conduct market research and find out about a customer's satisfaction with the airline's service.

(资料来源：http://www.en.m.wikipedia.org/wiki/In-flight_entertainment; http://www.cntraveler.com/stories/2014-07-17/future-of-in-flight-entertainment)

Notes

❶ In-flight entertainment (IFE) refers to the entertainment available to aircraft passengers during a flight.

句子大意：机上娱乐又可称作飞行娱乐，是指航空公司给旅客在客机上使用的娱乐方式。IFE是机上娱乐in-flight entertainment的缩写。

❷All performances were designed to become media events within themselves, not specifically to entertain passengers.

句子大意：所有的演出旨在产生轰动效应，而并不是为了娱乐旅客而进行的。

media event(s)媒介事件，是指那些令国人乃至世人屏息驻足的电视直播的历史事件，也就是大家常说的"重大新闻事件"。

❸Most major commercial airlines throughout the world are now flying with fold-up, swing-out, or seatback mounted LCD video screens.

句子大意：如今，全世界的主要航空公司都在客舱里安装了可折叠的、可移动的屏幕或是在前排座椅靠背内安装内嵌屏幕。

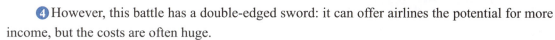

❹However, this battle has a double-edged sword: it can offer airlines the potential for more income, but the costs are often huge.

句子大意：然而，这场战役同时也是一把双刃剑。它给航空公司提供更多收入潜力的同时花费也是巨大的。

其中，battle指的是前文提到的新一代娱乐系统变革。

New Words and Expressions

controversy	[ˈkɒntrəvɜːsɪ]	n. 争议；(公开的)争论
exact	[ɪgˈzækt]	adj. 精密严谨的；确切的
live	[lɪv]	adj. 活的；直播的；现场的
media	[ˈmiːdɪə]	n. 传播媒介；(medium的复数)媒体；新闻媒介
option	[ˈɒpʃən]	n. 选择权；可选物
storage	[ˈstɔːrɪdʒ]	n. 存储；仓库；储藏所
distort	[dɪˈstɔːt]	v. 扭曲；使失真；曲解
audio-on-demand	[ˈɔːdɪəʊɒndɪˈmɑːnd]	n. 声音点播
video-on-demand	[ˌvɪdɪəʊɒndɪˈmɑːnd]	n. 影视点播
commercial airline	[kəˈmɜːʃ(ə)l][ˈeəlaɪn]	商业航空公司
fold-up	[ˈfəʊldʌp]	adj. 适于折叠的；可折拢的
swing-out	[ˈswɪŋˈaʊt]	摇动式
LCD video screen	[ˈvɪdɪəʊ][skriːn]	液晶显示屏
generation	[ˌdʒenəˈreɪʃən]	n. 一代；产生
satellite	[ˈsætəlaɪt]	n. 卫星
abundance	[əˈbʌndəns]	n. 充裕，丰富

119

innovative	['ɪnəvətɪv]	adj. 革新的,创新的
fast-forward	['fɑːst'fɔːwəd]	vi. 快进
leading-edge	['liːdɪŋedʒ]	adj. 尖端的,前沿的；领先优势的
availability	[əˌveɪlə'bɪlətɪ]	n. 可用性；有效性；实用性
scan	[skæn]	v. 扫描；浏览
merchandise	['mɜːtʃəndaɪs;-z]	n. 商品,货物
duty-paid	['djuːtɪ'peɪd]	adj. 已完税的；已纳税的
swipe	[swaɪp]	vt. 刷……卡
built-in	[ˌbɪlt'ɪn]	adj. 嵌入的
double-edged	['dʌbl'edʒd]	adj. 双刃的
sophisticated	[sə'fɪstɪkeɪtɪd]	adj. 复杂的；精致的
recoup	[rɪ'kuːp]	v. 收回；恢复；偿还；扣除
pay-per-view	['peɪpəvjʊ]	adj. 按次计费的
boost	[buːst]	v. 促进；增加

Part E
Supplementary Reading

Try to discuss:
1. Do you know some famous tourist attractions in Shanghai?
2. How much do you know about Shanghai's food and people?

Shanghai

　　Located in the Yangtze River Delta, Shanghai sits in the middle portion of the Chinese coast. Shanghai is the largest Chinese city by population and the largest city proper by population in the world. It is also a global financial center, and a transport hub.

　　Shanghai is a popular tourist destination renowned for its historical landmarks such as The Bund, City God Temple and Yu Garden as well as the extensive Lujiazui skyline and major museums including the Shanghai Museum and the China Art Museum. It has been described as the "showpiece" of the booming economy of mainland China.

　　Shanghai was the largest and most prosperous city in the Far East during the 1930s, and rapid re-development began in 1990s. This is exemplified by the Pudong District, which became a pilot area for integrated economic reforms. By the end of 2009, there were 787 financial institutions, of which 170 were foreign-invested. In 2009, the Shanghai Stock Exchange ranked third among worldwide stock exchanges in terms of trading volume. In September 2013, with the backing of Chinese Premier Li Keqiang, the city launched the China (Shanghai) Pilot Free-Trade Zone—the first free-trade zone in mainland China. The Zone introduced a number of pilot reforms designed to create a preferential environment for foreign investment.

Due to its cosmopolitan history, Shanghai has a blend of religious heritage as shown by the religious buildings and institutions still scattered around the city. Taoism has a presence in Shanghai in the form of several temples, including the City God Temple, at the heart of the old city, and a temple dedicated to the Three Kingdoms general Guan Yu. The Wenmiao is a temple dedicated to Confucius. Buddhism has had a presence in Shanghai since ancient times. Longhua temple, the largest temple in Shanghai, and Jing'an Temple, were first founded in the Three Kingdoms period.

Shanghai is one of the leading air transport gateways in Asia. The city has two commercial airports: Shanghai Pudong International Airport and Shanghai Hongqiao International Airport. Pudong Airport is the main international airport, while Hongqiao Airport mainly operates domestic flights with limited short-haul international flights.

(资料来源：http://en.wikipedia.org/wiki/Shanghai)

参考译文

上 海

上海位于中国东部海岸线的正中间，地处长江三角洲。它是中国人口最多的城市，亦是世界上最大的城市之一，市区总人口数量世界第一。上海同时也是全球金融中心和交通枢纽。

作为一个热门的旅游胜地，上海拥有很多著名的历史地标：外滩、城隍庙、豫园以及陆家嘴一望无垠的天际线和一些著名的博物馆，如上海博物馆和中国美术馆。它被誉为是中国大陆经济蓬勃发展的"展示品"。

在20世纪30年代，上海就是远东地区规模最大、最繁华的城市，其重新快速发展始于20世纪90年代。浦东新区的开发，成为试验区综合经济改革的成功案例。截至2009年底，共有787家金融机构在此落户，其中170家来自外商投资。2009年，上海证券交易所的交易量排名世界第三。2013年9月，在李克强总理的支持下，上海启动了中国（上海）试点自由贸易区项目，该项目是中国大陆地区的第一个自由贸易区。上海自由贸易区出台了多项改革试点，旨在为外商的投资创造更优越的环境。

得益于其国际化的历史背景,上海在宗教继承方面呈现出多样化的特点,这点可通过散落在城市各个角落的宗教建筑和机构得到佐证。其中,道教的历史可追溯到现存的一些寺庙,如位于老城区中心的城隍庙,以及纪念三国时期武将关羽的关帝庙。文庙则是为供奉孔子的。佛教在上海历史最悠久,龙华寺是上海最大的寺庙,与静安寺一样,最早修建于三国时期。

上海是中国的航空枢纽之一,拥有两座国际机场:上海浦东国际机场和上海虹桥国际机场。浦东机场主要面向国际航线,虹桥机场主要面向国内航班,同时也兼顾部分短途国际航线。

Cabin Service English

Unit 10

Duty-free Sale

- Part A   Useful Words and Expressions
- Part B   Dialogues
- Part C   Public Announcements
- Part D   Work-task
- Part E   Supplementary Reading

Students will be able to:
memorize the words and expressions about duty-free sale in the cabin;
make up the dialogues about duty-free sale service in the cabin;
obtain and improve public announcements skills about duty-free sale;
know about general information about duty-free sale service;
introduce Los Angeles.

Suggested Hours: *4 class hours*

Part A
Useful Words and Expressions

Please list as many expressions about duty-free sale as possible.

_____
_____

- duty-free/tax-free
- duty-free catalogue
- cash
- credit card
- check
- traveler's check
- RMB
- US dollar
- Euro
- Diner's Club
- Master
- Visa
- American Express
- Union Pay
- We have a wide selection on board today.
- If there is anything that interests you, please feel free to contact us.
- What would you think of a silk tie?
- Excuse me, Madam. Would you like any duty-free goods?
- Excuse me, Sir. Can I interest you in any duty-free items?
- Would you like to purchase any duty-free items, Sir?
- We provide duty-free sales after the meal service.
- The duty-free goods magazine in the rear pocket shows our selection.
- For more information on... please refer to the duty-free catalogue.
- How would you like to pay? Cash or credit card?
- Have you got any small change?
- This credit card has expired. Is there another way you can pay? Or do you have another card you can use?
- Here are the duty-free items you have bought. Please check the receipt/your items.
- Please press your password/enter your pin number and sign your name on the receipt.

Culture Tips

➤ Each country has a currency in which the prices of goods and services are quoted.
➤ People in different countries use different currencies as well as different languages.

Unit 10　Duty-free Sale

The translator between different currencies is the exchange rate. An exchange rate is the price of one currency in terms of another.

➢ Because of trade, travel, and other transactions between individuals and business enterprises of different countries, it becomes necessary to convert money into the currency of other countries in order to pay for goods or services in those countries.

➢ Common currency symbols

—U.S. Dollar　　　　　　USD　　　　　　U.S./ $
—Renminbi Yuan　　　　　CNY　　　　　　RMB/ ¥
—Euro　　　　　　　　　 EUR　　　　　　€
—Japanese Yen　　　　　　JPY　　　　　　¥
—Pound　　　　　　　　　GBP　　　　　　£

Cabin Term

Checked Baggage / Luggage　托运行李

释义：check一般指登记签到的含义，比如入住酒店多使用check in 来表达办理入住的含义。Checked Baggage是指托运行李，国内航空公司一般提供20kg/人、40cm×60cm×100cm /件的免费托运行李额度。

◉ Match phrases or sentences in column B to the situations in column A.

Column A	Column B
1. Before duty-free sales service.	a. Here are the duty-free items you have bought. Please check your items.
2. During duty-free sales service.	b. The duty-free goods magazine in the rear pocket shows our selection.
3. After duty-free sales service.	c. Would you like any duty-free goods?
4. On a domestic flight.	d. I'm sorry, in-flight duty-free sales services are not available.
5. Collect money from passengers.	e. How would you like to pay?
6. Ask passengers paying method.	f. Have you got any small change?

◉ Make up a dialogue about duty-free sales service in the cabin.

Part B
Dialogues

(CA=Cabin Attendant, PAX=Passenger)

1

CA: Good afternoon. May I interest you in any duty-free items?
PAX: Yes. Can I have a look at the Levis watch?
CA: Certainly, Sir. Here you are.
PAX: That's lovely. Do you have the same watch in white?
CA: Let me check. I am sorry. A limited stock of each colour is available. The white is very popular today. We only have light or dark brown left.
PAX: Oh, I see. I have no interest in the brown one. Thank you.
CA: I'm sorry about that. You may browse through the in-flight duty-free magazine located in the seatback pocket in front of you. If there is anything that interests you, please feel free to contact us.
PAX: Yes. Thank you.

2

PAX: Can I have a bottle of Chanel No. 5, please?
CA: Chanel No. 5, the spray one?
PAX: Yes. How much is that?
CA: That's £76, Sir.
PAX: I'll take it. Would it be possible for me to pay with Japanese Yen?
CA: I'm afraid that we can't accept Japanese Yen for the purchase. You need to pay for it in US dollars. Or you may pay by credit card.
PAX: Well, I'll pay for it in US dollars. What's the exchange rate between UK pound and US dollar?
CA: Our exchange rate today makes 1 UK pound equal to 1.6 US dollars. So it comes to 123 US dollars.
PAX: Here's 130 dollars. Keep the change.
CA: No, thanks. We don't accept tips. It's a pleasure to serve you. Here is your change. Thank you just the same.

3

PAX: Excuse me, I want to buy something for a man who doesn't smoke or drink. What would you recommend?

Unit 10 Duty-free Sale

CA: What would you think of a silk tie?
PAX: I have no idea about it. I heard lots about cloisonné. How about a pair of cloisonné sleeve buttons?
CA: I'm sorry, Madam. Cloisonne' sleeve buttons are not available on board.
PAX: What a pity. May I see the silk tie?
CA: Of course. After you've made your selection, you can purchase the items from the duty-free trolley.
PAX: Thank you, I will take it. May I use my credit card?
CA: Yes. We accept credit card for duty free purchases.
PAX: Here you are.
CA: Excuse me, but this credit card has expired. Is there another way you can pay? Or do you have another card you can use?
PAX: Oh, I took the wrong one. Sorry to trouble you.
CA: It doesn't matter.

(*A cabin attendant comes with a trolley along the aisle.*)
PAX: Miss. Can I spare you a minute?
CA: Yes. How may I assist you, Sir?
PAX: Could you recommend something as a gift for my wife?
CA: Certainly! We have fragrance, make-up sets, lipsticks and silk scarves.
PAX: Chinese silk scarves? That sounds wonderful.
CA: How do you like this one, Sir? It's a traditional design and has bright colors.
PAX: Yes, I like it. By the way, where was it made?
CA: It was made in Hangzhou. The city is famous for silk products.
PAX: How much is it?
CA: Only ten US dollars.
PAX: Could you give me a discount if I buy more than one?
CA: I am afraid I can't give you any discount. All the items we sell on board are marked prices.

PAX: Excuse me, Miss, do you sell duty-free items on board?
CA: Yes, we provide duty-free sales after the meal service.

127

PAX: Can I purchase duty-free liquor and tobacco on board?

CA: Certainly. We stock all the major alcohol brands and cigarettes brands. For more information on alcohol products and cigarettes products, please refer to the duty-free catalogue.

PAX: They are all my favorite well-known international brands. Are they with high prices?

CA: They are all duty-free goods and save 15% to 40% on the suggested retail price of various items.

PAX: Great. I really want to spoil myself with duty-free products. Please give me 3 cartons of Camel cigarettes and 2 bottles of Johnnie Walker.

CA: I'm sorry, Sir. As far as I know, visitors to Hongkong are allowed 400 cigarettes or 50 cigars and alcoholic beverage not exceeding 1,000 cc. If you go over your allowance, you may have to pay duty. For passengers who are in transit, please note that liquid, aerosol and gel items purchased onboard must be kept in a sealed bag with receipts. Please keep your boarding pass and get these items ready for inspection at the security check.

PAX: Thank you for reminding me. Two cartons of Camel cigarettes and one bottle of Johnnie Walker, please. Do you accept cash?

CA: Yes, Sir. All major currencies in cash are accepted as payment onboard.

6

CA: Excuse me, Sir. May we invite you to take a look at our redesigned and updated on board sales catalogue? You will be surprised by the selection of products and well-known brands available at competitive prices.

PAX: Well, I'd love to. But I want to buy some on my return flight. I don't want to carry my purchases with me throughout my trip.

CA: Don't worry, Sir. We offer top quality duty-free products. We can deliver your duty-free purchases on your return flight. Home Delivery Service is provided now. More than 200 duty-free items marked with a Home Delivery icon are available both on board and for home delivery. The icons below will tell you where products can be delivered. So you will not Miss out on your favorite item in-flight.

PAX: You said it. Let me see. You have better prices.

CA: Yes. Our duty-free goods for sale on board are around 20%~25% cheaper than equivalent products down on the ground in Europe.

PAX: I want Pandora Sterling Silver Bracelet set and Estee Lauder Purse Spray collection. How much is it altogether?

CA: It is 136 US dollars altogether.

PAX: I'm awfully sorry, I didn't have enough US dollars to pay them. Can I pay in Euro traveler's check?

CA: I'm sorry. We don't accept that kind of traveler's check. We accept credit cards and major currencies.

Unit 10　Duty-free Sale

New Words and Expressions

interest	['ɪntrɪst]	v.	使感兴趣；使参与
lovely	['lʌvlɪ]	adj.	美丽的，极好的，可爱的
limited	['lɪmɪtɪd]	adj.	有限制的；少的；见识不广的
stock	[stɒk]	n.	股票，股份；库存
popular	['pɒpjʊlə]	adj.	流行的；受欢迎的
browse	[braʊz]	v.	随便看看；浏览
exchange rate	[ɪks'tʃeɪndʒ][reɪt]		汇率；兑换率
come to	[kʌm][tuː]		想起；共计
change	[tʃeɪndʒ]	n.	零钱；变化；换洗衣物
cloisonné	[klɒɪ:'zɒneɪ]	n.	(法)景泰蓝瓷器
purchase	['pɜːtʃəs]	n.	购买；紧握
		v.	购买；获得
expired	[ɪks'paɪəd]	adj.	过期的；失效的
fragrance	['freɪgr(ə)ns]	n.	香味，芬芳
make-up set	[meɪkʌp][set]		化妆品套装
lip-stick	['lɪpstɪk]	n.	口红；唇膏
scarves	[skɑːvz]	n.	围巾；领带(scarf的复数)
traditional design	[trə'dɪʃənəl][dɪ'zaɪn]		传统图案
discount	['dɪskaʊnt]	n.	折扣；贴现率
major	['meɪdʒə]	adj.	主要的
retail price	['riːteɪl][praɪs]		零售价
spoil	[spɒɪl]	vt.	溺爱
receipt	[rɪ'siːt]	n.	收据；发票
currency	['kʌrənsɪ]	n.	货币；通货
competitive price	[kəm'petətɪv][praɪs]		[物价]竞争价格
equivalent	[ɪ'kwɪvələnt]	adj.	等价的，相等的

● Role play the cabin attendant's responses.

CA: _____.
PAX: Can I have a look at the perfume?
CA: _____.
PAX: How much is it?
CA: _____.
PAX: May I use credit card?
CA: _____.

> CA: _____.
> PAX: Please give me 3 cartons of Camel cigarettes.
> CA: _____.
> PAX: Oh, thank you for reminding me.
> CA: _____.
> PAX: I'll pay for it in Japanese Yen. What's the exchange rate?
> CA: _____.
> PAX: Thank you very much.

Discuss the following questions.

1. When a passenger would like to buy a bottle of whisky but it has sold out. How would you explain to the passenger?
2. When a passenger wants to buy too many duty-free cigarettes on board, what advice would you give to him?
3. When a passenger plans to buy something typically Chinese such as cloisonné or a Tang Horse, which you don't carry on board, what would you say to him?
4. A passenger wants to pay in Euro travelers' checks for the duty-free items, but you don't accept them. What would you say to him?
5. When a passenger asks you to give him a discount, what would you say to him?

Make up dialogues based on the following situations.

1. Jill is a cabin attendant. She is introducing duty-free sale service to a passenger.
2. A passenger has no idea about the duty-free items prices in Japanese Yen. Jill is explaining exchange rate to him.
3. Shirley is a purser of the flight, and she is telling the duty-free related regulations to a passenger who wants to buy too many duty-free items.

Translate the following sentences into English.

1. 机上付款时接受所有的主要货币。
2. 我们不接受那种旅行支票。
3. 今天航班上备有各种各样的商品。
4. 对不起,女士,您需要免税品吗?
5. 用餐服务后我们进行免税品销售。
6. 前方座椅口袋里的免税品杂志有商品的介绍。
7. 这个信用卡已经过期了,您有其他方式或者其他信用卡支付吗?
8. 您想用哪种方式付款?现金还是刷卡?
9. 这是您买的免税物品,请您检查一下。
10. 请输入您的密码,并在收据上签上您的名字。

Unit 10　Duty-free Sale

Part C
Public Announcements

Duty-free Sales

Good morning, ladies and gentlemen,

In an effort to further meet your traveling needs, we are pleased to offer you a wide selection of duty-free items. A brochure featuring these items is located in your seat pocket. All items are priced in US dollars. Please check with your cabin attendant for prices in other currencies. Most major currencies and US dollar travelers' checks are accepted for your purchases. The major credit cards are also accepted.

Thank you!

In-flight Duty-free Goods Sales Service

Ladies and gentlemen,

For passengers who are interested in purchasing duty-free items, we will begin our in-flight sales service very soon.

Our duty-free goods catalog, with product information, can be found in the seat pocket in front of you. For your convenience, we accept both cash and major international credit cards.

For passengers with connecting flights, please note that liquid items purchased onboard are subject to *Safety Regulations on Prohibiting Liquid Items* onboard. Please feel free to contact any of our flight attendants for detailed information.

Thank you!

Duty-free Items Sales Closed

Ladies and gentlemen,

Our duty-free shop will be closed shortly. If you have any interest in our duty-free items, please contact the attendant now.

Thank you for your cooperation.

Duty-free Items Sales Halted

Ladies and gentlemen,

According to _____ (country) customs regulations, in-flight duty-free sales service is now suspended.

Thank you for your understanding and cooperation!

Duty-Free Sale(To Australia)

Ladies and gentlemen,

We are pleased to offer you a wide selection of exclusive duty-free items which are available on our flight. The prices are in US dollars. Please ask our flight attendants for prices in other currencies. We also accept credit cards. For more information, the duty-free catalog is in the seat pocket in front of you.

Passengers continuing to other cities, please follow the rules of The Australian Government to make sure that your liquid duty-free items are less than 100 milliliter and must be in a zip-lock transparent plastic bag, otherwise it will be taken by the security check. If you have any questions, please contact flight attendants.

Thank you!

New Words and Expressions

further	[ˈfəːðə]	adv.	进一步地
selection	[sɪˈlekʃən]	n.	选择，挑选
brochure	[ˈbrəʊʃə(r)]	n.	手册，小册子
customs	[ˈkʌstəmz]	n.	海关；习惯
exclusive	[ɪkˈskluːsɪv]	adj.	高级的；新式的
milliliter	[ˈmɪlɪliːtə]	n.	毫升
zip-lock	[ˈzɪplˈɒk]	n.	封锁
transparent	[trænsˈpærənt]	adj.	透明的
plastic	[ˈplæstɪk]	adj.	塑料的

Speaking Practice

Practice making public announcements about duty-free sales with these alternatives.

- China
- UK
- USA
- Japan
- France

● **Please read following sentences in the right tone(′ for stress, ↗ for rising tone, ↘ for falling tone).**

1. In an effort to ′ further ↗ meet your traveling needs ↘, we are ′ pleased ↗ to offer you a wide ′ selection of duty-free items.↘
2. A brochure ↗ featuring these items is ′ located in your seat pocket.↘
3. All items ↗ are ′ priced in US dollars.↘
4. If you have any ′ interest ↗ in our duty-free items ↘, please contact the attendant now.↘
5. Please ↗ ask our flight attendants for ′ prices in other currencies.↘

● **Translate the following expressions into English and practice making public announcement about duty-free sales.**

- 免税品销售
- 各种货品均以美元标价
- 购物指南放置在座椅口袋中
- 接受现金和主要的国际信用卡
- 请咨询乘务员
- 《禁止携带液体类物品乘坐飞机的规定》
- 容积小于100mL
- 放置在密闭的透明塑料袋内
- 被当地安检没收
- 提供各种免税商品

Part D
Work-task

📋 **Try to discuss:**
1. What do you know about duty-free sale?
2. What can passenger buy on board?

Duty-free Sale

  Airlines, like any business are looking for ways to increase their revenue. One of the primary sources of revenue for airlines is the in-flight duty-free shop. However, not all carriers provide the sale of certain duty-free items on international flights. In most countries, tax does not have to be paid on goods which are being exported. Accordingly, the goods can leave the country tax-free or the tax can be reclaimed later. Travelers are allowed to import the goods into the country to which they are travelling, as long as the amount of these goods does not exceed the set "duty-free" allowance.❶

Airlines vary in their approach to in-flight duty-free sales. The traditional duty-free items are cigarettes and alcohol, perfumes, airline memorabilia, gadgets and gifts, food, and beauty products. Some airlines attach a great deal of importance to this source of income; indeed, in some cases crew members are given incentives in order to encourage sales. The cabin attendants hand out brochures or price lists describing the items available and then make the sales from a rolling cart which they pass through the aisle of the aircraft. Since the key product suppliers on the duty-free catalogs are well-known companies and strong brand names such as Chanel, Dior, Gucci, Marlboro, Olympus, Sony, Swatch, etc. As a result it seems to passengers that it is less necessary to worry about the quality of these brand name products.❷ Besides, as the term "duty-free" implies to shoppers, there is a price advantage in comparison to prices charged by other retailers. The in-flight shoppers have the benefit from both the brand name products as well as the duty-free prices, and which decreases their feelings of risk.❸

After the sale, cabin attendants are also responsible for keeping the proper records for all such transactions. As well as being involved with on board purchasing, a competent flight attendant has to be familiar with a variety of on-board services, ranging from reclining seats to the entertainment facilities.❹

(资料来源：http://www.getreadytofly.com.br/book.html)

Notes

❶Travelers are allowed to import the goods into the country to which they are travelling, as long as the amount of these goods does not exceed the set "duty-free" allowance.

句子大意：旅客携带的物品只要没有超过免税额度是可以带入境的。

这里"import the goods"并不是真正的进口物品，而是指把物品带入境的意思。

❷Since the key product suppliers on the duty-free catalogs are well-known companies and strong brand names such as Chanel, Dior, Gucci, Marlboro, Olympus, Sony, Swatch, etc. As a result it seems to passengers that it is less necessary to worry about the quality of these brand name products.

句子大意：因为在免税品目录上出现的产品都是世界闻名的公司出产并且都是诸如香奈尔、迪奥、古驰、万宝路、奥林巴斯、索尼、斯沃琪等国际大牌。在旅客看来完全没有必要担心这些品牌产品的质量问题。

其中，"key product"是拳头产品的意思。

"it is necessary to do sth"是非常常见的句型，表示有必要做某事。less意思为较小地，加在necessary，与之前的句式意思刚好相反，表示没有必要。

❸The in-flight shoppers have the benefit from both the brand name products as well as the duty-free prices, and which decreases their feelings of risk.

句子大意：旅客可以在享受大牌的同时又节省了开支。低廉的价格让旅客降低了风险感。

❹As well as being involved with on board purchasing, a competent flight attendant has to be familiar with a variety of on-board services, ranging from reclining seats to the entertainment facilities.

句子大意：一名称职的乘务员不仅能胜任机上免税品销售，同时也能熟识小到调座椅靠背、使用机上娱乐设施的各种服务。

其中，"on-board services"意为"机上服务"，有时也用"in-flight services"。

New Words and Expressions

carrier	['kærɪə(r)]	n. 承运人；载体
export	[ek'spɔːt]	n. 出口；出口商品
reclaim	[rɪ'kleɪm]	vt. 开拓；回收再利用
allowance	[ə'laʊəns]	n. 津贴，零用钱；允许；限额
perfume	['pɜːfjuːm]	n. 香水；香味
memorabilia	[memərə'bɪlɪə]	n. 大事记；值得纪念的事物
gadget	['gædʒɪt]	n. 小玩意；小器具；小配件
incentive	[ɪn'sentɪv]	n. 动机；刺激
transaction	[træn'zækʃən]	n. 交易；事务；办理

Part E
Supplementary Reading

Try to discuss:
1. Do you know some famous tourist attractions in Los Angeles?
2. How much do you know about Los Angeles's history?

Los Angeles

Los Angeles, located in southwestern California, is the second largest city in the United States and the largest city in the western United States. It is often called the "City of Angels" and covers an area of about 1,215 square kilometers.

Los Angeles is one of America's important industrial and commercial centers, it is also the center of international trade, science and education, entertainment and sports. Meanwhile, it is one of the major bases of the United States' petrochemical, marine, aerospace, and electronics industries. It also has many world-renowned higher education institutions, such as California Institute of Technology, UCLA, University of Southern California, Pepperdine University, etc.

Historically, Los Angeles once belonged to 3 countries. In 1781, Los Angeles became a Spanish colony. In 1821, it became a colony of Mexico. In 1846, Mexico failed in the Mexican-American War and later ceded California to the United States, thus Los Angeles became a US territory. Geographically, except for hills, Los Angeles has a flat terrain with an average elevation of 84 meters. The highest point is Mount Elsie, which is about 1,548 meters high. Los Angeles has a temperate Mediterranean climate, being mild throughout the year. It is generally dry all year round, but it rains slightly more in winter. The annual precipitation (mainly raining in winter) is about 378mm. The average maximum temperature is 23.3℃, and the average minimum temperature is 13℃.

From the perspective of culture, Hollywood is the entertainment center of Los Angeles. It takes about 40 minutes to reach Hollywood from the city by bus. Since the first film company was established here in 1911, the area has quickly become the world's film center. Los Angeles is  the second largest market for modern art in the United States (follow behind New York). More than 150 art galleries and numerous museums have jointly created a contemporary art palace. In the field of sports, the Los Angeles Angels is a major league baseball team belonging to the Pacific Coast League. The Los Angeles Lakers is a basketball club, founded in Minneapolis in 1947 and won six championships in eight consecutive years from 1947 to 1954.

The main attractions of Los Angeles are: Oweila Street, Griffith Park, Los Angeles Symphony Orchestra, Hollywood, Universal Studios, Los Angeles Disneyland, Santa Monica, etc. In November 2018, Los Angeles ranked as one of the world's first-tier cities. On December 26, 2019, it ranked 5th in the list of the top 500 global cities.

(资料来源：https://baike.so.com/doc/2934628-3096512.html)

参考译文

洛 杉 矶

洛杉矶，位于美国加利福尼亚州西南部，是美国第二大城市，也是美国西部最大的城市，常被称为"天使之城"。洛杉矶面积约1215km^2，城市中心坐标为北纬34°03′、西经118°15′。

洛杉矶是美国重要的工商业、国际贸易、科教、娱乐和体育中心之一，也是美国石油化工、海洋、航天工业和电子业的主要基地之一。洛杉矶还拥有许多世界知名的高等教育机构，比如加州理工学院、加州大学洛杉矶分校、南加州大学、佩珀代因大学等。

历史上，洛杉矶曾隶属于3个国家。1781年，洛杉矶成为西班牙殖民地；1821年，洛杉矶归属墨西哥；1846年，美墨战争中墨西哥失败，后将加利福尼亚州割让给美国，洛杉矶成为美国领土。地理上，洛杉矶除局部为丘陵外，全市地势平坦，平均海拔为84m，最高点是埃尔西峰，高约1548m。洛杉矶属于温带地中海型气候，全年气候温和。大体上终年干燥少雨，只是在冬季降雨稍多。年降水量约378mm，以冬季降雨为主。平均最高气温23.3℃，平均最低气温13℃。

文化领域，好莱坞是洛杉矶的娱乐中心，从市区坐公共汽车约40分钟即可到达好莱坞。自从1911年在此成立了第一家电影公司后，该地迅速成为世界的电影中心。洛杉矶是美国现代艺术作品第二大交易市场（仅次于纽约）。150余所艺术画廊以及众多的博物馆共同打造了一座当代艺术的殿堂。体育领域,洛杉矶天使队是一支美国职棒大联盟的球队,主场位于美国加利福尼亚州的洛杉矶,隶属于太平洋海岸联盟。洛杉矶湖人队是一支位于美国加利福尼亚州洛杉矶的篮球俱乐部,1947年成立于明尼阿波利斯,1947—1954年的八年内六夺总冠军。

　　洛杉矶的主要景点有:欧威拉街、格里菲斯公园、洛杉矶交响乐团、好莱坞、环球影城、洛杉矶迪士尼乐园、圣塔莫尼卡等。2018年11月,世界城市排名发布,洛杉矶进入世界一线城市行列。2019年12月26日,位列2019年全球城市500强榜单第5名。

Cabin Service English

Unit 11

Delays

* Part A Useful Words and Expressions
* Part B Dialogues
* Part C Public Announcements
* Part D Work-task
* Part E Supplementary Reading

Students will be able to:
memorize the words and expressions about delay reasons;
make up the dialogues about delay;
obtain and improve public announcements skills about delay;
know about general information about delay and related procedures;
introduce Beijing Daxing International Airport.

Suggested Hours: *4 class hours*

Part A
Useful Words and Expressions

◉ **Please list as many reasons and regretful expressions for the delay as you can.**

_____

_____

- aircraft late arrival
- bad/unfavorable weather conditions
- air traffic control
- airport runway congestion
- mechanical problems
- waiting for a late passenger
- waiting for cargo or passengers' baggage to be loaded
- waiting for in-flight catering
- We have to wait till the fog lifts.
- I'm afraid we have to wait until …
- We're waiting for the clearance from the air traffic control tower
- We need to wait for the aircraft ahead of us to take off
- We can't take off because …
- I'm really sorry to tell you that our flight has been delayed due to …
- The ice on the runway has been cleared.
- The airport is closed due to poor visibility.
- We'll be leaving as soon as boarding is completed.
- Thank you for your patience.
- Thank you for your understanding and cooperation.
- Hopeful it won't take long.
- All the overnight accommodation will be provided by our airline.

Culture Tips

➢ An acronym is an abbreviation formed from the initial components in a phrase or a word. For instance, the National Aeronautics and Space Administration is known more commonly by its acronym, NASA.

➢ In English and most other languages, such abbreviations historically had limited use. But because the computer age has provided the world with an abundance of new acronyms, they became much more common in the 20th century so it is vital to know how to use acronyms appropriately. However, when cabin attendant is providing cabin service, it is not advised to use acronym.

> Avoid using casual language on board:
—OMG   Oh My god!
—ASAP   As soon as possible.
—BRB   Be right back.
—BBS   Be back soon.
—BTW   By the way.
—YW   You're welcome.

Cabin Term

Hand baggage / Carry-on luggage   手提行李

释义：Carry on 意为随身携带的，Carry-on luggage 用来表示手提行李。国内航空公司一般为乘客提供1件/人、5kg/件、20cm×40cm×55cm/件的免费手提行李额。

● Match phrases or sentences in column B to the situations in column A.

Column A	Column B
1. Air traffic control	a. We will be leaving as soon as weather conditions improved.
2. Passengers' late arrival	b. We will depart as soon as the boarding is completed.
3. Bad weather conditions	c. We are waiting for the departure clearance from the Air Traffic Tower.
4. Mechanical problems	d. We are waiting in line for take-off.
5. Aircraft's late arrival	e. Our departure will be delayed due to a minor mechanical problem with this aircraft.
6. Airport runway congestion	f. The aircraft has not arrived due to unfavorable weather condition enroute.

● Make up a dialogue about explaining causes for the delay.

Part B
Dialogues

(CA=Cabin Attendant, PAX=Passenger)

PAX: Excuse me, Miss, why aren't we leaving yet? It's already past the scheduled departure time.
CA: I'm awfully sorry to tell you that our flight has been delayed due to the unfavorable weather conditions.

Unit 11 Delays

PAX: You must be kidding. It is sunny outside!
CA: Yes Sir. The weather conditions are fine over our airport, but they are unfavorable on flight route. For the sake of safety, we have to wait for the further weather report.
PAX: How long are we going to wait here?
CA: I'm afraid we have to wait until the weather improves.
PAX: That's too bad! I do hope the plane will take off soon.

2

PAX: I've been wondering why our plane hasn't taken off yet. What's the hold-up?
CA: We're waiting for a few more passengers to come on board. We'll be leaving as soon as boarding is completed.
PAX: How irritating! Can't we just leave them behind?
CA: I understand how you feel, but all passengers who have checked in must be on board. So we could do nothing for the moment but to wait for a few more minutes. Hopefully it won't take long. Sorry for the inconvenience.

3

PAX: Miss! Could you come here a second?
CA: What's the matter?
PAX: How long has the flight been delayed? When will we be landing on earth?
CA: I'm sorry. We have been delayed for about two and half hours. We still have another 90 minutes to fly.

PAX: OMG. Could you tell me what the weather will be like when we arrive at the destination?
CA: According to the present weather report, it is 3 degrees below zero and it's snowing there.
PAX: Will the snow let up before our arrival?
CA: No. The weather forecast says it's going to snow all day.
PAX: What a bore!
CA: Well, perhaps you'll have a white Christmas there.
PAX: Yes. That will be terrific.

4

PAX: Miss, I'm really worried about landing at an alternate airport. Why can't we land at Beijing Capital International Airport? My friends are meeting me there.
CA: We're extremely sorry for causing you inconvenience. Beijing Capital International Airport has been closed due to thick fog. I'm afraid we have no choice about it. We have to land at Tianjin Binhai International Airport.
PAX: Oh, Dear.

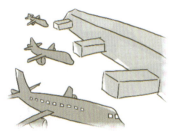

5

PAX: Excuse me. Could you tell me how long we'll have to stay at the alternate airport?

CA: It's hard to say. We'll have to wait until the weather in Shanghai has improved. There is a possibility that our plane is going to stay overnight at the airport.

PAX: If that happens who will arrange our accommodation here?

CA: Don't worry. All the overnight accommodation will be provided by our airlines.

6

PAX: Miss, I'm sorry to trouble you, but I've got a question.

CA: Yes. What can I do for you?

PAX: You see Beijing is my transit airport and I have a connecting flight to Xi'an there. But it seems that our flight could not reach Beijing on time. I will fail to catch my connecting flight. So could you tell me what I can do about my connecting flight?

CA: I am awfully sorry about the inconvenience caused by the delay. As far as I know, if you Miss an onward connecting flight due to our fault, you'll be arranged to take the next available flight to the destination.

PAX: Thank you.

New Words and Expressions

scheduled	['ʃedju:ld]	adj. 预定的
unfavorable	['ʌn'feɪvərəbl]	adj. 不宜的
hold-up	[həʊldʌp]	n. 停顿；耽误
irritating	['ɪrɪteɪtɪŋ]	adj. 令人不愉快的
Forecast	['fɔ:kɑ:st]	n. 预测；预想
Terrific	[tə'rɪfɪk]	adj. 极好的；非常的；可怕的
alternate	['ɔ:ltəneɪt]	adj. 交替的；轮流的
accommodation	[ə,kɒmə'deɪʃən]	n. 住处，住宿
connecting flight	[kə'nektɪŋ][flaɪt]	转接航班

Role play the cabin attendant's responses.

PAX: Why haven't we taken off yet?
CA: _____.
PAX: How long will the delay last?
CA: _____.
PAX: What a bore!

> PAX: What are we waiting for?
> CA: _____.
> PAX: You must be kidding. Can't we leave them behind?
> CA: _____.
> PAX: I hope this will not take too much time.
> CA: _____.

◉ **Discuss the following questions.**

1. The plane is delayed because of bad weather at the airport. The delay will be 15 minutes. Please explain the situation to the passengers.
2. The plane will be delayed because several passengers who have checked in are late in arriving. Please give the reason for the delay.
3. Make an announcement about the weather condition at your base city.
4. The plane is going to stay overnight at a diversionary airport. The passengers want to know who will pay for their accommodation. What would you say to them?

◉ **Make up dialogues based on the following situations.**

1. Jill is a cabin attendant. She is making an explanation to a passenger that the flight is delayed due to bad weather conditions.
2. The flight is delayed due to the air traffic control. Jill is a cabin attendant. Please explain the reason to the passenger.
3. Shirley is a purser of the flight, and she is trying to calm down the passengers who are restless for the delay.

◉ **Translate the following sentences into English.**

1. 恐怕我们要等到跑道上的积冰清理完毕。
2. 恐怕我们要等到前面的飞机起飞之后。
3. 我们在旅客登机结束之后出发。
4. 机场因天气原因关闭。
5. 我们排队等待起飞,感谢您的耐心等待。
6. 我们的飞机由于小的机械故障而延误,感谢您的理解与支持。
7. 由于航路天气不好我们不能起飞。
8. 机场因能见度低而关闭。
9. 请问我们将要在备降机场待多久呢?
10. 所有的过夜住宿将由我们航空公司提供。

Part C
Public Announcements

Mechanical Problems

Ladies and gentlemen,

This is your (chief) purser speaking. The Captain has informed us that our departure will be delayed due to a minor mechanical problem with this aircraft. Our maintenance staff is working diligently to solve this issue.

As your safety is our primary concern, please remain in your seat. Further information will be given as soon as possible.

Thank you for your understanding and patience!

Deicing Delay

Ladies and gentlemen,

This is your purser speaking. The Captain has informed us that this aircraft will need deicing prior to departure. Our ground staff is working diligently on this, please remain in your seat.

Thank you for your understanding.

Notes

Deicing

Aircraft deicing and anti-icing is required in winter time when frost, snow, and ice can form on the wings and fuselage of an aircraft. Such a layer of frost or ice on aircraft surfaces influences the aircraft's aerodynamic properties which may cause a loss of lift that could result in a crash.

飞机起飞是靠机翼在空气中相对运动形成的升力，升力的大小依机翼的形状而变化，附着在飞机表面的冰、雪、霜等污染物会直接导致飞机的空气动力特性的改变，这种改变也是造成空难的主要原因之一，所以飞机起飞时，机翼表面不能有任何附着物。除冰是指除去飞机表面附着的霜、冰、雪，以提供清洁外表的航空器的工作程序。

Unit 11　Delays

Return / Diverted Flight

Ladies and gentlemen,

　　May I have your attention please.

　　Due to bad weather, we are going to return / divert to _____ airport. (we will fly directly to _____ airport.)

　　Further information will be given to you after landing. We apologize for the inconvenience caused.

　　Thank you!

Waiting for Transit Passengers

Ladies and gentlemen,

　　We are currently waiting for several transfer passengers to join us. During this short delay, please remain in your seat.

　　Thank you!

Waiting for Takeoff

Ladies and gentlemen,

　　This is your purser speaking. The Captain has informed us that due to_____.(There are still _____ aircraft currently waiting ahead of us.)The departure time will be in approximately_____ minutes. Further information will be given you as soon as possible. (We will be serving _____ during this period.)

　　Thank you for your patience!

Address to the Transit Passengers after Delay

Ladies and gentlemen,

　　We are sorry for the delay of our flight due to _____.

　　Those who planned to transfer at this airport, please contact any flight attendant. We will contact our ground staff.

　　After landing, they will assist you with your connecting flight. If you require any further assistance, you are welcomed to contact us.

　　Thank you for your understanding and cooperation!

Overnight

Ladies and gentlemen,

　　We are sorry to inform you that due to _____, our flight has been canceled. We will have to stay overnight at _____ airport. Please take your overnight articles with you as you leave the aircraft. Hand baggage may be left on board, but take valuables with you.

　　(Please have your passport ready to go through entry and customs formalities in the waiting hall.)

The flight will take off at _____ (AM/PM) tomorrow.

(Further information will be given to you in the terminal building. We apologize for the inconvenience caused.)

Thank you!

New Words and Expressions

mechanical	[məˈkænɪkl]	adj. 机械的；呆板的
minor	[ˈmaɪnə]	adj. 较小的
maintenance	[ˈmeɪntɪnəns]	n. 维持，保持；维修
solve	[sɒlv]	v. 解决
staff	[stɑːf]	n. 职员
deicing	[ˌdiːˈɪsɪŋ]	n. 除冰
prior to	[ˈpraɪə(r)][tuː]	在……之前
diligently	[ˈdɪlɪdʒəntlɪ]	adv. 勤勉地
divert	[daɪˈvɜːt]	v. 转移；使……欢愉
cancel	[ˈkænsəl]	v. 取消
overnight	[ˌəʊvəˈnaɪt]	adj. 一整夜的

Speaking Practice

● **Practice making public announcements about overnight with these alternatives.**
- bad/unfavorable weather conditions
- air traffic control
- mechanical trouble/problems
- passenger late arrival
- airport runway congestion
- beverages
- breakfast
- lunch
- dinner
- snack

● **Please read following sentences in the right tone(′ for stress, ↗ for rising tone, ↘ for falling tone).**

1. We are sorry to ′inform you that ↘ due to bad weather ↘, our flight has been canceled.
2. Please take your overnight ′articles with you ↘ as you ′leave the aircraft.

3. Hand baggage may be left ↗ on board, ↘ but take ↗ valuables ↗ with you.
4. Further ↗ information will be given to you ↘ in the terminal building. We ↗ apologize ↘ for the ↗ inconvenience caused.
5. Those who planned to ↗ transfer at this airport ↘, please ↗ contact any flight attendant.

◉ **Translate the following expressions into English and practice making public announcement about delays.**
- 天气不利
- 航空管制
- 机械故障
- 等待旅客
- 推迟起飞
- 深表歉意
- 感谢您的理解与配合
- 地面工作人员
- 过夜物品
- 航站楼

Part D
Work-task

> **Try to discuss:**
> 1. What do you know about delays?
> 2. What are common reasons of flight delays?

Delay

A flight delay is when an airline flight takes off and/or lands later than its scheduled time. The Federal Aviation Administration (FAA) considers a flight to be delayed when it is 15 minutes later than its scheduled time.❶ A cancellation occurs when the airline does not operate the flight at all for a certain reason. When flights are canceled or delayed, passengers may be entitled to compensation due to rules obeyed by every flight company.❷ This rule usually specifies that passengers may be entitled to certain reimbursements, including a free room if the next flight is the day after the canceled one, a choice of reimbursement, rerouting, phone calls, and refreshments.

Much as we dislike delays, we cannot avoid them, even in the most well-run airlines.

Airlines cannot afford to maintain a spare aircraft to cater for unforeseen technical problems unless it is a very large operator. So if your airplane has a technical problem, inevitably there would be delays. It would be cumulative because the same aircraft will be used for later flights. The next time you are told of a technical delay, think of safety. Would you rather have the engineers rectify the defects thus delaying your flight, or would you risk your life with a problematic airplane?

In many other regions of the world, air spaces are also getting very congested as well. Most delays are attributed to obtaining air traffic clearances along common routes during the peak times.❸

Passengers themselves often delay flights too. If a passenger with no check-in baggage fails to turn up at the stipulated time, he would be left behind. However, on international flights, passengers who have checked in with bags and failed to show up, either because they were so engrossed with their duty free shopping or got lost in the complex terminal, the flight cannot depart unless their check-in bags are off-loaded.

Modern planes are safe and can withstand most weather conditions, but storms such as blizzards, hurricanes and tornadoes will cancel flights. Flights are also delayed due to poor weather like snow, heavy rain, and microburst activities in the vicinity of thunderstorms or thick fog. In such situations, aircraft may be subjected to holding in the air for weather improvement or air traffic controllers may impose wider separation between aircraft for safety reasons.❹

(资料来源:http://www.askcaptainlim.com/-air-travel-flying-49/466-what-causes-flight-delays.html)

Notes

❶ The Federal Aviation Administration (FAA) considers a flight to be delayed when it is 15 minutes later than its scheduled time.

句子大意:美国联邦航空管理局规定航班到达时间比预定时间晚15分钟以上即为延误。

美国联邦航空管理局(Federal Aviation Administration),缩写为FAA。

❷ When flights are canceled or delayed, passengers may be entitled to compensation due to rules obeyed by every flight company.

句子大意:当航班取消或延误时,旅客可以根据航空公司的规定而获得赔偿。

其中,"be entitled to"的意思是有权;有……的资格。

❸ Most delays are attributed to obtaining air traffic clearances along common routes during the peak times.

句子大意:大多数航班延误的原因是在高峰期获取放行许可。

"be attributed to"的意思是归因于……

❹ In such situations, aircraft may be subjected to holding in the air for weather improvement or air traffic controllers may impose wider separation between aircraft for safety reasons.

句子大意: 在这些情况下,飞机只能在空中盘旋等待天气状况改善或是出于安全考虑等待管制员加大飞机间的飞行间隔。

Situations 用复数指代上文出现的天气状况。

New Words and Expressions

Federal Aviation Administration (FAA)	['fedərəl][eɪvɪeɪʃən][əd,mɪnɪ'streɪʃən]	美国联邦航空管理局
entitle to	[ɪn'taɪtl][tuː]	拥有……的权利
compensation	[,kɒmpen'seɪʃən]	n. 补偿;赔偿金
specify	['spesɪfaɪ]	v. 详细说明;指定;阐述
reimbursement	[,riːɪm'bəːsmənt]	n. 偿还;赔偿;偿付
rerouting	[,rɪə'ruːtɪŋ]	n. 重编路由
well-run	['wel'rʌn]	adj. 经营良好的
afford	[ə'fɔːrd]	v. 花费得起;承担得起(后果)
spare	[speə]	adj. 备用的;多余的;闲置的
unforeseen	[,ʌnfɔːr'siːn]	adj. 无法预料的
technical	['teknɪkl]	adj. 技术的;专业的
operator	['ɒpəreɪtə(r)]	n. 操作员;管理者
inevitably	[ɪn'evɪtəbli]	adv. 不可避免地
cumulative	['kjuːmjələtɪv]	adj. 累积的;渐增的;累计的
defect	['diːfekt]	n. 缺点;缺陷
problematic	[,prɒblə'mætɪk]	adj. 问题的;有疑问的
congest	[kən'dʒest]	v. 使充满;使拥塞
stipulated time	['stɪpjʊletɪd][taɪm]	[法] 约定期限
engross	[ɪn'grəʊs]	v. 使全神贯注
off-load	['ɒfləʊd]	vt. 卸货
withstand	[wɪð'stænd]	v. 抵挡;禁得起
blizzard	['blɪzəd]	n. 暴风雪,大风雪
hurricane	['hʌrɪkən]	n. 飓风;暴风
tornado	[tɔː'neɪdəʊ]	n. 龙卷风;旋风
microburst	[maɪkrəʊ'bəːst]	n. 小型爆发(射电),瞬间阵风
subject to	['sʌbdʒekt][tuː]	使服从;受……管制

Part E
Supplementary Reading

Try to discuss:
1. When did Beijing Daxing International Airport be built?
2. How much do you know about Beijing Daxing International Airport?

Beijing Daxing International Airport

Official name	Beijing Daxing International Airport
Airport opening	September 2019
Destination (in May 2020)	124
Total Area of Terminal (in September 2019)	70 thousand square meters
Passenger throughput (in 2019)	3.13 million
Air cargo throughput (in 2019)	7,362.3 tons
Runways	4
Runways Length (in September 2019)	Three: 3,800 meters; One: 3,400 meters
Aircraft Parking Bays (in 2019)	268
Flight courses (in May 2020)	328

Beijing Daxing International Airport (IATA: PKX; ICAO: ZBAD) is a super-large international transportation hub built between Daxing District, Beijing and Guangyang District, Langfang City, Hebei Province.

In the first phase of project, four runways and one dual-use runway (namely Nanyuan New Air Force Airport) has be constructed. The terminal has an area of 700,000 square meters, and the passenger flow reaches 45 million.

On December 26, 2014, Beijing Daxing International Airport commenced building. On September 29, 2018, the hangar of China Eastern Airlines Base at Beijing Daxing International Airport was officially capped. On May 13, 2019, the first test flight landed at this airport. On June 30, the terminal building was completed and accepted. On September 25, Beijing Daxing International Airport was officially put into operation.

The terminal is shaped like a phoenix spreading its wings, which has the shape of a five-pointed corridor, that is, a radial shape with 5 legs. This shape is completely centered on passengers. There are 82 gates in the entire terminal. A total of five rail lines in the new airport are integrated and arranged in a group on the periphery of the airport, running through the terminal area along the central axis of the new airport, namely, Jingba Intercity, Airport Express, R4/S6, reserved line and Langzhuo Intercity.

The completion of Beijing Daxing International Airport has greatly eased the shortage of airspace resources faced by Beijing Capital International Airport, making Beijing the second city in China to face the challenge of "one city, two airports" after Shanghai.

(资料来源:https://baike.so.com/doc/7363933-7631068.html)

参考译文

北京大兴国际机场

机场名称	北京大兴国际机场
启用时间	2019年9月
通航城市(截至2020年5月)	124个
航站楼总面积(截至2019年9月)	70万m²
客运量(2019年)	313.5074万人次
货运量(2019年)	7362.3t
跑道数量	4条
跑道长度(截至2019年9月)	3条3800m;1条3400m
停机位数量(2019年)	268个
航线数量(截至2020年5月)	328条

北京大兴国际机场(IATA代码:PKX;ICAO代码:ZBAD),是建设在北京市大兴区与河北省廊坊市广阳区之间的超大型国际航空综合交通枢纽。

机场主体工程占地多在北京境内,第一期工程建设4条跑道及1条军民两用跑道(即空军南苑新机场)。航站楼面积为70万m²,客流达到4500万人次。

2014年12月26日,大兴国际机场破土动工。2018年9月29日,北京大兴国际机场东航基地机库正式封顶。2019年5月13日,北京大兴国际机场试飞正式开始,第一架试飞飞机降落大兴国际机场。6月30日,大兴国际机场航站楼竣工验收。8月26日,北京大兴国际机场圆满完成ⅢB(3B)进近着陆、HUD RVR75m起飞和国产四级A-SMGCS系统试飞项目。9月25日,北京大兴国际机场正式投入运营。

北京新机场航站楼形如展翅的凤凰,与T3航站楼"一"字造型不同,新机场是五指廊的造型,即5条腿的放射形,这个造型完全以旅客为中心。整个航站楼有82个登机口。新机场共有5条轨道线路在机场外围整合并列为一组,沿新机场中轴贯穿航站区,依次分别是京霸城际、机场快轨、R4/S6、预留线和廊涿城际。

北京大兴机场的建成,大大缓解了北京首都国际机场面临的空域资源紧张局面,使北京成为继上海之后中国第二个面对"一市双场"挑战的城市。

Unit 12

Turbulence

* Part A Useful Words and Expressions
* Part B Dialogues
* Part C Public Announcements
* Part D Work-task
* Part E Supplementary Reading

Students will be able to:

memorize the words and expressions about turbulence;

make up the dialogues about turbulence;

obtain and improve public announcements skills about turbulence;

know about general responsibilities of a cabin attendant;

introduce Hong Kang International Airport.

Suggested Hours: *4 class hours*

Unit 12　Turbulence

Part A
Useful Words and Expressions

◉ **Please list as many words related to turbulence as you can.**

- turbulence
- moderate turbulence
- severe turbulence
- sudden turbulence
- airsick
- airsickness bag
- waste bag
- seat pocket
- vomit
- fasten seat-belt
- seat-belt sign
- keep seat-belt fastened
- return to your seat
- remain in your seat
- If you feel airsick, please use the airsickness bag.
- The seat-belt sign is on, could you please return to your seat?
- We advise you to keep your seat-belt fastened as a precaution against sudden turbulence.
- We advise you to use the extension belt for your baby.
- Our plane is very bumpy at the present. Please keep your seat-belt fastened. Please be seated and fasten your seat-belts.
- Refrain from using the lavatories until the seat-belt sign goes off.
- Lavatories may not be used at this time.
- When you are using the lavatory, please hold the handle tightly.
- Our aircraft is experiencing some moderate rough air and it is expected to last for some time.
- Please take extra care if you are having meals.
- For the time being, cabin service will be suspended.
- We apologize for the inconvenience caused.
- If you have any concerns, please contact our flight attendants.
- Thank you for your understanding.
- Thank you for your cooperation.

153

Culture Tips

➢ Before taking off and landing, and whenever the pilot considers it necessary in the interest of safety, each passenger on board shall occupy a seat with their seat-belt properly secured.

➢ The seat-belt sign should not be left on during the entire flight if the air is smooth. This diminishes its effectiveness as a warning function. Passengers also tend to respond more to seat-belt compliance announcements made by the flight crew.

➢ While seat-belt sign stays on during the crossing of the mountain of range, passengers must remain in their seat with their seat-belts fastened and cabin crew must be secured in their jump seats with full harness. If passengers do not comply with the advisory to remain seated, cabin crew should reaffirm the PA announcement.

➢ Prevention is important. Injuries are far less likely to occur to passengers who are secured with their seat-belt fastened than to those who are not. The best defense to turbulence related injuries is to ensure persons on board are buckled-up.

Cabin Term

Emergency Landing / Emergency Ditching   紧急着陆/水上迫降

释义：Emergency Landing是指紧急着陆，在陆地上着陆。而Emergency Ditching指的是水上迫降，其中ditch含有（飞机）迫降、摆脱、逃离等含义。

◉ **Match phrases or sentences in column B to the situations in column A.**

Column A	Column B
1. Light turbulence	a. Please keep your seat-belt fastened, as a precaution against sudden turbulence.
2. Moderate turbulence	b. Please take care if you are having meals.
3. Severe turbulence	c. When you are using lavatory, please hold the handle tightly.
4. Sudden turbulence	d. Cabin service will be suspended during this time.
5. After turbulence	e. If you feel airsick, please use the airsickness bag located in the seat pocket in front of you.

Unit 12　Turbulence

◉ **According to the pictures given below, please discuss with your partner what had happened on board.**

Part B
Dialogues

(CA=Cabin Attendant, PAX=Passenger)

CA: Sir, the captain has switched the seat-belt sign on. Could you please return to your seat?
PAX: Yeah, I know. I'm fine.
CA: Sir, you must return to your seat now. We're expecting turbulence.
PAX: Don't worry. It'll be fine.
CA: It could get really rough. Nobody is allowed to stand in the cabin during the period. You must return to your seat and strap in.
PAX: Look. I'm fine. Don't worry.
CA: Sir. The aircraft may drop hundreds of feet without any warning, for your safety, now, sit down!

CA: Excuse me, Sir, the seat-belt sign is still on. Please keep the seat-belt fastened.
PAX: Yes, I know. I'm strapped in.
CA: Your son must be strapped in, too.
PAX: I can hold him on my lap.
CA: I'm sorry, Sir. It's not secure for him. You have to use the extension belt. Let me assist you.
PAX: Oh, for goodness sake! He'll scream the place down.
CA: Sir, we're expecting some turbulence very soon. Strap him in now. It's for his safety.
PAX: All right. I will do it.

155

3

CA: Yes, Madam. Is there anything I can do for you?
PAX: When will you provide meal service?
CA: We've been informed by our captain just now, we'll meet some strong headwinds, so there'll be moderate to severe turbulence. If that happens, the meal service will be delayed. I suggest you to fasten your seat-belt for any unforeseen turbulence. After that, we'll start meal service.

PAX: I see.

4

CA: Ladies and gentlemen, we are entering an area of turbulence. So please fasten your seat-belts. Use of the lavatories has been suspended. (to a passenger standing in the aisle) Sir, please return to your seat.
PAX: I will fasten my seat-belt after using the lavatory.
CA: The use of lavatory will be suspended during turbulence. You need to return to your seat and fasten your seat-belt.
PAX: I can't wait. I will fasten my seat-belt right after using the lavatory.
CA: If you insist on using the lavatory, please do hold the bars tightly while in the lavatory.
PAX: I got it.

5

PAX: Yes? Is there anything wrong?
CA: Sir, sorry to interrupt you. We have been informed just now that we may experience turbulence due to strong wind. So if you want to sleep, please fasten your seat-belt as a precaution against sudden turbulence. Even when the fasten seat-belt sign comes on, we won't need to wake you up.

PAX: Thank you for reminding me.
CA: If there is anything we can do for you, please press the call button.

6

CA: Excuse me, Madam. You look restless. May I bring you a glass of water?
PAX: Thank you. I feel nervous. I'm afraid that I'm going to suffer from airsickness.
CA: Please calm down. There is an airsickness bag in the seat pocket in front of you. Once you want to vomit,

you may use it.

PAX: What a shame. I am afraid of flying!

CA: Take it easy. According to the study, one in 10 of us is afraid of flying.

PAX: Really? You are so nice to tell me this. Can I have some more airsickness bags in case of turbulence happening?

CA: Sure. I will bring you more in a few seconds.

New Words and Expressions

expect	[ɪkˈspekt]	v.	期望；预料
rough	[rʌf]	adj.	粗糙的，崎岖不平的
strap	[stræp]	v.	用带子系
drop	[drɒp]	v.	落下；跌倒；下降
extension	[ɪkˈstenʃən]	n.	延长
for goodness sake	[fə(r)][ˈgʊdnɪs][seɪk]		天哪；务请；看在老天爷分上
scream the place down	[skriːm][ðə][pleɪs][daʊn]		拼命叫喊
headwind	[ˈhedwɪnd]	n.	顶头风，逆风
moderate	[ˈmɒdərət]	adj.	温和的，中等的
severe	[sɪˈvɪə(r)]	adj.	严峻的；剧烈的
precaution	[prɪˈkɔːʃən]	n.	预防措施
restless	[ˈrestləs]	adj.	焦躁不安的
airsickness	[ˈeəsɪknəs]	n.	晕机
vomit	[ˈvɒmɪt]	v.	呕吐；喷出

⦿ **Role play the cabin attendant's responses.**

CA: _____.
PAX: I want to use the lavatory.
CA: _____.
PAX: I can take care of myself.
CA: _____.
PAX: No problem. I will do it.

CA: _____.
PAX: I feel nervous. This is my first flight.
CA: _____.
PAX: I'm afraid that I'm going to suffer from airsickness.
CA: _____.
PAX: Oh, that's very kind of you. Thank you.

Discuss the following questions.

1. The plane is entering an area of turbulence. Please inform the passengers of this situation.
2. Due to the turbulence, the use of the lavatory is suspended. Please make an explanation to the passengers.
3. The flight is experiencing turbulence. The meal service will be put off. Please make an explanation to the passengers.
4. A passenger is suffering from airsickness due to turbulence. Please calm her down.
5. How do you deal with service spills or other mishaps happen for which the Airline may be responsible?
6. How would you deal with passenger spills or other incidents for which the Airline is not responsible?

Make up dialogues based on the following situations.

1. Jill is a cabin attendant. The plane is expecting a sudden turbulence, she persuades a passenger to strap in as a precaution.
2. The flight is experiencing turbulence. The use of the lavatory is suspended. Jill is a cabin attendant, please explain the reason to the passenger.
3. Shirley is a purser of the flight, and she is trying to calm down the passenger who is suffering from airsickness due to turbulence.

Translate the following sentences into English.

1. 我们遇到了严重颠簸，请您坐在椅子上并系好安全带。
2. 如果您感到晕机并且想呕吐，请使用呕吐袋。
3. 直到安全带指示灯熄灭后您才能使用卫生间。
4. 当您使用卫生间时，请抓紧扶手。
5. 飞机正遇到中等强度的气流，预计将持续一段时间。
6. 如果您正在用餐，请多加小心。
7. 客舱服务要暂停。
8. 给您带来不便我们深表歉意。
9. 如果您有任何问题，请联系我们的乘务员。
10. 我们的飞机目前非常颠簸，请系好安全带。

Unit 12 Turbulence

Part C
Public Announcements

Turbulence

Ladies and gentlemen,

We are encountering turbulence. For your safety and comfort, please remain seated and fasten your seat-belt. Toilets are not in use. If you feel airsick, please use the airsickness bag located in the seat pocket in front of you.

(Cabin service will be suspended during this period.)

Thank you.

Turbulence (Suspension of Cabin Service)

Ladies and gentlemen,

We are currently experiencing some turbulence. For your safety, please return to your seat and fasten your seat-belt. Refrain from using the lavatories until the seat-belt sign goes off. Cabin service will be suspended during this time.

Thank you for your understanding.

Moderate Turbulence

Ladies and gentlemen,

Our aircraft is experiencing some moderate turbulence and it is expected to last for some time. (The captain has informed us that we will pass through an area of rough air in _____ minutes, and the moderate turbulence will last for _____ minutes.)

Please be seated and fasten your seat-belts. Do not use the lavatories. Please take extra care if you are having meals. For the time being, cabin service will be suspended.

Thank you.

Severe Turbulence

Ladies and gentlemen,

We have encountered some strong turbulence. Please take your seat and fasten your seat-

159

belt. Do not use the lavatories.

Cabin service will be suspended during this period.

After Severe Turbulence

Ladies and gentlemen,

The aircraft has experienced some severe turbulence. We apologize for the inconvenience caused. If you have any problems, please contact us.

Thank you for your understanding and cooperation.

New Words and Expressions

encounter	[ɪnˈkaʊntə(r)]	v. 遭遇；邂逅；遇到
avoid	[əˈvɔɪd]	v. 避免
regret	[rɪˈgret]	v. 对……感到后悔
currently	[ˈkʌrəntli]	adv. 当前，目前
extra	[ˈekstrə]	adj. 额外的

Speaking Practice

◉ **Practice making public announcements about turbulence with these alternatives.**
- turbulence
- moderate turbulence
- severe turbulence
- sudden turbulence

◉ **Please read following sentences in the right tone(′ for stress, ↗ for rising tone, ↘ for falling tone).**

1. We are ′ encountering turbulence. ↘

2. For your ′ safety ↗ and comfort ↘, please remain ′ seated ↘ and ′ fasten your seat-belt.

3. If you feel ′ airsick ↘, please use the airsickness bag ↗ located in the seat pocket ↘ in front of you.

4. Cabin service will be ′ suspended ↘ during this period.

5. Refrain from using the ′ lavatories ↗ until the seat-belt sign goes off. ↘

◉ **Translate the following expressions into English and practice making public announcement about turbulence.**
- 就座
- 系紧安全带
- 晕机袋

- 客舱服务暂停
- 洗手间暂停使用
- 感谢理解
- 经历颠簸
- 返回到座位
- 安全带指示灯熄灭
- 就餐时请格外小心

Part D
Work-task

📋 **Try to discuss:**
1. Have you ever experienced any turbulence?
2. Are you afraid of turbulence?

Turbulence

Turbulence is the leading cause of in-flight injuries. There are countless reports of occupants who were seriously injured while moving about the passenger cabin when clear air turbulence is encountered.❶ Many passengers do not understand the effects of turbulence, or that an encounter with turbulence may occur without warning.

Turbulence or rough air can be subdivided into visible and invisible causes. Clouds, especially thunderstorms, create turbulence of varying severity. Thunder clouds, or cumulonimbus clouds are filled with parcels of air moving up and down at great speeds and often contain ice crystals as well as rain drops.❷ These particles can be seen by the aircraft's radar enabling the flight crews to avoid the storms and hence the turbulence.❸

Based on the level of turbulence described, the crew should be aware of the appropriate actions to be taken with regard to service duties and passenger management. Service may continue during light turbulence; however the service of all hot beverages should stop. Cabin crew should complete a seat-belt compliance check to ensure passengers are fastened and the cabin is secure. During a turbulence encounter above light, it is important to secure the cabin and galley when conditions permit.

However, the most appropriate first response by cabin crew might be self-preservation. Cabin crew can increase risk and compromise their personal safety by attempting to adhere to routine procedures normally performed on all flights such as the seat-belt compliance checks, rather than responding in accordance with the level and intensity of turbulence.❹

GUIDANCE

FOR

TURBULENCE MANAGEMENT

161

Another example that poses risk is on a short flight cabin crew often feel the pressure to complete a service and therefore are less cautious with their own personal safety than on a longer flight with no time constraints. Cabin crew should always secure themselves, sit down and fasten their seat-belt immediately when turbulence levels are a risk to personal safety.

CONDITIONS INSIDE THE AIRCRAFT		
LIGHT	MODERATE	SEVERE
• Liquids are shaking but not splashing out of cups. • Carts can be maneuvered with little difficulty. • Passengers may feel a light strain against seat-belts.	• Liquids are splashing out of cups. • Difficulties to walk or stand with out balancing or holding on to something. Carts are difficult to maneuver. • Passengers feel definite strain against seat-belt.	• Items are falling over unsecured, objects are tossed about. • Walking is impossible. • Passengers are forced violently against seat-belts.

(资料来源:http://www.casa.gov.au/scripts/nc.dll?WCMS:STANDARD:1001:pc=PC_91477; IATA guidance-on-turbulence-management)

Notes

❶ There are countless reports of occupants who were seriously injured while moving about the passenger cabin when clear air turbulence is encountered.

句子大意:无数的报道称由于客机在空中遇到晴空湍流,导致在客舱里走动的旅客受伤严重。

clear air turbulence:晴空湍流。

❷ Thunder clouds, or cumulonimbus clouds are filled with parcels of air moving up and down at great speeds and often contain ice crystals as well as rain drops.

句子大意:充满气块的雷暴云或积雨云快速上下移动,并通常含有冰晶体以及雨滴。

积雨云也叫雷暴云,是积状云的一种。积雨云和雷暴都是影响飞行安全的危险天气。积雨云属于强对流云,它伴随大风、龙卷、雷暴、冰雹、阵雨等天气现象,雷暴是积雨云发展旺盛的产物。在积雨云中有强电场,当电压达到一定的范围,就形成放电,即闪电。由于电场的作用,积雨云中产生强磁场。飞机误入积雨云中时,容易遭雷击,或在强磁场的作用下,指针摇摆不定或一直指向磁场方向,导致指针暂时失灵。积雨云中有强烈的上升和下沉气流,飞机

误入时会造成颠簸。超过机翼所能承载的重量时,机翼有可能折断,造成飞行事故。

❸ These particles can be seen by the aircraft's radar enabling the flight crews to avoid the storms and hence the turbulence.

句子大意:机组人员通过雷达可以看到这些云块,继而避开雷暴,避免遇到颠簸。

❹Cabin crew can increase risk and compromise their personal safety by attempting to adhere to routine procedures normally performed on all flights such as the seat-belt compliance checks, rather than responding in accordance with the level and intensity of turbulence.

句子大意：如果乘务员不考虑自身安全,只是按照日常惯例来进行诸如旅客安全带检查的工作,而没有根据颠簸的强度进行调整的话,她们受伤的风险会增加。

rather than 而不是。

New Words and Expressions

occupant	['ɒkju:pənt]	n.	乘客
subdivide	[sʌbdɪ'vaɪd]	v.	把……再分
invisible	[ɪn'vɪzəb(ə)l]	adj.	无形的,看不见的
severity	[sɪ'verɪtɪ]	n.	严重;严格;猛烈
thunder cloud	['θʌndə][klaʊd]	n.	雷暴云
cumulonimbus	[ˌkju:mjʊləʊ'nɪmbəs]	n.	[气象] 积雨云
parcel	['pɑ:s(ə)l]	n.	[气象] 气块
compliance	[kəm'plaɪəns]	n.	顺从,服从;承诺
self-preservation	[self,prezə'veɪʃən]	n.	自卫本能,自我保护
constraint	[kən'streɪnt]	n.	约束;限制
splash	[splæʃ]	v.	泼洒;刊登
maneuver	[mə'nʊvə]	v.	演习;调遣
strain	[streɪn]	n.	拉紧;负担

Part E
Supplementary Reading

📋 **Try to discuss:**

1. How much do you know about Hong Kong International Airport?
2. What makes Hong Kong International Airport different from other major airports in the world?

Hong Kong International Airport

Official name	Hong Kong International Airport
Airport opening	July 1998
Connectivity	Over 100 airlines operate flights to about 180 locations worldwide, including 44 destinations on the Chinese Mainland
Total airport site area	1,255 hectares
Passenger throughput (in 2013)	59.9 million
Air cargo throughput (in 2013)	4.12 million tons
Flight handling capacity	65 flights per hour at peak hours
Terminals	Two (Terminal 1 and Terminal 2)
Runways	Two (South and North Runways)
Runway length	3,800 meters
Aircraft Parking Bays	Passenger apron: 59 frontal stands, 27 remote stands; Cargo apron: 41 stands; Long Term: 23 stands; Maintenance: 14 stands
Airport workforce	Over 65,000

Hong Kong International Airport (HKIA, IATA: HKG; ICAO: VHHH) is the main airport in Hong Kong Special Administrative Region (HKSAR). It is located on the island of Chek Lap Kok, so the airport is also known as Chek Lap Kok Airport.

HKIA is the world's busiest cargo gateway and one of the world's busiest passenger airports. In 2013, 59.9 million passengers used HKIA and 4.12 million tons of air cargo passed through Hong Kong. HKIA is connected to about 180 destinations, including 44 in the Mainland, through over 1,000 daily flights by more than 100 airlines.

Since commencing operation in July 1998, HKIA adheres to four principles—Safety, Operation Efficiency, Customer Convenience, and Environment. This commitment has earned HKIA the recognition as the world's best airport over 50 times.

HKIA is a gateway of China. It is closely connected to Mainland, especially the Pearl River Delta (PRD). Every day, cross-boundary coaches carry passengers on about 550 scheduled trips linking HKIA with over 110 PRD cities and towns.

(资料来源：http://www.hongkongairport.com/eng/business/about-the-airport/welcome.html; http://www.aci.aero/)

参考译文

香港国际机场

机场名称	香港国际机场
启用时间	1998年7月
航空网络	超过100家航空公司提供前往全球约180个航点的航班,其中44个位于中国内地
机场总面积	1255hm^2
客运量(2013年)	5990万人次
货运量(2013年)	412万t
跑道容量	繁忙时段每小时65架次
航站楼数量	两座(1号航站楼和2号航站楼)
跑道数量	两条(南跑道和北跑道)
跑道长度	3800m
停机位数量	客机坪:59个廊前停机位,27个远端停机位; 货机坪:41个停机位; 长期:23个停机位; 维修:14个停机位
机场员工数量	65000多人

香港国际机场(英文缩写HKIA,IATA代码:HKG;ICAO代码:VHHH)是香港特别行政区的主要机场。机场坐落于赤鱲角,因此也被称为赤鱲角机场。

香港国际机场时世界上最繁忙的货运枢纽,也是全球最繁忙的客运机场之一。2013年,香港国际机场的总客运量达到5990万人次,总货运量达到412万t。香港国际机场连接全球约180个航点,其中中国内地城市44个。超过100家航空公司在香港国际机场运营,每天提供超过1000个航班。

自从1998年7月启用以来,香港国际机场坚持"安全、运营效率、顾客服务及环境"四大原则,先后50余次被推举为全球最佳机场。

香港国际机场是通往中国内地的门户,与中国内地,尤其是珠三角地区联系紧密。香港国际机场开通了跨境客车,往返于机场和110多个珠三角城镇,每天开出定期班次约550班。

Cabin Service English

Unit 13

Weather and Time

✦ Part A Useful Words and Expressions ✦ Part B Dialogues
✦ Part C Public Announcements ✦ Part D Work-task
✦ Part E Supplementary Reading

Students will be able to:
memorize the words and expressions about weather and time;
make up the dialogues about talking about weather and time in the cabin;
obtain and improve public announcements skills about weather and time;
know about jet lag;
introduce Heathrow Airport.

Suggested Hours: *4 class hours*

Unit 13　Weather and Time

Part A
Useful Words and Expressions

◉ **Please list as many expressions about weather and time as you can.**

_____

_____

- foggy
- rainy
- cool
- stormy
- weather forecast
- temperature
- below zero
- on schedule
- ahead of schedule
- behind schedule
- time difference
- jet lag
- What's the weather like today? / How's the weather like?/ What will be the weather like when we arrive there?
- It's raining/snowing heavily, the ground temperature is… degrees Centigrade/Fahrenheit.
- It's almost cloudy, and the chance of rain is 70%.
- What's the weather like today?
- It's raining/snowing heavily.
- We will arrive tomorrow at 7:00 a.m. local time.
- According to the latest weather forecast, it's sunny in Seoul.
- It doesn't seem to be stopping. I'll tell you if there is any change.
- The estimated arrival time is 6:00 a.m. local time.
- It is colder in London than in Beijing. Please put on coat.
- The flight time today is ten hours and twenty-five minutes.
- There is a two-hour time difference between Beijing and Sydney.
- Beijing is 12 hours ahead of New York.

Culture Tips

➢ To save energy, about 110 countries, including America and Australia, have implemented the Daylight Saving Time (DST) or Summer Time, which is an hour earlier than the Standard Time.

> China implemented the Daylight Saving Time (DST) from year 1986 to 1991.
> Avoid using casual language to inform passengers of time and weather:

—big wind
—big rain
—many clouds
—fall rain
—blow wind

> People rarely use "weather" as subject when they talk about weather, they would prefer to use "it" as subject instead, such as:

—It is sunny/fine/windy/snowy.

> Here are some common words used to describe the weather:

—cold/hot/warm/sunny/cool/foggy/rainy/snowy/humid/windy/stormy
—showers/typhoon/tornado/hurricane/thunderstorm/hailstorm/blizzard

> Ways to describe time:

—11:45 p.m.: eleven forty five in the evening; quarter to twelve; eleven forty five p.m.
—10:30 a.m.: ten thirty in the morning; half past ten in the morning; ten thirty a.m.
—2:15 p.m.: two fifteen in the afternoon; a quarter past two in the afternoon; two fifteen p.m.
—08:50 a.m.: eight fifty in the morning; ten to nine in the morning; eight fifty a.m.

Cabin Term

On schedule 正班飞行/**Ahead of schedule** 提前飞行/**Behind schedule** 晚点飞行

航班计划(Schedule)是规定正班飞行的航线、机型、班次和班期时刻的计划。正班飞行(On schedule)是按照对外公布的班期时刻表进行的航班飞行。在中国，正班飞行完成的周转量和运输量占全部航空运输周转量运输量的90%左右。正班飞行的航线、机型、班次和班期时刻，实际上就是航空公司向社会承诺提供的航空运输服务产品，从这个意义上说，航班计划是航空公司最重要的生产作业计划。从飞机调配、空勤组排班到座位销售、地面运输服务组织、航空公司运输生产过程的各个环节，都要依据航班计划进行组织与安排。

◉ **Match phrases or sentences in column B to the situations in column A.**

Column A	Column B
1. Inquiry about arrival time	a. It takes about 13 hours.
2. Inquiry about weather	b. There is still an hour and a half.
3. Inquiry about flight time	c. It's clear and sunny.
4. Inquiry about time difference between two cities	d. It's International Date Line.
5. Adjust one's watch	e. Most people experience it and it'll last several days.
6. Jet lag	f. Put it 2 hours forward.
	g. City A is 2 hours ahead of city B.

Unit 13　Weather and Time

⦿ **Make up a dialogue about weather and time in the destination city between cabin attendant and passenger.**

Part B
Dialogues

(CA=Cabin Attendant, PAX=Passenger)

PAX: Miss, when will we arrive at Sydney?
CA: There is still an hour and a half.
PAX: What's the weather like there?
CA: According to the latest weather forecast, it's clear and plenty of sunshine; the ground temperature there is 35 degrees Centigrade.
PAX: 35 degrees? Oh, it's really hot. It's minus 5 degrees Centigrade in Beijing when we left yesterday.
CA: Yes. Australia is in the Southern Hemisphere. The climate there is quite different from that in Beijing. It's in February, the hottest season in Sydney.
PAX: Well, I know it's warm there in February, but I don't expect it's so hot. Perhaps I'll have a hot winter holiday. Thank you so much.
CA: You are welcome.

PAX: Miss, could you come here a minute?
CA: Of course. What's the matter?
PAX: I'm worrying about the weather in Seoul. What will the weather be like when we arrive there?
CA: According to the latest weather report, it's raining in Seoul.
PAX: Is it raining hard? Will it stop when we arrive?
CA: Well, no, it's not raining hard. There're only scattered showers. But the rain doesn't seem to be stopping. I'll tell you if there is any change.
PAX: That's too bad. Are we going to arrive on schedule? Is it going to be all right for landing?
CA: Yes, of course. The visibility is not so poor. Besides, the flight crew is very experienced. They will make a safe landing. Please don't worry.
PAX: Thank you. I feel better now. Please tell me if it stops raining.

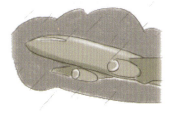

CA: You are welcome. I will.

3

PAX: Miss, could you tell me what the weather will be like when our plane arrives at Paris?
CA: According to the present weather report, it's mostly cloudy and an isolated shower is developing in the west, the chance of rain is 70%.
PAX: Oh, no. It's raining again. Why is it always raining when I travel there? Is it rainy in summer?
CA: Well, Paris experiences the typical Western European oceanic climate. Summer comes in July and lasts till August. Rainfall is not frequent although the occasional and unexpected shower could disturb the tourists at any time. However, the city witnesses more than 8 hours of sunshine per day.

PAX: How irritating!
CA: Perhaps it could be very romantic traveling in rainy Paris.
PAX: Well, I hope so. Wish it's a sunny day tomorrow. Thanks a lot.
CA: You are welcome. Hope you have a happy journey.

4

CA: Excuse me, Madam. Did you press the call button?
PAX: Yes. How long does it take from Beijing to Los Angeles?
CA: It takes about 13 hours.
PAX: When will we arrive?
CA: The estimated time of arrival is 6:00 a.m. local time.
PAX: What's the time difference between Beijing and Los Angeles?
CA: 16 hours. Beijing is 16 hours ahead of Los Angeles.
PAX: 16 hours?
CA: Yes. That means when it is 6:00 a.m. in Los Angeles, it is 11:00 p.m. in Beijing, the same day as we leave Beijing.
PAX: Thank you.
CA: You are welcome.

5

PAX: Excuse me. May I trouble you for a moment?
CA: Sure. How can I assist you?
PAX: What's the time difference between Shanghai and the United States?
CA: Well, Sir, in China we only have one time zone, that is Beijing Standard Time.

PAX: Only one time zone?

CA: Yes. But in the United States different places have different times as the country runs across several time zones.

PAX: Ok. Then what is the time difference between Beijing and New York?

CA: About 13 hours. New York is 13 hours ahead of Beijing, but one day behind. That means when we arrive at 1:00 a.m. in New York, it is 2:00 p.m. in Beijing.

PAX: But on the same day?

CA: Yes. And from the second Sunday in March to the first Sunday in November, the time difference is 12 hours.

PAX: Why?

CA: In North America they change time twice a year, 1 hour forward in spring and 1 hour back in fall.

PAX: So complicated! Thank you for your patience.

CA: You are welcome.

6

PAX: Excuse me. Could you spare me a few minutes?

CA: Certainly. What can I do for you?

PAX: I'm totally confused. What time and what date is it?

CA: It is Saturday, 28th June and 1:30 in the morning, Beijing local time.

PAX: But my watch is showing Friday, 27th June and 1:30 in the afternoon.

CA: Yes, Beijing is 12 hours ahead of New York, because we cross the International Date Line.

PAX: Then how can I adjust my watch to Beijing time?

CA: Please put it 12 hours forward for Beijing.

PAX: OK. I think I suffer from jet lag. I'm feeling so drained but cannot get to sleep.

CA: Yes. Most people experience jet lag when they travel long distances and cross into a different time zone. Symptoms usually include fatigue and trouble sleeping. It might last several days for the body to overcome the jet lag caused by the time difference.

PAX: Yeah. It is a small price to pay to travel around the world. Anyway, thanks a lot.

CA: You are welcome. If you have any problems, please press the call button.

New Words and Expressions

degree	[dɪˈgriː]	n. 程度；等级；度
centigrade	[ˈsentɪgreɪd]	n. 摄氏度
minus	[ˈmaɪnəs]	adj. 负的
hemisphere	[ˈhemɪˌsfɪə]	n. 半球
Seoul	[səʊl]	n. 首尔

scattered	['skætəd]	adj. 分散的，散乱的
shower	['ʃaʊə]	n. 阵雨；淋浴
schedule	['ʃedjuːəl]	n. 时刻表
visibility	[ˌvɪzɪ'bɪlətɪ]	n. 能见度
oceanic	[ˌəʊʃɪ'ænɪk]	adj. 海洋的；广阔无垠的
occasional	[ə'keɪʒənəl]	adj. 偶尔的
witness	['wɪtnɪs]	v. 目击，见证
irritating	['ɪrɪteɪtɪŋ]	adj. 气人的，使愤怒的
time zone	[taɪm][zəʊn]	n. 时区
complicated	['kɒmplɪkeɪtɪd]	adj. 难懂的，复杂的
confused	[kən'fjuːzd]	adj. 困惑的
International Date Line	[ɪntə'næʃənəl][deɪt][laɪn]	国际日期变更线
jet lag	[dʒet][læg]	飞行时差反应
drain	[dreɪn]	v. 耗尽；使流出
symptom	['sɪmptəm]	n. 症状

Role play the cabin attendant's responses.

PAX: Excuse me. What time and what date is it?
CA: _____.

PAX1: But my watch is showing a different time.
CA: _____.

PAX: Then how can I adjust my watch to Beijing time?
CA: _____.

PAX: OK. Thanks for your help.

PAX: Miss, I'm worrying about the weather in Seoul. What will the weather be like when we arrive there?
CA: _____.

PAX: Will it stop when we arrive?
CA: _____.

PAX: That's too bad. Are we going to arrive on schedule?
CA: _____.

PAX: Thank you. Please tell me if it stops raining.
CA: _____.

Discuss the following questions.

1. On an international flight from New York to Beijing, how would you tell passengers to adjust their watches?
2. Make an announcement about the weather condition at your base city.

3. The plane will land at an alternate airport because the destination airport has been closed due to bad weather, how would you explain to passengers?

◉ **Make up dialogues based on the following situations.**
1. Maria is a cabin attendant. She is trying to help a passenger from Beijing adjust his watch before the flight landing at New York.
2. A passenger is wondering the weather condition at the destination city. A cabin attendant comes towards him and informs him the latest weather information.

◉ **Translate the following sentences into English.**
1.这里的秋天多雾而且凉爽。
2.这里的春天多雨。
3.据天气预报报道,明天会有暴风雨。
4.温度是零下3℃。
5.我们会准时/推迟抵达。
6.今天会是怎样的天气?
7.现在下着大雨/大雪。
8.我们将在明天当地时间早上7点抵达。
9.根据最新的天气预报,首尔天气晴朗。
10.看起来雨还没停,如果天气有什么变化我会告诉你的。

Part C
Public Announcements

Ladies and gentlemen,
   Our flight is expected to arrive at _____ airport at _____ a.m. / p.m.. The ground temperature is _____ degrees Centigrade or _____ degrees Fahrenheit. The weather there is _____.
   Thank you!

173

Time (International Long Route)

Good morning (afternoon/evening), ladies and gentlemen,

We will be landing at _____ airport at _____ a.m. / p.m. Beijing time or _____ a.m. / p.m. local time. The ground temperature is _____ degrees Centigrade or _____ degrees Fahrenheit. The weather there is _____.

Thank you!

Arrival Time Is Behind Schedule

Ladies and gentlemen,

Due to a strong adverse wind on route, the estimated arrival time will be _____ minutes behind schedule. Please fasten your seat-belt.

Thank you!

Fly Directly

Ladies and gentlemen,

We regret to inform you that due to unfavorable weather in _____ airport, we'll be landing in _____ airport instead. We expect to land in about _____ hour(s) and _____ minutes and shall keep you updated. We appreciate your understanding and apologize for any inconvenience caused.

Thank you.

Route and Service Instruction (International)

Ladies and gentlemen,

There is a _____ hour time difference between _____ and _____. We are expected to arrive at our destination at approximately _____ (a.m. / p.m.) on (date) local time.

This is a non-smoking flight. Smoking or using e-cigarettes anywhere in the aircraft is against the law. For your safety, please always keep your setbelt fastened while seated in case of turbulence.

Thank you!

New Words and Expressions

fahrenheit	['færənhaɪt]	adj. 华氏的；华氏温度计的
International Long Route	[ɪntə'næʃənəl][lɒŋ][ruːt]	国际长途航线
adverse	['ædvɜːs]	adj. 相反的；不利的
estimated	['estɪmeɪtɪd]	adj. 估计的；预计的

updated	[ʌpˈdeɪtɪd]	adj. 更新的
time difference	[taɪm] [ˈdɪfrəns]	n. 时差
destination	[ˌdestɪˈneɪʃən]	n. 目的地,终点
e-cigarette	[ɪˌsɪgəˈret]	n. 电子烟

Speaking Practice

◉ **Try to work out.**

1. When it is 4 o'clock in the afternoon in Beijing, what time is it in London?
2. When it is 9 o'clock in the morning in London, what time is it in New York?
3. When it is 9 o'clock in the morning in Beijing, what time is it in Paris?

◉ **Study the following ways of expressing time differences.**

+	−
2 hours ahead	1 hour behind
forward	backward
put your watch forward	put your watch backward
wind your watch forward	wind your watch backward

◉ **Practice making public announcements about Time with these alternatives.**

- Harbin / 1:10 / 24 / 75/sunny
- Tianjin / 7:00 / 22 / 72/foggy
- Wuhan/ 10:30/ 38/ 100/muggy
- Paris/ 6:50/ 9/ 48/rainy
- Chicago / 8:20 / 19 / 66/cool

◉ **Please read following sentences in the right tone(′ for stress, ↗ for rising tone, ↘ for falling tone).**

1. Our ′ flight is expected ↗ to arrive at the Tianjin Binhai Airport ↘ at 5 p.m. ↘
2. The weather is ′ sunny there. ↘
3. The ground ′ temperature is 36 degrees ↗ centigrade. ↘
4. Due to a strong adverse wind on route ↘ , the ′ estimated arrival time ↗ will be ′ 30 minutes behind schedule. ↘
5. Your cooperation ↗ will be ′ much appreciated. ↘

◉ **Translate the following expressions into English.**

- 多雾天气
- 阴雨天气
- 天气预报
- 大雨
- 大雪

- 预期抵达时间
- 飞行时间
- 时差
- 天气凉爽
- 当地时间

Part D
Work-task

Try to discuss:
1. Do you know why there is jet lag?
2. What advices would you give to your passengers to reduce jet lag?

Jet Lag

What is jet lag?

Jet lag is a physiological condition which results from alterations to the body's circadian rhythms resulting from rapid long-distance (east–west or west–east) travel on a (typically jet) aircraft.❶

What factors cause jet lag?

The main, but not the only cause of jet lag is crossing time zones. Children under three don't seem to suffer jet lag badly, as they are more adaptive and less set in their ways. Adults who adjust readily to changes of routine also seem to suffer less from jet lag. Those who are slaves to a fixed daily routine are often the worst sufferers.

The second one is your pre-flight condition. If you're over-tired, excited, stressed, nervous, you are more likely to suffer from it. The wise traveler who wants to get the most out of a trip has a good night's sleep prior to departure.

The third one is lack of exercise. Lack of exercise is one of the worst aspects of long-haul flying. It makes the flight uncomfortable and sets you up for a longer period of jet lag afterwards. Do stretching exercises in your seat, especially for the legs, and if possible go for walks up and down the aisle. If you have a spare seat next to you, try to get your feet up. Get off the plane whenever possible at stopovers and do some exercises.❷

How to reduce jet lag?

Tip 1: Pre-flight. Before departing, make sure you have all your affairs in order. Get plenty of exercise in the days prior to departure and try to avoid sickness such as the flu, colds and so on. Get a good night's sleep just prior to departure.

Tip 2: Drinking fluids. The dry air in aircraft causes dehydration. Drinking plenty of non-alcoholic fluids counters this. Water is better than coffee, tea and fruit juices.

Tip 3: Sleeping aids. Blindfolds and ear plugs are all useful in helping you get quality sleep while flying. Kick your shoes off to ease pressure on the feet (some airlines provide slippers, and many experienced travelers carry their own).

Tip 4: Exercise. Get as much exercise as you can. Walking up and down the aisle, standing for spells, and doing small twisting and stretching exercises in your seat all help to reduce discomfort, especially swelling of legs and feet.❸ Get off the plane if possible at stopovers, and do some exercises or take a walk.

Tip 5: Showers. During extended stopovers on a long-haul flight, showers are sometimes available. A shower not only freshens you up but gets the muscles and circulation going again and makes you feel much better for the rest of the flight.❹

Tip 6: Sleeping pills (don't!). Some people use sleeping tablets to try to ease jet lag. This is a dangerous approach as sleeping pills cause a sleepy state with little or no natural body movement, and it is well known that prolonged immobility during flight can lead to fatal blood clots.❺

(资料来源：http://en.wikipedia.org/wiki/Jet_lag; http://www.nojetlag.com/jetlag1.html)

Notes

❶ Jet lag is a physiological condition which results from alterations to the body's circadian rhythms resulting from rapid long-distance (east–west or west–east) travel on a (typically jet) aircraft.

句子大意：坐飞机（通常是喷气式飞机）长途飞行（东向西或西向东），会导致生理节奏的改变，从而造成生理上的不适，这就是时差反应。

❷ Get off the plane whenever possible at stopovers and do some exercises.

句子大意：只要可能，在经停的机场都要下飞机活动一下。

其中，"whenever possible"意为"只要可能，"例如：

Whenever possible, try to look at the bright side. 只要可能，都应试着看看光明的一面。

❸ Walking up and down the aisle, standing for spells, and doing small twisting and stretching exercises in your seat all help to reduce discomfort, especially swelling of legs and feet.

句子大意：在客舱通道上走动走动，从座椅上站起来伸展活动一下，或坐在座位上做些扭身子和舒展的活动，这些都有助于减少飞行期间的身体不适感，尤其是腿和脚的肿胀感。

❹ A shower not only freshens you up but gets the muscles and circulation going again and makes you feel much better for the rest of the flight.

句子大意：淋浴不仅可以使你精神焕然一新，还可以让肌肉更放松，血液循环更流畅，从而保证你在接下来的旅程中感觉更舒适。

其中,"freshen"是由形容词"fresh"加后缀"en"变成动词而来的,类似构词法的例子还有shorten(变短)、brighten(变明亮)、widen(变宽)。freshen常和介词up搭配,意为"使鲜艳;使干净",如:

My mother asks me to freshen vegetables up by putting them into water.

妈妈让我把蔬菜浸入水中以保持新鲜。

❺ This is a dangerous approach as sleeping pills cause a sleepy state with little or no natural body movement, and it is well known that prolonged immobility during flight can lead to fatal blood clots.

句子大意:这是一种危险的方法,因为安眠药会促使人进入一种少动或者不动的睡眠状态;而我们都知道,坐飞机长时间身体保持不动,会很容易在体内引发致命的血液凝块。

New Words and Expressions

physiological	[ˌfɪziə'lɒdʒɪkəl]	adj.	生理学
alteration	[ˌɔːltə'reɪʃən]	n.	改变;变更
circadian	[sə:'keɪdɪən]	adj.	与生理节奏有关的
rhythm	['rɪðəm]	n.	节奏
adaptive	[ə'dæptɪv]	adj.	适应的
sufferer	['sʌfərə]	n.	患者;受害者
stressed	[strest]	adj.	紧张的;感到有压力的
long-haul	['lɒŋ'hɔːl]	adj.	长途的
affair	[ə'feə]	n.	事件,事情
flu	[fluː]	n.	流感
fluid	['fluːɪd]	n.	流体;饮料
dehydration	[ˌdiːhaɪ'dreɪʃən]	n.	脱水
counter	['kaʊntə]	v.	反击;反对
blindfold	['blaɪndfəʊld]	n.	眼罩;障眼物
ease	[iːz]	v.	减轻,缓和
slippers	['slɪpəz]	n.	拖鞋
twisting	['twɪstɪŋ]	n.	扭转;缠绕
swelling	['swelɪŋ]	n.	肿胀;膨胀
freshen	['freʃən]	v.	使清新;使新鲜
circulation	[ˌsə:kjʊ'leɪʃən]	n.	血液流通;传播
tablet	['tæblɪt]	n.	药片
prolonged	[prə'lɒŋd]	adj.	延长的;拖延的
immobility	[ˌɪməʊ'bɪlətɪ]	n.	不动,固定
clot	[klɒt]	n.	血块;凝块

Part E
Supplementary Reading

> **Try to discuss:**
> 1. How much do you know about Heathrow Airport?
> 2. Why do you think Heathrow Airport can handle the largest number of international passengers in the world?

Heathrow Airport

Official name	London Heathrow Airport
Airport opening	1946
Connectivity	82 airlines operate flights to 180 destinations in 85 countries
Total airport site area	1,227 hectares
Passenger throughput (in 2016)	75.71 million
Air cargo throughput (in 2013)	1.42 million tons
Number of flights (in 2013)	Annual 469,552; Daily average 1,286
Terminals	Five (Terminal 1, 2, 3, 4 and 5)
Runways	Two (Northern and Southern)
Runway length	Northern 3,902 meters; Southern 3,658 meters
Number of aircraft stands	Aircraft stands served by an airbridge 125; Remote stands 49; Cargo stands 12
Airport workforce	Over 76,600

London Heathrow Airport (IATA: LHR; ICAO: EGLL) is a major international airport in West London, England, United Kingdom.

Heathrow is the busiest airport in the United Kingdom and also the busiest airport in Europe by passenger traffic. In 2013, 72.3 million passengers traveled through Heathrow, making the airport the third busiest airport in the world in total passenger traffic after Hartsfield-Jackson Atlanta International Airport and Beijing Capital International Airport. Heathrow Airport handles more international passengers than any other airport around the globe. Of its 72.3 million passengers in 2013, 7% (5 million) were domestic travelers and 93% (67.3 million) were international travelers.

Heathrow Airport has two parallel east-west runways and five passenger terminals, numbered 1 to 5. Terminal 5, opened in 2008, was voted Best Airport Terminal in Skytrax World Airport Awards from 2012 to 2014.

(资料来源：http://www.heathrowairport.com/about-us/company-news-and-information/; http://en.wikipedia.org/wiki/London_Heathrow_Airport; http://www.aci.aero/)

参考译文

希思罗机场

官方名称	伦敦希思罗机场
启用时间	1946年
航空网络	82家航空公司运营前往85个国家的180个航点的航班
机场总面积	1227hm^2
客运量（2016年）	7571万人次
货运量（2013年）	142万t
航班数（2013年）	469552班，日均1286班
航站楼数量	5座（1号、2号、3号、4号和5号航站楼）
跑道数量	两条（北跑道和南跑道）
跑道长度	北跑道3902m；南跑道3658m
停机位数量	125个廊前停机位；49个远端停机；12个货运停机位
机场员工数量	76600多人

伦敦希思罗机场（IATA代码：LHR；ICAO代码EGLL）是一座位于英国伦敦西部的重要国际机场。

希思罗机场是英国最繁忙的机场，同时也是欧洲客运量最大的机场。2013年，希思罗机场的客运量达7230万人次，排名全球第三，仅次于美国亚特兰大哈兹菲尔德—杰克逊国际机场和中国北京首都国际机场。希思罗机场接待的跨境旅客数量位居全球第一。在2013年处理的7230万人次客运总量中，7%（500万人次）为国内旅客，93%（6730万人次）为国际旅客。

希思罗机场共有两条平行的东西向跑道和5座客运航站楼，即1~5号航站楼。5号航站楼于2008年启用，2012—2014年连续3届在五星航空公司（Skytrax）世界机场大奖中被评选为最佳机场航站楼。

Cabin Service English

Unit 14

Dealing with Health Issues

* Part A Useful Words and Expressions
* Part B Dialogues
* Part C Public Announcements
* Part D Work-task
* Part E Supplementary Reading

Students will be able to:
memorize the words and expressions about dealing with health issues;
make up the dialogues about health issues in the cabin;
obtain and improve public announcements skills about dealing with health issues;
know about first aid;
introduce Frankfurt Airport.

Suggested Hours: *4 class hours*

Part A
Useful Words and Expressions

◉ Please list as many expressions about dealing with health issues in the cabin as you can.

_____
_____

- flu
- fever
- headache
- stomachache
- toothache
- nose bleed
- running nose/runny nose
- nose-drop/eye-drop
- painkiller
- bandage
- gauze
- Do you feel dizzy?
- Are you feeling better?/Are you feeling well now?
- Are you allergic to any medicine?
- Do you suffer from high blood pressure?
- How long have you been like this?
- Have you brought any medicine yourself?
- Because of a change in air pressure, you are suffering from an earache.
- You may take a nap after taking the medicine. I'll bring you a blanket.
- Have you ever suffered from airsickness before?
- Do you have a stomachache/ headache/ toothache?
- I'll bring you a cup of warm water immediately.
- Please tell us if you need any assistance.
- If you still don't feel well, please don't hesitate to let us know.
- I'm sorry to tell you that there is no doctor or nurse on board.

Culture Tips

➢ Here are some common illness on board:
—flu/fever/high blood pressure/diabetes/allergy/heart attack
➢ Here are some common symptom on board:

—headache/stomachache/toothache/heartburn/asthma/nose bleed/vomit/running nose/diarrhea/indigestion

➤ Due to a recent illness, injury, surgery or hospitalization, some passengers may need special medical consideration when they travel. In this case, a Passenger Medical Clearance (MEDA) Form should be completed by the passenger's attending doctor. The purpose of the MEDA Form is to enable airline, in conjunction with doctor, to determine the passenger's fitness to travel.

Cabin Term

Airsickness 晕机/**Dizzy** 晕眩的/**Vomit** 呕吐

晕动病是因汽车、轮船或飞机运动时所产生的颠簸、摇摆或旋转等任何形式的加速运动,刺激人体的前庭神经而发生的疾病。该病常在乘车、航海、飞行和其他运行数分钟至数小时后发生。起初感觉上腹不适,继有恶心、面色苍白、出冷汗,随即有眩晕、精神抑郁、唾液分泌增多和呕吐。严重者可有血压下降、呼吸深而慢、眼球震颤。严重呕吐引起失水和电解质紊乱。症状一般在停止运行或减速后数十分钟和几小时内消失或减轻。经多次发病后,症状或可减轻,甚至不发生。

◉ **Match phrases or sentences in column B to the situations in column A.**

Column A	Column B
1. Suffering from airsickness	a. I'll get you the medicine for cold and a cup of water.
2. Falling down and get hurt in a jolt	b. You can relieve your earache through swallowing and by eating sweets.
3. One's ankle is sprained in a jolt	c. Let's move to the rear cabin and lie down there.
4. Suffering from ear drumming	d. I'll get you some airsick tablets.
5. Catching a bad cold	e. Let's wash the cuts and wrap it up.
6. Looking for a doctor	f. If there is a doctor among you, please contact us immediately.

◉ **Make up a dialogue about offering assistance to a passenger who is suffering from earache after take-off.**

Part B
Dialogues

(CA=Cabin Attendant, PAX=Passenger)

1

PAX: Miss, the plane is bumping badly, I'm very sick and dizzy and I feel like vomiting.

CA: Have you ever suffered from airsickness before? You're probably airsick.

PAX: Airsickness? It's my first time to take a plane. What shall I do now?

CA: You may need some airsickness tablets. I'll get you the tablets at once. May I assist you in reclining your seat-back so you can have a rest? If you want to vomit, please use the airsickness bag in the seat pocket in front of you. I will attend to it.

PAX: That's very kind of you.

2

CA: Madam, your face looks flushed. Are you feeling well?

PAX: I have high blood pressure and I feel short of breath now.

CA: I see. Do you need me to find a doctor among the passengers?

PAX: Thanks, but that would not be necessary.

CA: Madam, try to keep calm and unfasten your seat-belt and your tie. Have you brought any medicine with you?

PAX: Yes, it's in my coat pocket. Give me a cup of warm water, please.

CA: Certainly. I will take a cup of warm water for you very soon.

(*1 minute later.*)

CA: Here is a cup of water and a towel for you. Would you lie down for a moment and take a rest? This is the call button. If you still don't feel well, please don't hesitate to let us know.

3

PAX: Help!

CA: What's the matter with you, Sir?

PAX: I was going to the lavatory. There was a sudden jolt and I fell down and hurt myself.

CA: You've got a bump on your forehead, and some cuts here.

PAX: Really? Am I bleeding?

CA: Don't worry. The bleeding is controlled. Let's wash the cuts. I'll wrap it up with gauze. Would you please sit down and have a rest?

PAX: Ouch! My right ankle is hurting! It must be sprained too!

CA: If your right ankle is sprained, we will try to contact a doctor among our passengers. However, if that happens to be no doctor on board, we'll assist you to move to the rear cabin. There are some vacant seats there. I'll lift up the armrests so that you can lie down.

PAX: That'll be great.

4

PAX: Miss, My ears are ringing after take-off. It really hurts. What's wrong with me?

CA: Please don't worry. Because of a change in air pressure, you are suffering from an earache. You can relieve your earache by swallowing and by eating sweets. And you'll feel better when the plane stops climbing.

PAX: Ok, I'll have a try.

(*A few minutes later.*)

CA: Excuse me, Madam. Are you feeling better now?

PAX: Yes, much better. Thanks a lot.

5

CA: How may I best assist you, Sir?

PAX: I've got a headache, a sore throat and my nose is stuffed up. I also feel a chilly in both my hands and feet. I'm afraid I've caught a bad cold.

CA: Oh, that's too bad. We'll make an announcement to find out whether there is a doctor or a nurse among our passengers that can give you a hand.

PAX: Thanks a lot.

(*The purser made an announcement to look for medical assistance among the passengers. Unfortunately, there was no doctor or nurse on board.*)

CA: We can't find any medical worker on board. I think you'd better take some medicine for colds. And we also have nose-drops. You might as well try them.

PAX: Please give me an aspirin.

CA: I'll be right back.

(*1 minute later.*)

CA: Here is the medicine and a cup of water for you, Sir. May we remind you that before you take the medicine, you need to fill out the Exception Reguest Form?

PAX: That's OK.

CA: Would you like to read the instructions first to see whether it's suitable for you or not?

PAX: I usually take aspirin when I catch a cold.

CA: You may take a nap after taking the medicine. I'll bring you a blanket.

PAX: That would be very kind of you.

6

CA: Did you press the button, Madam?

PAX: Yes, I'm feeling nauseous. And I also have diarrhea and a headache. I wonder if I ate something bad yesterday.

CA: How long have you been like this? Have you taken any medicine?

PAX: About 2 hours. I've taken some medicine but still feel sick. Could you ask for a doctor?

CA: Sure. I'll look for a doctor immediately.

　　(*A few minutes passed*.)

CA: I'm sorry to tell you that there is no doctor or nurse on board. But we have informed the ground staff and they will send you to the hospital as soon as the plane lands. Is that all right?

PAX: Thanks a lot.

CA: You are welcome. If you still don't feel well, please don't hesitate to let me know.

New Words and Expressions

airsickness bag	['eəsɪknɪs][bæg]		呕吐袋
flushed	[flʌʃt]	adj.	脸发红的
pressure	['preʃə]	n.	压力
unfasten	[ˌʌn'fɑːsən]	v.	解开
jolt	[dʒəʊlt]	n.	颠簸, 摇晃
bump	[bʌmp]	n.	肿块, 隆起物
forehead	['fɒrɪd]	n.	前额
wrap	[ræp]	v.	包扎
gauze	[gɔːz]	n.	纱布
ankle	['æŋkl]	n.	脚踝
sprain	[spreɪn]	n.	扭伤
ear ringing	[ɪə]['rɪŋɪŋ]	n.	耳鸣
swallow	['swɒləʊ]	v.	吞咽
sore	[sɔː]	adj.	疼痛的
stuff	[stʌf]	v.	堵塞
nose-drop	['nəʊz'drɒp]	n.	滴鼻液
aspirin	['æspərɪn]	n.	阿司匹林
Exception Request Form	[ɪk'sepʃn][rɪ'kwest] [fɔːm]		免责单
nap	[næp]	n.	打盹儿
nauseous	['nɔːzɪəs]	adj.	令人作呕的, 厌恶的

● Role play the cabin attendant's responses.

PAX: Excuse me. I feel sick. I don't know what is going on.
CA: _____.
PAX: No, this is my first time to take a flight.
CA: _____.
PAX: I also have ear ringing.

Unit 14　Dealing with Health Issues

> CA: _____.
>
> PAX: Miss, I've got a splitting headache. I feel chilly in both my hands and feet.
> CA: _____.
> PAX: Can you get a cup of hot water for me?
> CA: _____.
> PAX: Yes. I feel better now. Thanks!

◉ Discuss the following questions.

1. A passenger says: "I am feeling sick and dizzy." How can you help an airsick passenger?
2. A passenger say: "I felt pains in my ears after take-off. What's the matter with me?" How can you help the passenger?
3. A passenger says: "I have a headache, a sore throat and my nose is stuffed up." How can you help the passenger?
4. A passenger is suffering from an acute medical condition. There is no doctor on board. What can you do to help him?
5. A passenger says: "there was a sudden jolt and I fell down and hurt myself." What do you do to help the passenger?

◉ Make up dialogues based on the following situations.

1. After take-off, the cabin attendant notices a passenger is uncomfortable, so she comes up to him and asks if she can offer some assistance.
2. A passenger feels sick, and she asks the cabin attendant for help.

◉ Translate the following sentences into English.

1. 她得了流感。
2. 她正发烧。
3. 您可以按压鼻子来止住鼻血。
4. 他流鼻涕了。
5. 您可以服用止痛药来缓解胃痛。
6. 您可以给他的胳膊打上绷带。
7. 我们备有滴鼻液。
8. 您如果想吐,可以使用您前面座椅后置物袋里的呕吐袋。
9. 我会用纱布来包裹。
10. 您感到眩晕吗?

187

Part C
Public Announcements

Call for Doctor

Ladies and gentlemen,

May I have your attention please.

There is a sick passenger on board. If there is a doctor or a nurse among you, please contact us by pressing the call button immediately.

Thank you!

Emergency Landing (Sick Passenger)

Ladies and gentlemen,

May I have your attention please.

There is a sick passenger on board, and the captain has decided to make an emergency landing at _____ airport. We expect to arrive there in _____ hour(s) and _____ minutes.

Thank you!

Request for Medical Assistance

Ladies and gentlemen,

May I have your attention please.

We have a passenger in need of medical attention. (A lady is going to give birth.) If there is any medical personnel on board, please identify yourself to the flight attendants immediately.

Thank you!

Medical Assistance Needed

Ladies and gentlemen,

May we have your attention please.

We urgently require the assistance of a medical doctor. If there are any medical personnel onboard, please make yourself known to one of our Cabin Crew. Thank you!

New Words and Expressions

emergency landing	[ɪˈmɜːdʒənsɪ][ˈlændɪŋ]	紧急着陆
give birth	[gɪv][bɜːθ]	v. 分娩
personnel	[ˌpɜːsəˈnel]	n. 人员；人事部门
identify	[aɪˈdentɪfaɪ]	v. 确定；识别
urgently	[ˈɜːdʒəntlɪ]	adv. 迫切地，紧急地
crew	[kruː]	n. 全体人员

Speaking Practice

◎ Match the most appropriate responses with the passengers' symptoms.

Column A	Column B
1. I've got terrible toothache.	a. Would you like me to get you an aspirin?
2. There's been an accident.	b. I'm afraid you're got a bad cold.
3. I've got a pain.	c. Have you suffered from heart attack before?
4. I've got sore throat.	d. Where is it exactly?
5. I'm feeling very dizzy.	e. What happened?
6. I've a pain in my chest.	f. Would you need some airsickness bag?
7. I feel very sick.	g. Have you suffered from airsickness before?

◎ Practice making public announcements about Emergency Landing (Sick Passenger) with these alternatives.
- Harbin / 2 / 30
- Tianjin / 1 / 20
- Wuhan / 2 / 45
- Paris / 4 / 10
- Chicago / 3 / 15

◎ Please read following sentences in the right tone(ˈ for stress, ↗ for rising tone, ↘ for falling tone).
1. May I ↗ have your ↗ attention please. ↗ / ↘
2. There is a ↗ sick passenger on board. ↘
3. We expect ↗ to arrive there ↘ in 3 hours and 20 minutes. ↘

4. We have a passenger ↘ in ↗ need of ↗ medical attention. ↘

5. If there is a ↗ doctor or a nurse among you ↘, please ↗ contact us ↗ by ↗ pressing the call button immediately. ↘

◉ **Translate the following expressions into English.**
- 处理
- 健康问题
- 过敏反应
- 流感
- 高血压
- 流鼻血
- 晕机药
- 呕吐袋
- 耳鸣
- 消化不良

Part D
Work-task

Try to discuss:
1. Have you ever received first aid training?
2. Do you know how to perform a first aid?

First Aid

First aid is the provision of initial care for an illness or injury. It is usually performed by non-expert (or sometimes by an expert in case of an emergency), but trained personnel to a sick or injured person until definitive medical treatment can be found. It generally consists of a series of simple and in some cases, life-saving techniques that an individual can be trained to perform with minimal equipment.❶

Flight attendant's duty is to offer immediate care to a passenger of an accident or sudden illness until professional care can be obtained. It is given in order to prevent death or further injury. It may mean the difference between life and death, or temporary and permanent disability.❷

Listed below are six basic rules for performing first aid in-flight.
- Keep calm and find out the injuries or sudden cause of illness.
- Find out exactly what happened. Information may be obtained from the customer, friends, family or witnesses.
- Put on latex gloves before doing first aid, particularly when treating an open wound.

- Check for an emergency medical alert emblem or other identification, such as a card, bracelet or necklace to provide information on the customer's condition (have a witness when searching for identification).❸
- If customer's condition appears serious, do not hesitate to request medical assistance from a doctor that may be on board.
- Treat injuries in order of their importance.

Once emergency measures have been taken to ensure the customer's safety, at least one flight attendant continues first aid treatment while another flight attendant tells all pertinent information to the captain. The captain will determine if an unscheduled landing is necessary, based on the flight attendant's assessment of the situation.

Anytime first aid is administered in-flight, a Report of Irregularity must be completed. It always obtains the information about the event, such as customers' full name, address and phone number, customers' medical history, the treatment given to the customer and his responses.❹

(资料来源：http://www.flightattendantcabincrewtraining.com/firstaid.htm; http://en.wikipedia.org/wiki/First_aid#Key_skills)

Notes

❶ It generally consists of a series of simple and in some cases, life-saving techniques that an individual can be trained to perform with minimal equipment.

句子大意：急救通常包括一系列简单的，但在某些情况下能起到救命作用的技术，人们通过培训，可以利用最少量的设备，对患者实施急救。

❷ It may mean the difference between life and death, or temporary and permanent disability.

句子大意：这可能意味着生和死，或临时伤残与永久伤残之间的差异。

❸ Check for an emergency medical alert emblem or other identification, such as a card, bracelet or necklace to provide information on the customer's condition (have a witness when searching for identification).

句子大意：检查旅客是否随身携带紧急医疗警报标识或其他证件，如卡片、腕带或项链，用以确认旅客的身份及健康信息（寻找此类证件时，应确保有第三者在场）。

❹ It always obtains the information about the event, such as customers' full name, address and phone number, customers' medical history, the treatment given to the customer and his responses.

句子大意：事故报告书通常包括对该事故的描述，如旅客的全名、家庭住址、电话号码、过往的病史、对旅客实施的急救手段以及患者的反应。

New Words and Expressions

provision	[prəʊ'vɪʒən]	n. 提供,准备;条款
initial	[ɪ'nɪʃəl]	adj. 最初的
expert	['ekspɜːt]	n. 专家
definitive	[dɪ'fɪnɪtɪv]	adj. 决定性的;最后的
consist	[kən'sɪst]	v. 由……组成
technique	[tek'niːk]	n. 技巧,技术
individual	[ˌɪndɪ'vɪdjʊəl]	n. 个人,个体
injury	['ɪndʒərɪ]	n. 伤害,损害
temporary	['tempərərɪ]	adj. 暂时的,临时的
permanent	['pɜːmənənt]	adj. 永久的,永恒的
disability	[ˌdɪsə'bɪlətɪ]	n. 残疾
latex	['leɪteks]	n. 乳胶
gloves	[glʌvz]	n. 手套
wound	[waʊnd]	n. 创伤,伤口
emblem	['embləm]	n. 象征;徽章
identification	[aɪˌdentɪfɪ'keɪʃən]	n. 鉴定,识别
bracelet	['breɪslɪt]	n. 腕带;手镯
necklace	['neklɪs]	n. 项链
measure	['meʒə]	n. 措施;测量
pertinent	['pɜːtɪnənt]	adj. 相关的,中肯的
determine	[dɪ'tɜːmɪn]	v. 确定;决定
assessment	[ə'sesmənt]	n. 评定;估价
Report of Irregularity	[rɪ'pɔːt][əv][ɪˌregjʊ'lærətɪ]	事故报告书
response	[rɪ'spɒns]	n. 响应;反应

Unit 14 Dealing with Health Issues

Part E
Supplementary Reading

> **Try to discuss:**
> 1. How much do you know about Frankfurt Airport?
> 2. What factors make Frankfurt an airport with the most international destinations?

Frankfurt Airport

Official name	Frankfurt Airport
Airport opening	July 1936
Connectivity	264 destinations in 113 countries
Total airport site area	2,100 hectares
Passenger throughput (in 2013)	58 million
Air cargo throughput (in 2013)	2.1 million tons
Number of flights (in 2013)	472,692
Terminals	Three (Terminal 1, Terminal 2 and Lufthansa First Class Terminal)
Runways	Four (North, South, West and Northwest)
Runway length	Runway North: 4,000 meters; Runway South: 4,000 meters; Runway West: 4,000 meters; Runway Northwest: 2,800 meters
Aircraft Parking Bays	188
Airport workforce	Approx. 75,000

Frankfurt Airport (IATA: FRA; ICAO: EDDF) is a major international airport located in Frankfurt, the fifth-largest city of Germany and one of the world's leading financial centers.

Handling 58 million passengers in 2013, Frankfurt Airport is by far the busiest airport by passenger traffic in Germany, the third busiest in Europe after London Heathrow Airport and Paris-Charles de Gaulle Airport and the 12th busiest worldwide. With a freight throughput of 2.1 million metric tons in 2013, it is also the busiest airport in Europe by cargo traffic. As of winter 2012/2013, Frankfurt Airport served 264 destinations in 113 countries, making it the airport with the most international destinations in the world.

Frankfurt Airport has two large main passenger terminals (1 and 2) and a much smaller dedicated First Class Terminal which is operated and exclusively used by Lufthansa. Frankfurt Airport has four runways of which three are arranged parallel in east-west direction and one in south-north direction.

(资料来源：http://www.fraport.com/en/investor-relations/financial-and-air-traffic-figures/traffic-figures.html; http://www.frankfurt-airport.com/content/frankfurt_airport/en/business_location/facts_figures.html; http://en.wikipedia.org/wiki/Frankfurt_Airport)

参考译文

法兰克福机场

官方名称	法兰克福机场
启用时间	1936年7月
航空网络	113个国家的264个航点
机场总面积	2100hm^2
客运量（2019年）	7056万人次
货运量（2019年）	3187万t
航班数（2019年）	513912
航站楼数量	3座（1号航站楼、2号航站楼和汉莎航空头等舱航站楼）
跑道数量	4条（北跑道、南跑道、西跑道和西北跑道）
跑道长度	北跑道：4000m； 南跑道：4000m； 西跑道：4000m； 西北跑道：2800m
停机位数量	188个
机场员工数量	约75000人

法兰克福机场（IATA代码：FRA；ICAO代码：EDDF）是一座位于德国法兰克福的主要国际机场。法兰克福为德国第五大城市，并且是世界主要经济中心之一。

法兰克福机场2013年接待旅客5800万人次，客运量位列德国各机场第一位，在欧洲仅次于伦敦希思罗机场和巴黎夏尔·戴高乐机场位居第三，全世界排名第十二位。法兰克福机场2013年货运量达210万t，位居欧洲第一位。截至2012—2013年冬季，法兰克福机场开通了前往113个国家的264个航点的航班，国际航点数量位居世界第一。

法兰克福机场有两座大型客运航站楼，即1号和2号航站楼，以及一座较小的头等舱专用航站楼，由汉莎航空运营并专门使用。法兰克福机场有4条跑道，其中3条为东西向的平行跑道，1条为南北向跑道。

客舱服务英语(第2版)

Unit 15

Cabin Service English

Safety & Emergency I

* Part A Useful Words and Expressions
* Part B Dialogues
* Part C Public Announcements
* Part D Work-task
* Part E Supplementary Reading

Students will be able to:

memorize the words and expressions about the emergency equipment in the cabin;

make up the dialogues about emergency equipment in the cabin;

obtain and improve public announcements skills about depressurization, fire in the cabin and fire extinguished;

know about some emergency equipment in the cabin;

introduce The Terracotta Warriors and Horses

Suggested Hours: *4 class hours*

Unit 15 Safety & Emergency I

Part A
Useful Words and Expressions

◉ **Please list as many names of emergency equipment in the cabin and the related words and expressions as you can.**

_____

_____

- life vest / life jacket
- oxygen mask
- seat-belt
- put on life jacket
- slip it over your head
- inflate the life jacket by pulling down the tab
- blow into the tubes / mouthpieces
- pull the oxygen mask towards you
- place the oxygen mask over your nose and mouth
- fasten / unfasten your seat-belt
- insert the link into the buckle
- put out the link
- Slip the life jacket over your head, secure the straps around your waist and tie them securely.
- Place the mask over your mouth and nose, and slip the elastic band over your head.
- Please put your oxygen mask on as quickly as possible.
- Please be seated and fasten your seat-belt.

Culture Tips

➤ When explaining something complicated in the cabin, e.g. the use of emergency equipment, the emergency evacuation procedure, it is strongly recommended that cabin attendants use logical connectors (逻辑连接词) to make the explanation more explicit and understandable.

➤ In oral English, logical connectors are connective words or phrases that indicate the relationship between or within a sentence or a group of sentences. Here list some frequently used logic connectors:

—**Sequence**: first, second, firstly, secondly, first of all, next, then, before, after, as soon as, finally, eventually, in the end…

—**Time**: now, later, afterward, then, subsequently, soon, meanwhile, at last…

—**Space**: above, behind, below, under, nearby, ahead, next to, adjacent to, in front of, close to…

—**Addition**: and, besides, also, too, in addition, moreover, what's more, furthermore…

—**Alternative**: or, nor, on the other hand…
—**Cause**: because, for, as, since, because of, due to, owing to, as a result of…
—**Effect**: so, thus, therefore, hence, consequently, accordingly, as a result…
—**Contrast**: but, yet, however, instead, still, while, whereas, on the contrary, rather than…
—**Concession**: although, though, even though, in spite of…
—**Exemplification**: for example, for instance, such as…
—**Comparison**: like, likewise, similarly…
—**Condition**: if, if not, if necessary, in that case, otherwise…

Cabin Term

Life vest/Life jacket　救生衣

救生衣又称救生背心，是一种救护生命的服装，设计类似背心，采用尼龙面料或氯丁橡胶、浮力材料或可充气的材料、反光材料等制作而成。一般使用年限为5~7年，是船上、飞机上的救生设备之一。穿在身上具有足够的浮力，使落水者头部能露出水面。充气救生衣主要由密封充气式背心气囊、微型高压气瓶和快速充气阀等组成，在有掉入水中可能性的工作中经常使用。正常情况下（未充气），整个充气式救生衣如同带状穿戴、披挂在人的肩背上，由于体积小巧，不妨碍人们的作业自由；一旦落入水中遇到危险时，可根据水的作用自动膨胀充气（全自动充气救生衣），或用手拉动充气阀上的拉链（手动充气救生衣），便会在规定时间完成充气，产生8~15kg的浮力，向上托起人体，使不慎落水者头、肩部露出水面，及时获得安全保护。

◉ **Match the logical connectors in Column A to the sentences in Column B.**

Column A	Column B
1. Time	a. Due to a mechanical fault, the cabin pressure has reduced.
2. Contrast	b. To inflate the life jacket, you can pull the tab or blow into the mouthpieces.
3. Cause	c. We are experience turbulence, so please be seated and fasten your seat-belt.
4. Effect	d. The safety demonstration will begin soon.
5. Space	e. First of all, pull the oxygen mask towards you.
6. Alternative	f. Your life jacket is located under your seat.
7. Sequence	g. But remember: do not inflate your life jacket in the cabin.

◉ **Make up a dialogue about showing passengers how to use the emergency equipment in the cabin by using the logical connectors mentioned above as many as possible.**

Unit 15   Safety & Emergency I

Part B
Dialogues

(CA=Cabin Attendant, PAX=Passenger)

1

(*Before the safety demonstration*)
PAX: Miss, where can I find my life jacket?
CA: It is located under your seat in a pouch. You can reach and use it in an emergency.
PAX: And how can I use it?
CA: Don't worry. The safety demonstration will begin shortly. Please listen carefully. Our cabin attendants will show you how to use the life jacket in detail.
PAX: Thanks.
CA: You are welcome.

2

(*After the life jacket demonstration*)
PAX: Miss, could you tell me how to use my life jacket? I'm not quite sure about the life jacket demonstration.
CA: Certainly. Let me show you. When you are required to put on the life jacket, slip it over your head. Secure the straps around your waist and tie them securely.
PAX: OK. How can I inflate it?
CA: You can inflate it by pulling these tabs down, or you can blow into the mouthpieces. But remember don't inflate it in the cabin.
PAX: It doesn't seem that complicated. Thank you, Miss!
CA: You are welcome, Sir.

3

(*After the oxygen mask demonstration*)
PAX: I'm sorry, Miss, but can you show me that again, please? I'm not quite clear.
CA: Certainly, let me show you again. First of all, pull the oxygen mask towards you. Then place the mask over your mouth and nose, and slip the elastic band over your head. After that, just breathe normally.
PAX: Thank you, Miss!
CA: You are welcome, Sir.

4

(*To passengers in the cabin*)
CA: Ladies and gentlemen, due to a mechanical fault, the cabin pressure has reduced.

Please pull the oxygen mask over your nose and mouth.

(*To the lady in the cabin who hasn't put her mask on*)

CA: Madam, please put your oxygen mask on as quickly as possible.

PAX: I have to help my son first. He is too young to put it on by himself.

CA: Put your own mask first, please!

PAX: Thank you for reminding me.

5

(*To passengers in the cabin*)

CA: Ladies and gentlemen, we are entering an area of turbulence. Please be seated and fasten your seat-belt.

(*To the passenger walking in the aisle*)

CA: Please return to your seat, Sir.

PAX1: But I have to go to toilet.

CA: Sorry, Sir. We are experiencing turbulence, so please return to your seat as quickly as possible. The use of lavatories has been suspended.

PAX1: Oh, I see. Thank you.

PAX2: Miss, may I have a cup of tea? I'm thirsty.

CA: Sorry, Sir. During the turbulence, the cabin service has been suspended. I'll get one for you as soon as the turbulence stops.

PAX2: It's very kind of you.

PAX3: Miss, the turbulence makes me sick. I want to vomit.

CA: Please use the airsickness bag in the seat pocket in front of you. I'll attend to the bag after the turbulence.

PAX2: Thanks.

6

(*The lavatory is on fire. To passengers in the cabin*)

CA: A fire has broken out in the lavatory. We ask you to remain calm as we extinguish it.

(*The cabin attendants put the fire out immediately, and a passenger runs out of the lavatory.*)

CA: What happened in the lavatory, Sir?

PAX: I smoked in the lavatory and it got the lavatory on fire accidentally.

CA: For the sake of safety, smoking on board is strictly forbidden, especially in the lavatory. It's very dangerous.

PAX: I'm extremely sorry. It's my fault.

Unit 15   Safety & Emergency I

New Words and Expressions

pouch	[paʊtʃ]	n.	袋子
in detail	[ɪn]['diːteɪl]		详细地
waist	[weɪst]	n.	腰,腰部
tie	[taɪ]	v.	系;打结;连接
inflate	[ɪn'fleɪt]	v.	充气
tab	[tæb]	n.	悬垂物
mouthpiece	['maʊθpiːs]	v.	吹口
elastic	[ɪ'læstɪk]	adj.	有弹性的
band	[bænd]	n.	带子
breathe	[briːð]	v.	呼吸
normally	['nɔːməlɪ]	adj.	正常的,一般的
mechanical fault	[mɪ'kænɪkəl][fɔːlt;fɒlt]		机械故障
attend to	[ə'tend][tuː]		处理
break out	[breɪk][aʊt]		爆发
extinguish	[ɪk'stɪŋgwɪʃ]	v.	熄灭
accidentally	[æksɪ'dentəlɪ]	adv.	意外地;偶然地
fault	[fɔːlt; fɒlt]	n.	错误

● **Role play the cabin attendant's responses.**

PAX: Where can I find my life jacket?
CA: _____.

PAX: Could you tell me how to use it?
CA: _____.

PAX: After putting it on, how can I inflate it?
CA: _____.

(*During turbulence*)
CA: _____.

PAX1: But my kid has to go to the lavatory.
CA: _____.

PAX1: Oh, I see. Thank you.
PAX2: The turbulence makes me sick. I want to vomit.
CA: _____.

PAX2: Thank you.

201

◉ **Discuss the following questions.**

1. What is the life jacket demonstration for?
2. How would you teach passengers to inflate their life jackets?
3. How would you teach passengers to make use of the oxygen mask?
4. The plane is entering an area of turbulence. Please inform the passenger of this situation.
5. The lavatory is on fire. After extinguishing it, what would you say to passengers on board?

◉ **Make up dialogues based on the following situations.**

1. Sandra is a cabin attendant in charge of the economy class. She is ready to help the passenger who has difficulty in using the emergency equipment.
2. The plane is entering an area of turbulence. The cabin attendant asks the passengers in the aisle to be seated and fasten his seat-belt.
3. The purser is talking to a passenger who smoked in the lavatory.

◉ **Translate the following sentences into English.**

1. 您的救生衣位于您座椅下方的口袋内。
2. 当您被要求穿上救生衣时,将其从头部套下穿好。
3. 您可通过拉充气阀门为救生衣充气,也可通过人工充气管用嘴向内充气。
4. 首先,用力向下拉氧气面罩,接着将面罩罩在口鼻处并将带子套在头上。
5. 将连接片插入锁扣内以系紧安全带。
6. 解开时,先将锁扣打开,拉出连接片。
7. 您可以在紧急情况下使用它。
8. 女士,请您尽快戴好您的氧气面罩。
9. 女士们先生们,我们正在经历颠簸,请坐好并系好您的安全带。
10. 为保证飞行安全,机上禁止吸烟。

Part C
Public Announcements

Unit 15   Safety & Emergency I

Depressurization

Ladies and gentlemen,

Due to a loss of cabin pressure, we are making a rapid but controlled descent. The descent will last for a few minutes until our airplane reaches a safer altitude.

During this period, please use your oxygen mask. When you see the oxygen mask, pull it down, place it over your nose and mouth, and breathe normally. Adjust the strap to secure the mask. Secure your own mask before assisting your child or others. Please breathe through the oxygen mask until you are advised to remove it.

Thank you!

Oxygen Mask

Ladies and gentlemen,

We will now explain the use of the oxygen mask.

Your oxygen mask is in the compartment over your head and it will appear automatically when needed. If you see the mask, pull it towards you firmly to start the flow of oxygen. Place the mask over your nose and mouth, slip the elastic band over your head. Within a few seconds the oxygen flow will begin. Secure your own mask before assisting your child or others. Oxygen will be flowing although the bag does not inflate.

Thank you!

Seat-Belt

Ladies and gentlemen,

We will now explain the use of the seat-belt.

This is your safety belt on your seat. To fasten your seat-belt, insert the link into the main buckle. To be effective, the seat-belt should be fastened tight and low. When you wish to unfasten the seat-belt, lift the flap and pull out the link.

Thank you!

Fire in the Cabin

Ladies and gentlemen,

A minor fire has broken out in the _____ of the cabin, and we are trying to put it out. Passengers sitting around the fire, please move to a safe seat. All other passengers, please do not leave your seats.

Thank you!

Life Vest

Ladies and gentlemen,

We will now explain the use of the life vest.

Your life vest is located under your seat. To put the vest on, slip it over your head. Secure the straps around your waist and tie them securely.

To inflate the lie jacket, pull the tab. Do not inflate it while you are in the cabin. If your life vest is not inflated enough, you can also inflate it *manually* by blowing into the tube on either side.

Thank you!

New Words and Expressions

depressurization	[diːˌpreʃəraɪˈzeɪʃən]	n. 失压
rapid	[ˈræpɪd]	adj. 快速的
descent	[dɪˈsent]	n. 下降
altitude	[ˈæltɪˌtjuːd]	n. 海拔；高度
remove	[rɪˈmuːv]	v. 摘下；脱下
automatically	[ˌɔːtəˈmætɪkli]	adv. 自动地；机械地
firmly	[ˈfɜːmli]	adv. 坚定地；坚固地
safety belt	[ˈseɪfti][belt]	安全带
buckle	[ˈbʌkl]	n. 带扣
fasten	[ˈfɑːsn]	v. 系紧
manually	[ˈmænjʊəli]	adv. 手动地

Speaking Practice

⦿ **Practice making public announcements about Five in the Cabin with these alternatives.**
- front
- middle
- rear
- Beijing Capital International Airport
- Shanghai Pudong International Airport
- Xi'an Xianyang International Airport
- Hong Kong International Airport
- John F.kennedy International Airport

⦿ **Please read following sentences in the right tone. (′ for stress, ↗ for rising tone, ↘ for falling tone)**

1. We will now ↗′ explain the use of the oxygen mask. ↘
2. Due to a ′ loss of cabin pressure ↘, we are making a rapid ↗ but controlled descent. ↘
3. When you see the oxygen mask ↗, pull it down ↘ place it over your nose ↗ and mouth ↘, and breathe normally. ↘
4. ′ Secure your own mask ↗ before ′ assisting your child or others. ↘
5. Your life vest is ′ located under your seat. ↘

Unit 15　Safety & Emergency I

◉ **Translate the following expressions into English and practice making public announcement about** *Depressurization.*
- 客舱压力
- 客舱失压
- 飞机快速下降
- 到达安全高度
- 摘下氧气面罩
- 着火
- 灭火
- 穿上救生衣
- 救生衣充气
- 将氧气面罩戴在口鼻处

Part D
Work-task

▣ **Try to discuss:**
1. Do you know any emergency equipment in the cabin?
2. Do you think it is necessary for cabin attendants to learn how to use the emergency equipment in the cabin? Why?

Emergency Equipment

One of the jobs that the cabin attendants must do in the cabin is to check all the emergency equipment. They have to make sure that all the equipment is in the correct location as well as in good working order. A qualified cabin attendant is well trained to use all the equipment in emergent situation. Some common emergency equipment is shown in the following table.

Equipment	Pictures	Description
Carbon Dioxide Extinguisher (CO_2 Extinguisher) 二氧化碳灭火瓶		CO_2 Extinguishers are designed for Class B and Class C fires.❶
Water Extinguisher 水灭火瓶		Water extinguishers are designed for Class A fires.❶

205

continued

Equipment	Pictures	Description
Dry Chemical Extinguisher 干粉灭火瓶		Dry Chemical Extinguishers are designed for Class A, B and C fires.❶
BCF (Halon) Extinguisher 海伦灭火瓶		BCF extinguishers are capable of fighting all types of fire (Class A, B, C and D) in the flight deck and passenger cabin.❶
Smoke Hood (Protective Breathing Equipment, PBE) 防烟面罩		Smoke hoods are protective head coverings which have a filter system that prevents wearer from breathing in unwanted smoke gases and particles generated in a fire. They may also incorporate a small oxygen generator.❷
Smoke Goggles 防烟护目镜		The smoke goggles can be found in the flight deck for use with smoke hood (PBE) when the aircraft is in fire.❸
Asbestos Gloves 石棉手套		The asbestos gloves are kept in the flight deck and the cabin to protect the user from heat or fire. They can be also used to handle hot or sharp object.❹
Crash Axe 应急斧头		Crash axes were provided to obtain emergency access. The handle is insulated to protect against electric shock. In compliance with anti-terrorism regulations and procedures, axes are no longer carried and have been replaced by insulated crowbars in the passenger cabin on most airplanes.❺
Life Raft 救生筏		The life raft is used in evacuation after an emergency ditching. The items in a life raft include survival kit, canopy, canopy pole, hook knife, sea anchor, heaving line, heaving ring, hand pump, locator light, emergency locator transmitter, etc.❻
Emergency Locator Transmitter (E.L.T) 应急定位发射器		Emergency locator transmitter is a radio-frequency transmitter used after an emergency landing or ditching that broadcasts signals to help rescuer find survivors.❼

(资料来源：www.skybrary.aero)

Notes

❶ CO₂ Extinguishers are designed for Class B and Class C fires. Water extinguishers are designed for Class A fires. Dry Chemical Extinguishers are designed for Class A, B and C fires. BCF extinguishers are capable of fighting all types of fire (Class A, B, C and D) in the flight deck and passenger cabin.

句子大意：二氧化碳灭火瓶用来扑灭B类和C类火。水灭火瓶用来扑灭A类火。干粉灭火瓶用来扑灭A、B和C类火。海伦灭火瓶可以扑灭驾驶舱和客舱中所有类型(A、B、C和D类)的火。

根据美国的分类，A类是指燃烧固体燃料的火；B类是指燃烧液体或液化燃料的火；C类是指燃烧气体燃料的火；D类是指燃烧可燃烧金属的火。

❷ Smoke hoods are protective head coverings which have a filter system that prevents wearer from breathing in unwanted smoke gases and particles generated in a fire. They may also incorporate a small oxygen generator.

句子大意：防烟面罩是保护性的头罩，其中装有过滤系统，用来防止佩戴者吸入由火焰燃烧产生的烟雾气体和颗粒。有的防烟面罩还装有小型的氧气发生器。

其中，which have a filter system为定语从句，修饰protective head coverings；that prevent wearer from breathing in unwanted some gases and particles为定语从句，修饰a filter system；generated in a fire为过去分词结构做后置定语，修饰unwanted smoke gases and particles，等同于that are generated in a fire。

❸ The smoke goggles can be found in the flight deck for use with smoke hood (PBE) when the aircraft is in fire.

句子大意：防烟护目镜一般存放在驾驶舱，当飞机起火时通常与防烟面罩一起使用。

❹ The asbestos gloves are kept in the flight deck and the cabin to protect the user from heat or fire. They can be also used to handle hot or sharp objects.

句子大意：石棉手套存放在飞机的驾驶舱和客舱中，用以保护使用者不受高温和火苗的伤害。石棉手套同样可以用来处理高温或尖锐物品。

❺ Crash axes were provided to obtain emergency access. The handle is insulated to protect against electric shock. In compliance with anti-terrorism regulations and procedures, axes are no longer carried and have been replaced by insulated crowbars in the passenger cabin on most airplanes.

句子大意：应急斧头用于开辟紧急通道。斧子把手经过绝缘处理，以保护使用者不受电击。目前，为了遵守反恐法规和程序，大多数飞机的客舱不再配备应急斧头，取而代之的是绝缘撬棍。

❻ The items in a life raft include survival kit, canopy, canopy pole, hook knife, sea anchor, heaving line, heaving ring, hand pump, locator light, emergency locator transmitter, etc.

句子大意：救生筏上的物品包括救生包、天棚、天棚柱、刀子、锚、手抓绳、手抓环、手动充气泵、定位灯、紧急定位发射器等。

❼ Emergency locator transmitter is a radio-frequency transmitter used after an emergency landing or ditching that broadcasts signals to help rescuer find survivors.

句子大意：紧急定位发射器是一种射频发射器，它在飞机紧急着陆或水上迫降后使用，发射出的信号能帮助救援人员找到幸存者。

New Words and Expressions

quali fied	[ˈkwɒlɪfaɪd]	adj.	合格的；有资格的
carbon dioxide	[ˈkɑːbən][daɪˈɒksaɪd]		二氧化碳
extinguisher	[ɪkˈstɪŋgwɪʃə]	n.	灭火器
chemical	[ˈkemɪkəl]	n.	化学制品
halon extinguisher	[ˈheɪlɑːn][ɪkˈstɪŋgwɪʃə]		海伦灭火器
capable	[ˈkeɪpəbəl]	adj.	有能力的
flight deck	[flaɪt][dek]		驾驶舱
hood	[hʊd]	n.	头罩
protective	[prəˈtektɪv]	adj.	防护的
covering	[ˈkʌvərɪŋ]	n.	遮盖物
filter	[ˈfɪltə]	n.	过滤器
gas	[gæs]	n.	气体
particle	[ˈpɑːtɪkəl]	n.	颗粒物
generate	[ˈdʒenəreɪt]	v.	产生
incorporate	[ɪnˈkɔːpəreɪt]	v.	包含
generator	[ˈdʒenəreɪtə]	n.	发生器
goggle	[ˈgɒgəl]	n.	护目镜
asbestos	[æzˈbestɒs; æs-; -təs]	n.	石棉
object	[ˈɒbdʒɪkt; -dʒekt]	n.	物体
crash axe	[kræʃ][æks]		应急斧子
axe	[æks]	n.	斧子
access	[ˈækses]	n.	通道
insulated	[ˈɪnsə,leɪtəd]	adj.	绝缘的
in compliance with	[ɪn][kəmˈplaɪəns][wɪð]		遵守
terrorism	[ˈterərɪzəm]	n.	恐怖主义
crowbar	[ˈkrəʊbɑː]	n.	铁锹
life raft	[laɪf][rɑːft]		救生筏
survival kit	[səˈvaɪvəl][kɪt]		救生包
canopy	[ˈkænəpɪ]	n.	天棚
pole	[pəʊl]	n.	杆
hook	[hʊk]	n.	钩
anchor	[ˈæŋkə]	n.	锚
heaving line	[hiːvɪŋ][laɪn]		系留绳

pump	[pʌmp]	n. 泵
locator	[ləʊˈkeɪtə]	n. 定位器
Emergency Locator Transmitter(ELT)	[ɪˈmɜːdʒənsɪ][ləʊˈkeɪtə][trænzˈmɪtə]	应急定位发射器
radio-frequency	[ˈreɪdɪəʊˈfriːkwənsɪ]	n. 射频
signal	[ˈsɪɡnəl]	n. 信号
rescuer	[ˈreskjʊə]	n. 救助者
survivor	[səˈvaɪvə]	n. 幸存者；生还者

Part E
Supplementary Reading

Try to discuss:
1. How much do you know about The Terracotta Warriors and Horses?
2. What factors make The Terracotta Warriors and Horses famous?

The Terracotta Warriors and Horses

Terracotta Warriors and Horses, also known as Qin Terracotta Warriors and Horses or Qin Warriors for short, are located in a place, 1.5 kilometers east of the Mausoleum of Qin Shihuang in Lintong District, Xi'an City, Shanxi Province. In 1987, the Mausoleum of the First Emperor of Qin Dynasty and the Terracotta Warriors and Horses Pit were approved by *UNESCO* to be included in the "World Heritage List" and were hailed as "the eighth wonder of the world".

According to *Records of the Historian*, the Prime Minister Li Si began to preside over the planning and design of the Mausoleum of the First Emperor of Qin Dynasty, and the General Zhanghan supervised the construction for 39 years. The Terracotta Warriors and Horses were built and buried in the burial pit at the same time as the Qin tomb was built. The Terracotta Warriors and Horses of the Qin Dynasty is a typical example of the burial of the terracotta warriors. The Qin figurines strictly imitate real objects, with the nature and characteristics of portrait sketches, and are superior in scale and momentum.

The Terracotta Warriors and Horses of Qin Shihuang accompany the burial pit from west to east, and the three pits are arranged in a pattern. The earliest discovered is the No. 1 warrior pit, which is rectangular in shape. There are more than 8,000 terracotta warriors and horses in the pit, with sloped doorways on all sides. There is one pit each on the left and right sides of Pit No. 1, called Pit No. 2 and Pit No. 3. Pit No. 1 is in the south, 216 meters long from east to west, 62 meters wide, and covers an area of 13,260 square meters. Pit No. 2 is 124 meters long from east to west, 98 meters wide, and covers an area of 6,000 square meters. Pit No. 3 covers an area of 520 square meters. A total of 800 warrior figurines, 18 wooden chariots and more than 100 pottery horses were unearthed. Based on the current arrangement of the terracotta warriors and horses, there may be 7,000 warriors in the three pits, 100 chariots, and 100 war horses. The pottery figurines are tall, generally around 1.8 meters.

The terracotta warriors and horses are distinguished from the identity, and there are mainly two categories: soldiers and military officials. General soldiers do not wear crowns, while military officials wear crowns. The crowns of ordinary military officials and generals are not the same, and even armors are different. Most of the terracotta warriors and horses are made by smelting and firing. The original terracotta warriors and horses had bright and harmonious paintings. During the excavation process, it was discovered that some of the terracotta warriors and horses still retained their bright colors when they were just unearthed, but they were oxidized by oxygen after being unearthed. The color disappears instantly in less than ten seconds and turns into white ash. All can see now is the remaining traces of painted painting.

(资料来源：https://baike.baidu.com/item/%E5%85%B5%E9%A9%AC%E4%BF%91/60649?fr=aladdin)

参考译文

西安兵马俑

兵马俑，即秦始皇兵马俑，亦简称秦兵马俑或秦俑，位于今陕西省西安市临潼区秦始皇陵以东1.5km处的兵马俑坑内。1987年，秦始皇陵及兵马俑坑被联合国教科文组织批准列入《世界遗产名录》，并被誉为"世界第八大奇迹"。

据《史记》记载：秦始皇陵由丞相李斯依惯例开始主持规划设计，大将章邯监工，修筑时间长达39年之久，兵马俑是在修筑秦陵的同时制作并埋入随葬坑内。秦兵马俑是以俑代人殉葬的典型，也是以俑代人殉葬的顶峰。秦俑严格地模拟实物，带有肖像写生的性质和特点，并且在规模和气势上更胜一筹。

秦始皇兵马俑陪葬坑坐西向东，三坑呈品字形排列。最早发现的是一号俑坑，呈长方形，坑里有8000多个兵马俑，四面有斜坡门道。一号俑坑左右两侧各有一个兵马俑坑，称二号坑和三号坑。一号坑在南，东西长216m，宽62m，面积为13260m²。二号坑东西长124m，宽98m，面积为6000m²。三号坑面积520m²。共出土武士俑800件，木质战车18辆，陶马100多匹。按兵马俑现有排列形式推算，这三个坑的武士俑可能有7000件，战车100辆，战马100匹。陶俑身材高大，一般在1.8m左右。

兵马俑从身份上区分，主要有士兵与军吏两大类。一般士兵不戴冠，而军吏戴冠，普通军吏的冠与将军的冠又不相同，甚至铠甲也有区别。兵马俑大部分是采用陶冶烧制的方法制成，当初的兵马俑都有鲜艳和谐的彩绘，发掘过程中发现有的陶俑刚出土时局部还保留着鲜艳的颜色，但是出土后由于被氧气氧化，颜色不到10s瞬间消尽，化作白灰。现在能看到的只是残留的彩绘痕迹。

Cabin Service English

Unit 16

Safety & Emergency II

* Part A Useful Words and Expressions
* Part B Dialogues
* Part C Public Announcements
* Part D Work-task
* Part E Supplementary Reading

Students will be able to:
memorize the words and expressions about the emergency evacuation;
make up the dialogues about the emergency evacuation;
obtain and improve public announcements skills about emergency landing and ditching;
know about general responsibilities of cabin attendants in an emergency evacuation;
introduce Westminster Abbey.

Suggested Hours: *4 class hours*

Part A
Useful Words and Expressions

◉ **Please list as many words, expressions and sentence patterns related to an emergency landing as you can.**

_____
_____

- emergency landing / ditching
- emergency exits
- escape slide
- evacuate / evacuation
- brace for impact / brace position
- inflate the life jacket
- leave the airplane from the exit nearest to you
- cross one's arms
- put your crossed arms on the seatback in front of you
- rest one's head on the crossed arms
- hold the brace position until the airplane comes to a complete stop
- leave everything behind
- take off anything sharp
- Our plane has eight emergency exits.
- Jump and slide down!
- Don't panic. /Don't worry. /Don't be scared.
- Stay calm. /Just calm down.
- Please obey/follow the instructions.
- Please unfasten the seat-belts and disembark the airplane as soon as possible.

Culture Tips

➢ When a cabin attendant requests passengers to do something in the cabin, the expressions she/he adopts should be determined by the specific situation in which the request is made.

➢ In most cases, when making a request, a cabin attendant is required to use interrogative sentences (疑问句). Besides, modal verbs (情态动词) like "may", "could" and "would" should be used to show courtesy. For example:

—**May I** have your attention, please?
—**Could you please** do me a favor?
—**Would you please** turn off your mobile phone?

—**Would you mind** changing seats with that lady?
> However, under some circumstances, e.g. emergencies or passengers not following advice, cabin attendants can use imperative sentences to make requests or give commands. For example:

—Please be seated and fasten your seat-belt.
—Please follow my instruction.
—Jump and slide down!
—Don't panic.

Cabin Term

Brace for impact/Brace position   防冲撞姿势

通常，当飞机紧急迫降前，都会有距离冲撞，机舱内产生强烈震动。这时，旅客需要采取正确的防冲撞姿势，避免或减少伤害。大多数旅客可以采用上身前倾、两臂伸直、双手交叉、紧紧抓住前排座椅靠背、头部紧贴两臂之间的防冲撞姿势，这样前排座椅与身体上部和大腿所在方向构成最稳定的三角形状，能有效地保护身体。但这是普通旅客应该采取的防冲撞姿势，并不适合孕妇等特殊人群。将头低下，两腿分开，两臂用力抱紧大腿，使身体尽可能地保持球形姿态是前排旅客最安全的姿态。这是因为坐在前排的旅客前方没有靠椅，空间较大，团成球状可以有效避免巨大惯性带来的伤害。由于身体原因，孕妇完成这些动作也比较困难，对她们来说，采取这种姿势防止冲撞是不适合的。特殊旅客，包括孕妇、肥胖者、高个者或者老人，因为身体原因很难做到普通旅客的防冲击姿势。这些特殊旅客需要调直座椅，挺直上身，两手用力抓住座椅的扶手，收紧下巴，全身绷紧，脚用力蹬地，这样也可以尽可能地将自己的身体固定在座椅上，以起到保护作用。在飞机触地前一瞬间，应全身紧迫用力，憋住气，使全身肌肉处于紧张对抗外力的状态，以防猛烈撞击。

Match Column A to column B to form a complete sentence.

Column A	Column B
1. May I	a. stow your tray table?
2. Please	b. passing it to me?
3. Would you mind	c. see your boarding pass, please?
4. Would you please	d. unfasten your seat-belt until the plane comes to a complete stop.
5. Please don't	e. use mobile phone during take off.

Make up a dialogue about making a request in the cabin.

Part B
Dialogues

(CA=Cabin Attendant, PAX=Passenger)

CA: Ladies and gentlemen, our plane will soon make an emergency landing because of the engine failure. Don't panic. Our captain has full competence to make a safe landing. Please obey our instructions.

PAX: Emergency landing? I've never experienced that before. It must be very dangerous.

CA: Don't worry, Sir. Our captain and his co-pilot are experienced and competent enough to cope with this situation and all our cabin attendants are well trained to assist you.

PAX: I'm still terrified, but I believe that you can be relied on.

CA: We also need your cooperation, Sir. Just obey our instructions. Everything will be fine.

PAX: I hope so.

CA: Ladies and gentlemen, your life jacket is located under your seat. Please get your life jacket out of the pouch and slip it over your head. Then secure the straps around your waist and tie them securely. You can inflate your life jacket either by pulling these tabs down or blowing into the mouthpieces manually. Please remember, when you are outside the airplane, pull the red tabs down sharply to inflate your life jacket.

PAX: Yes, Miss.

CA: After putting on your life jacket, please return to your seat and fasten your seat-belts immediately. Ladies and gentlemen, our plane has eight emergency exits: two in the rear cabin, two in forward cabin and four in the middle. Please locate the exit that is nearest to you. After the aircraft has come to a full stop, please leave from the exit nearest to you.

(*To a passenger sitting beside the emergency exit*)

CA: After landing, please assist me by opening the exit and evacuating other passengers.

PAX: How can I assist you? I've never met with this situation before.

CA: Just follow the safety instruction in the seat pocket in front of you, Sir.

Unit 16   Safety & Emergency II

PAX: No problem, I'll try my best to assist you, Miss.
CA: Thank you so much, Sir!

4

CA: Attention, please. I will be explaining the bracing position. On the command of "Brace for Impact", please cross your arms, rest them on the seatback in front of you and then place your head on your arms. After the landing is made, the airplane may bounce several times. So please hold this position until the airplane has come to a complete stop. Then follow me.

PAX1: I can do this, but what about my kid? He is too young to touch the seatback in front of him.
   (*To the child*)
CA: Let me explain it to you. Just put your head between your legs with hands holding your ankles. Can you do this?
PAX2: Yes, that's easy. Thank you, Miss.

5

(*The plane has come to a complete stop*)
CA: Ladies and gentlemen, please unfasten your seat-belts and disembark from the airplane as soon as possible.
PAX: Where is my bag? I need to take my handbag with me. I have valuables in it!
CA: It's an emergency evacuation. Please leave everything behind and evacuate the airplane in this way.
PAX: But my bag…
CA: Evacuate! Evacuate!

6

CA: We will be evacuating the airplane using an escape slide. Please remove everything sharp on you and obey our instructions.

(*In front of the escape slide*)
PAX: Oh my Gosh! It's too high. I'm so terrified!
CA: Don't be scared, Sir. Please follow my instruction, jump and slide down!
PAX: It's horrible! Tell me again how to do this.
CA: Jump and slide down!

New Words and Expressions

| engine | ['endʒɪn] | n. 发动机 |
| failure | ['feɪljə] | n. 故障 |

215

panic	['pænɪk]	v.	惊慌
competence	['kɒmpɪtəns]	n.	资格；能力
obey	[ə'beɪ]	v.	服从；按照……行动
co-pilot	[kəʊ'paɪlət]	n.	副驾驶
competent	['kɒmpɪtənt]	adj.	胜任的；有能力的
cope with	[kəʊp][wɪð]		处理；应付
rely on	[rɪ'laɪ][ɒn]		依靠；依赖
evacuate	[ɪ'vækjʊeɪt]	v.	疏散；撤离
meet with	[miːt][wɪð]		经历；遭受
safety instruction	['seɪftɪ][ɪn'strʌkʃən]		安全须知
brace position	[breɪs][pə'zɪʃn]		防冲撞姿势
bounce	[baʊns]	v.	弹起
valuable	['væljʊəbl]	n.	贵重物品
escape slide	[i'skeɪp][slaɪd]		逃离滑梯
sharp	[ʃɑːp]	adj.	锋利的
terrified	['terɪfaɪd]	adj.	非常害怕的
horrible	['hɒrəbəl]	adj.	令人恐惧的

◉ **Role play the cabin attendant's responses.**

CA: _____.
PAX: The emergency landing must be dangerous.
CA: _____.
PAX: I hope we can be safe.
CA: _____.
PAX: Sure, I'll obey your instructions.

CA: _____.
PAX: Can you show me the brace position again?
CA: _____.
PAX: What about my kid? He can't put his arms on the seat.
CA: _____.
PAX: Thank you.

◉ **Discuss the following questions.**

1. The plane will make an emergency landing because of the sudden failure of an engine. Please inform the passengers of this situation.
2. The plane will make an emergency landing. Please inform the passengers how to escape from the emergency exits.

3. During an emergency landing, how do you instruct passengers to do "brace for impact"?
4. In an evacuation, a passenger tries to take his baggage. What do you say to stop him?
5. There will be an evacuation using an escape slide. How do you instruct the passengers?

◉ **Make up dialogues based on the following situations.**
1. Jenny is the chief purser of the flight. She is informing the passengers that the airplane will make an emergency landing.
2. The cabin attendants are instructing the passengers how to do "brace for impact".
3. In an evacuation, the cabin attendant is stopping a passenger who tries to take his baggage.

◉ **Translate the following sentences into English.**
1. 女士们、先生们，由于引擎故障，我们的飞机即将进近紧急迫降。
2. 女士们、先生们，本架飞机共有8个紧急出口：其中2个位于客舱后部，2个位于客舱前部，4个位于客舱中部。
3. 当飞机完全停稳后，请从最近的出口撤离。
4. 飞机着陆后，请协助我打开紧急出口并撤离旅客。
5. 当听到"防冲撞姿势"的指令时，请交叉双臂，放在前排座椅椅背上，并将头抵在手臂上。
6. 飞机着陆后可能会经历数次弹跳，请保持住防冲撞姿势，直至飞机完全停稳。
7. 请勿携带任何物品，由此通道撤离飞机。
8. 我们将使用应急滑梯撤离飞机，请脱下身上所有尖锐物品，遵从我们的指示。
9. 请根据我的指示跳上滑梯并滑下来！
10. 女士们、先生们，请解开安全带，并尽快撤离飞机。

Part C
Public Announcements

Emergency Landing

Ladies and gentlemen,

We will make an emergency landing in 15 minutes. All of our cabin attendants are well trained for this kind of situation, so please follow their instructions.

Please remain seated, place your seat in the upright position and secure the table in front of you.

When evacuating the airplane, you are not permitted to carry any hand baggage.

Thank you!

Ditching

Ladies and gentlemen,

We will make an emergency ditching in 15 minutes. All of our crew members are well trained for this kind of situation, so please follow their instructions.

After ditching, the airplane will keep floating in the water for more than 30 minutes. Life rafts will be deployed outside of each exit door. So please board the raft calmly under the direction of the crew member in charge.

When evacuating the airplane, you are not permitted to carry any hand baggage.

Thank you!

Preparation for Ditching

Ladies and gentlemen,

We will explain about personal preparations for your safety on ditching. So please follow our instructions.

First, remove all the sharp objects including shoes with high heels or metal attachments, dentures, pins, knives, pens and wrist watches. In addition, necklaces, earrings, and neckties are also recommended to be taken off. Then, hand them to the cabin attendants.

Place a cushion or a coat between the seat-belt and your body, and then fasten your seat-belt as tightly as possible.

Upon our instruction later, remove your eye glasses.

Put on your life jacket but do not inflate it until you have left the aircraft. Return seats and tables to the upright position. Place a pillow or blanket on your knees. Remain quiet and wait for further instructions from the cabin crew.

Thank you!

Bracing

Ladies and gentlemen,

We will show you two kinds of brace positions against the impact during emergency landing / ditching. Please read the *Safety Instructions* and take one of following positions fit for you.

The first brace position: Cross your arms, put your hands on the seatback in front of you, and place your head on your arms.

The second brace position: bend the upper part of your body forward as much as possible and clasp both ankles.

Take your brace position as soon as you hear the command of "brace for impact" and hold this position until the airplane comes to a complete stop.

Thank you!

Exit

Ladies and gentlemen,

Our cabin attendants will be pointing out the emergency exits. Our plane has eight emergency exits: two in the rear, two in front and four in the middle. Please locate the exit that is nearest to you and remember it. All exits are shown on the *Safety Instructions*.

After the airplane comes to a complete stop, evacuate from the exit nearest to you speedily. If that exit cannot be used, move quickly to another one.

Thank you.

New Words and Expressions

permit	[pəˈmɪt]	v. 许可；允许
float	[fləʊt]	v. 漂浮；浮动
deploy	[dɪˈplɔɪ]	v. 展开
board	[bɔːd]	v. 上（飞机、车、船等）
heel	[hiːl]	n. 脚后跟；鞋后跟
metal	[ˈmetəl]	v. 金属的
attachment	[əˈtætʃmənt]	n. 附件；配件
denture	[ˈdentʃə]	n. 假牙
pin	[pɪn]	n. 别针
wrist	[rɪst]	n. 手腕；腕关节
earring	[ˈɪərɪŋ]	n. 耳环
necktie	[ˈnektaɪ]	n. 领带
cushion	[ˈkʊʃən]	n. 垫子
pillow	[ˈpɪləʊ]	n. 枕头
blanket	[ˈblæŋkɪt]	n. 毯子

knee	[ni:]	n. 膝盖
upper	['ʌpə]	v. 上部的
clasp	[klɑ:sp]	v. 紧握；抱紧
speedily	['spi:dɪlɪ]	adv. 迅速地

Speaking Practice

◉ **Practice making public announcements about the following situations.**
- Emergency ditching
- Emergency landing
- Brace for impact/ Brace position
- Exits

◉ **Please read following sentences in the right tone.(′ for stress, ↗ for rising tone, ↘ for falling tone).**

1. Our cabin attendants will be ′ pointing out ↗ the emergency ′ exits. ↘
2. Please ′ locate the exit ′ that is nearest to you ↘ and remember it. ↘
3. After the airplane comes to a complete ′ stop, ′ evacuate from the exit ↗ nearest to you speedily. ↘
4. ′ All of our cabin attendants are well trained ↘ for this kind of ′ situation, so please ′ follow their instructions. ↘
5. Please remain ′ seated ↘, place your seat in the ′ upright position ↗ and ′ secure the table ↘ in front of you. ↘

◉ **Translate the following expressions into English and practice making public announcement about Emergency Landing or Ditching.**
- 紧急着陆
- 水上迫降
- 服从乘务员指令
- 移除尖锐物品
- 防冲撞姿势
- 飞机完全停止
- 离你最近的紧急出口
- 紧急撤离
- 在原座位坐好
- 展开救生筏

Part D
Work-task

📋 **Try to discuss:**
1. What role does a cabin attendant play in an emergency?
2. What qualities do you think should a cabin attendant have in dealing with emergencies?

Responsibilities of Cabin Attendants in an Emergency Landing

Besides providing passengers with high quality service in the cabin, one of the major responsibilities the cabin crew should take is to ensure the safety of the passengers, especially in an emergency.❶ Introduced in the ensuing paragraphs is what the cabin crew should do in an emergency landing.❷

- Safety briefing

As part of their pre-departure duties, the cabin crew will provide a safety briefing to passengers which will include the emergency evacuation of the aircraft.❸ This briefing will refer passengers to their individual *Safety Instructions* but will always include pointing out exit locations and floor path lighting for particular use in poor visibility.❹ Passengers seated in emergency exit rows at overwing exits where no cabin crew are located may be individually briefed on how to open these in the event of an emergency.❺

- Communication with the flight deck

When the flight deck is aware that they will be making an emergency landing, they will notify the cabin crew via the in-flight phone. When the cabin crew are notified, the lead flight attendant will ask the captain a series of questions that will be relayed to the other flight attendants.❻ Questions that will be asked include what type of emergency it is, if the evacuation will take place on land or water, what signals the captain will give to evacuate and how much time the cabin crew have to prepare the cabin.❼

- Preparing the cabin

The cabin crew must inform the passengers of the situation. Cabin crew will make a special announcement and proceed to show the passengers the proper brace positions such as crossing their arms on the seat in front of them and then placing their heads on their arms or wrapping their arms around their legs while they are in a seated position and putting their heads as far down as they are able to go.❽

- Evacuating passengers

Evacuation is normally ordered by the Captain. However, if communication with the flight crew is not possible and the situation in the cabin is judged by the senior cabin crew member to be incompatible with any delay, then they are trained to make the evacuation order themselves once the aircraft has come to a complete stop.❾ In these circumstances, they are responsible for assessing immediate danger such as external fire or engines still running before any exit is opened.❿ Cabin crew supervising exits must also secure the exit until the slide (if the exit is so equipped) inflates and block the exit from use in the event of a slide malfunction.⓫ They are also expected to motivate passengers using appropriate shouted commands and, if necessary, physical action, to exit quickly and to leave behind personal possessions, especially items in overhead lockers or under seats.⓬ Normally, the cabin crew will be the last to leave their exit; however, in practice they are trained to remain on board only to the point when they believe that by staying any longer they are putting their own lives at risk.⓭ Once they are out of the aircraft, they are trained to assist in moving passengers away from the aircraft to a position where they can be safely grouped together.⓮

(资料来源：http://www.skybrary.aero/index.php/Emergency_Evacuation_on_Land; http://www.ehow.com/list_6535269_flight-attendant-emergency-procedures.html)

Notes

❶ Besides providing passengers with high quality service in the cabin, one of the major responsibilities the cabin crew should take is to ensure the safety of the passengers, especially in an emergency.

句子大意：除了在客舱中为旅客提供优质服务，乘务员承担的一项重要职责就是确保旅客的安全，尤其是在紧急情况下。

其中，the cabin crew should take 为定语从句，修饰 one of the major responsibilities。

❷ Introduced in the ensuing paragraphs is what the cabin crew should do in an emergency landing.

句子大意：下文介绍紧急着陆情况下乘务员应该做哪些工作。

由于句子主语较长，故采用倒装结构，正常语序为：What the cabin crew should do in an emergency landing will be introduced in the ensuing paragraphs。

❸ As part of their pre-departure duties, the cabin crew will provide a safety briefing to passengers which will include the emergency evacuation of the aircraft.

句子大意：作为出发前的职责，乘务员会向旅客进行安全说明，内容会包括飞机紧急撤离。

其中，which will include the emergency evacuation of the aircraft 为定语从句，修饰 safety briefing。

❹ This briefing will refer passengers to their individual *Safety Instructions* but will always include pointing out exit locations and floor path lighting for particular use in poor visibility.

句子大意：安全说明会引导旅客阅读各自的《安全须知》，但也包括向旅客指出安全出口位置以及在能见度差的条件下使用特殊的地面路径灯光。

❺ Passengers seated in emergency exit rows at overwing exits where no cabin crew are located may be individually briefed on how to open these in the event of an emergency.

句子大意：机翼上紧急出口位置没有乘务员就座，乘务员会单独向坐在紧急出口位置一排的旅客介绍紧急情况下如何打开舱门。

Unit 16　Safety & Emergency II

其中，seated in emergency exit rows at overwing exits为过去分词结构，做主语passengers的后置定语，等于who are seated in emergency exit rows at overwing exits；where no cabin crew are located为定语从句，修饰overwing exits。

❻When the cabin crew are notified, the lead flight attendant will ask the captain a series of questions that will be relayed to the other flight attendants.

句子大意：当接到紧急降落通知时，乘务长会向机长问一系列问题，这些问题将传达给其他乘务员。

其中，when the cabin crew are notified为时间状语从句；that will be relayed to the other flight attendants为定语从句，修饰a series of questions。

❼Questions that will be asked include what type of emergency it is, if the evacuation will take place on land or water, what signals the captain will give to evacuate and how much time the cabin crew have to prepare the cabin.

句子大意：乘务长向机长提出的问题包括：这是什么样的紧急情况？在陆地上还是水上撤离旅客？机长会对紧急疏散发出什么样的信号？乘务员有多少时间做准备工作？

❽Cabin crew will make a special announcement and proceed to show the passengers the proper brace positions such as crossing their arms on the seat in front of them and then placing their heads on their arms or wrapping their arms around their legs while they are in a seated position and putting their heads as far down as they are able to go.

句子大意：乘务员会播报一段特殊情况广播词，接着会向旅客演示正确的防冲撞姿势，例如将交叉的双臂放在前方座位上，然后将头放在双臂上；或者坐在座位上用双臂抱紧双腿，并将头尽可能低下。

❾However, if communication with the flight crew is not possible and the situation in the cabin is judged by the senior cabin crew member to be incompatible with any delay, then they are trained to make the evacuation order themselves once the aircraft has come to a complete stop.

句子大意：但是，如果与驾驶舱无法取得联系，客舱的情况由资深的乘务员判断已经不能再耽误，那么一旦飞机完全停止，乘务员立即按照训练要求发出撤离命令。

❿In these circumstances, they are responsible for assessing immediate danger such as external fire or engines still running before any exit is opened.

句子大意：在这样的情况下，乘务员负责在打开紧急出口前评估即时的危险，例如舱外是否起火，发动机是否仍在运转。

⓫Cabin crew supervising exits must also secure the exit until the slide (if the exit is so equipped) inflates and block the exit from use in the event of a slide malfunction.

句子大意：负责安全出口的乘务员必须守好舱门直至滑梯（如果飞机配有滑梯）充气完毕；如果滑梯出现故障，乘务员应阻止旅客使用。

其中，supervising exists 为现在分词做后置定语修饰主语cabin crew，等同于who supervise exits。

⓬They are also expected to motivate passengers using appropriate shouted commands and, if necessary, physical action, to exit quickly and to leave behind personal possessions, especially items in overhead lockers or under seats.

句子大意：乘务员还被要求使用适当的呼喊口令，并且在需要的情况下使用肢体动作促使旅客快速撤离，在撤离的过程中不携带个人物品，尤其是头顶行李箱或座位下的物品。

其中，using appropriate shouted commands and, if necessary, physical action 为现在分词结构做方式状语；if necessary 意为"如果需要的话"，为插入语。

⑬ Normally, the cabin crew will be the last to leave their exit; however, in practice they are trained to remain on board only to the point when they believe that by staying any longer they are putting their own lives at risk.

句子大意：正常情况下，乘务员会最后离开客舱。但事实上，乘务员的训练要求他们在确信继续留在客舱会威胁自身生命安全时离开客舱。

其中，when they believe that by staying any longer they are putting their own lives at risk 为定语从句，修饰 point；that by staying any longer they are putting their own lives at risk 为宾语从句。

⑭ Once they are out of the aircraft, they are trained to assist in moving passengers away from the aircraft to a position where they can be safely grouped together.

句子大意：一旦离开飞机，乘务员需按照训练要求帮助旅客远离飞机到能将旅客安全集合的位置。

其中，once they are out of the aircraft 为时间状语从句；where they can be safely grouped together 为定语从句，修饰 a position。

New Words and Expressions

ensue	[ɪnˈsjuː]	v.	接着发生
safety briefing	[ˈseɪftɪ][ˈbriːfɪŋ]		安全说明
pre-departure	[priːˈdɪpɑːtʃə]	adj.	行前的；出发前的
overwing	[ˌəʊvəˈwɪŋ]	adj.	机翼上的
individually	[ˌɪndɪˈvɪdjʊəlɪ]	adv.	个别地；单独地
brief	[briːf]	v.	向……说明
aware	[əˈweə]	adj.	意识到的
via	[ˈvaɪə]	prep.	通过；经由
in-flight	[ˈɪnˈflaɪt]	adj.	在飞行中的
relay	[ˈriːleɪ]	v.	转达
proceed to	[prəˈsiːd][tuː]		继续
proper	[ˈprɒpə]	adj.	适当的
senior	[ˈsiːnɪə]	adj.	资深的；高级的
incompatible	[ɪnkəmˈpætɪbəl]	adj.	不相容的
responsible	[rɪˈspɒnsɪbəl]	adj.	负责的
immediate	[ɪˈmiːdɪət]	adj.	直接的；立即的
external	[ɪkˈstɜːnəl]	adj.	外部的；外面的
supervise	[ˈsuːpəvaɪz]	v.	监督；管理

malfunction	[mæl'fʌŋkʃən]	n. 故障
motivate	['məʊtɪveɪt]	v. 激发
physical	['fɪzɪkəl]	adj. 身体的
possession	[pə'zeʃən]	n. 财产；所有物
item	['aɪtəm]	n. 物品
in practice	[ɪn]['præktɪs]	实际上；事实上
at risk	[æt][rɪsk]	处于危险中

Part E
Supplementary Reading

Try to discuss:

1. Suppose the destination of the flight is England, what places of interest would you like to introduce to the passengers on board?
2. How much do you know about the Westminster Abbey?

Westminster Abbey

Westminster is the home of the British Parliament for more than a thousand years. It is one of the most beautiful parts of London.

An early English king, Sebert, built the first abbey and palace at Westminster near the Thames, in the 7th century. Four hundred years later, King Edward decided to make the abbey the biggest and most important in the country. Since the 11th century, all the kings of England have been crowned in Westminster Abbey.

At the north end of the Houses of Parliament is another big tower—the famous clock tower known as Big Ben. Big Ben is really the name of the bell inside. It is named after Sir Benjamin Hall, who was in charge of the new parliament building in 1859.

Big Ben has been chiming out for more than a century. It started chiming on June 11, 1859. The clock that regulates the chiming of Big Ben keeps good time. In 1939, the Royal Astronomer made a 290-day check on the performance of the clock. He found that during this test the margin of error was less than two-tenths of a second in 24 hours on 93 days and greater than one second only on 16 of the 290 days.

(资料来源：http://en.wikipedia.org/wiki/ Westminster_Abbey)

威斯敏斯特大教堂

威斯敏斯特区是一千年来英国的议会所在地，也是伦敦最美的地区。

一位早期的英国国王塞伯特于7世纪在泰晤士河附近的威斯敏斯特建造了第一座教堂和宫殿。四百年后，英国国王爱德华决定把它建成全国最大、最重要的教堂。自11世纪以来，所有的英国国王都是在威斯敏斯特教堂进行加冕的。

在议会大厦的北端，有一座高塔，这就是有名的"大本钟"。"大本"实际上是塔内那口大钟的名字。而这口钟又是根据本杰明·霍尔爵士的名字命名的。1859年，他负责建造这座新的大厦。

大本钟从1859年6月11日开始鸣响，到现在已有一个多世纪了。钟塔里的钟很准时。1939年，皇家天文学家对钟进行290天的检测。其结果显示在检测期间的93天里，它每24h的误差小于2/10s。总共290天里，只有16天它的误差每24h大于1s。

Cabin Service English

Unit 17

Before Landing

* Part A Useful Words and Expressions
* Part B Dialogues
* Part C Public Announcements
* Part D Work-task
* Part E Supplementary Reading

Students will be able to:

memorize the words and expressions about before landing;

make up the dialogues about before landing;

obtain and improve public announcements skills about Customs Form and preparations before landing;

know about how to fill out Customs Form;

introduce Beijing Local Snack.

Suggested Hours: *4 class hours*

Part A
Useful Words and Expressions

◉ Please list as many situations and the related ways of communication in the cabin before landing as you can.

_____

_____

- tray table
- seatback/seat-belt /life jacket /oxygen mask
- seatback
- electronic devices
- laptop computer
- CD player
- iPad
- scheduled arrival time
- delay
- checked baggage/hand baggage /carry-on baggage
- overhead compartment/ locker
- Baggage Claim Area
- public transportation
- subway / metro
- taxi
- limousine
- switch off electronic devices
- catch flight
- make connection
- go through entry formalities in the arrival hall
- The Customs Form is for your declaration of luggage.
- fill out / fill in / complete Customs Form
- go through Customs, Immigration and Quarantine (CIQ)
- Would you please stow your tray table?
- Would you please put your seatback to the upright position?
- Would you please switch your laptop computer off?
- It will take you one hour to get downtown.
- You can get your checked baggage at the Baggage Claim Area.
- You need to go to the Domestic Departure Hall to make your connection.
- The information desk in the terminal hall will be able to assist you.

Unit 17　Before Landing

Culture Tips

> Before entering or leaving a foreign county, passengers have to fill out different kinds of forms, e.g. Arrival Card, Departure Card and Customs Form. To complete these forms, passengers are required to fill in their personal information, e.g. name, date of birth, sex, nationality, and country of residence.

— Name: usually Family/last name, middle name and given/first name are required. Most Chinese people only have family name (姓) and given name (名).

— Date of Birth: China uses "YYYY-MM-DD" date format, while some other countries use "MM-DD-YY(YY)" or "DD-MM-YY(YY)" date format (YYYY means four-digit year, YY means two-digit year, MM means two-digit month, and DD means two-digit day).

— Sex: male or female.

— Nationality: the country or region that issues your passport, e.g. Chinese.

— Country of residence: the country where you currently live.

> Other personal information used in Arrival Card, Departure Card and Customs Form may include passport number, place of issue, date of issue, expiry date, occupation, residential address, place of birth, etc.

Cabin Term

Fill in/Fill out/Complete Customs Form　填写海关申请表

报关(Customs Declaration)是指进出口货物装船出运前，向海关申报的手续。按照我国海关法规定：凡是进出国境的货物，必须经由设有海关的港口、车站、国际航空站，并由货物所有人向海关申报，经过海关放行后，货物才可提取或者装船出口。旅客行李申报单，是外国短期旅客、华侨、外籍华人，因公、因私短期进出境的中国籍居民携带的货币、金银及其制品、旅行自用物品、耐用消费品等物品向海关申报时所用的申报单。

◉ **Victor White is an American Studying in China. Match the items in Column A to his personal information in Column B.**

Column A	Column B
1. Date of birth	a. Victor
2. Sex	b. White
3. Family name	c. Male
4. Country of residence	d. 04-05-1987
5. Given name	e. U.S.
6. Nationality	f. Chinese

◉ **The following picture is a sample of US I-94 Arrival/Departure Card. Try to fill in the card with your personal information.**

1. Family Name	
2. First (Given) Name	3. Birth Date (DD/MM/YY)
4. Country of Citizenship	5. Sex (Male of Female)
6. Passport Issue Date (DD/MM/YY)	7. Passport Expiration Date (DD/MM/YY)
8. Passport Number	9. Airline and Flight Number
10. Country Where You Live	11. Country Where You Boarded
12. City Where Visa Was Issued	13. Date Issued (DD/MM/YY)
14. Address While in the United States (Number and Street)	
15. City and State	
16. Telephone Number in the U.S. Where You Can be Reached	
17. E-mail Address	

CBP Form I-94(05/08)

Part B
Dialogues

(CA=Cabin Attendant, PAX=Passenger)

1

CA: Excuse me, Sir. Would you please return your seatback to the upright position and stow your tray table? We'll be landing soon.

PAX: All right.

(a moment later)

PAX: Miss, I've tried, but I can't stow my tray table. It's my first time to travel by plane.

CA: Let me assist you. You just put the tray table upright and turn this knob tightly. Now it is stowed properly.

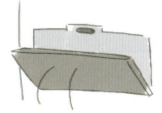

2

CA: Excuse me. Would you please switch your laptop computer off? We will be landing in a few minutes.

PAX: I'm dealing with an urgent assignment. I promise I'll switch it off in five minutes.

Unit 17　Before Landing

CA: I can understand that, Madam. But when the plane is going to land, all the electric devices should be switched off to comply with the regulations.
PAX: Alright, Miss. I'll switch it off right away.

PAX: Miss, could you tell me when we'll be landing at Shanghai Hongqiao International Airport?
CA: The scheduled arrival time is 6:25 p.m., but due to the delay caused by mechanical problem, our plane won't arrive at Hongqiao Airport until 7:30 p.m..
PAX: Seven thirty? I've been wondering if I can catch Flight CA 1528 to Tianjin today. The flight will depart at 9:45 p.m. from Hongqiao Airport.
CA: After we arrive, it will take you about two hours to go through the entry formalities in International Arrival Hall. Then you need to go to the Domestic Departure Hall to make your connection. That means time is pressing.
PAX: So do you think I have to change my flight?
CA: Yes, Madam. I think so.

PAX: Excuse me, Miss. Could you tell me where I can get my checked baggage after arrival?
CA: Yes, you can get your checked baggage in the Baggage Claim Area.
PAX: But where is the Baggage Claim Area?
CA: The Baggage Claim Area is in the Arrival Hall. After you go through the Immigration, you will see the Baggage Claim Area.

PAX: After I arrive at the Baggage Claim Area, how can I get my checked baggage?
CA: You can pick up your checked baggage from the carousel. The notice in the Baggage Claim Area will tell you the number of the carousel which the baggage from our flight will be put on.
PAX: Thank you.

PAX: Miss, would you mind telling me how I can get downtown from the airport?
CA: Not at all. You can take a taxi or the subway. And you can take the limousine as well.
PAX: Could you give me any suggestions?
CA: Taxi is the fastest and most convenient one, but the most expensive. It will take you longer to get to the downtown by subway, but it's much

|231

cheaper. I recommend you to take the limousine. It's cheaper and fast.
PAX: Then how long will it take to get to downtown?
CA: Roughly an hour.
PAX: And where can I get the information on the limousine?
CA: The information desk in the terminal building will be able to assist you.
PAX: Thank you so much for your advice.

6

CA: Excuse me, Sir. This is your Customs Form. Would you please fill it out before we arrive?
PAX: Oh, what is it for?
CA: The Customs Form is for your declaration of luggage. You should list all the dutiable items in this form.
PAX: I see. I'll give it back to you as soon as I complete it.
CA: Please keep your declaration form and other forms with you. You'll need them when you go through the Customs, Immigration and Quarantine.

New Words and Expressions

knob	[nɒb]	n.	旋钮
depart	[dɪˈpɑːt]	v.	离开；出发
go through	[gəʊ][θruː]		通过
entry formality	[ˈentrɪ][fɔːˈmælɪtɪ]		入境手续
international	[ɪntəˈnæʃənəl]	adj.	国际的
domestic	[dəˈmestɪk]	adj.	国内的
Baggage Claim Area	[ˈbægɪdʒ][kleɪm]		行李认领处
immigration	[ɪmˈgreɪʃən]	n.	移民局
carousel	[ˌkærəˈsel]	n.	行李传送带；传播
subway	[ˈsʌbweɪ]	n.	地铁
limousine	[ˈlɪməzɪn]	n.	机场巴士
dutiable	[ˈdjuːtɪəbəl]	adj.	应纳税的；应征税的
quarantine	[ˈkwɒrəntiːn]	n.	检疫

Role play the cabin attendant's responses.

PAX: Miss, could you tell me where I can get my checked baggage?
CA: _____.
PAX: But where can I find the Baggage Claim Area?
CA: _____.
PAX: After arriving at the Baggage Claim Area, how can I get my checked baggage?

CA: _____.
PAX: Miss, would you tell me how to get downtown?
CA: _____.
PAX: Which one is faster, taxi or subway?
CA: _____.
PAX: How long will it take to downtown?
CA: _____.

Discuss the following questions.

1. It is a few minutes before landing. A passenger doesn't put his seatback upright, and doesn't stow his tray table, either. What would you say to him?
2. A passenger says: "Where can I get my checked baggage?" How would you help him?
3. A passenger says: "It's my first time at this airport. Can you suggest how I can get downtown?" What would you say to him?
4. When a passenger wonders why he needs to fill out a Customs Form, how would you explain to him?
5. A passenger has just filled out several forms. He asks: "When do I need these forms? Do I need to return them to you?" What would you say?

Make up dialogues based on the following situations.

1. Nancy is a cabin attendant. She is asking one of the passengers to switch his iPad off before landing.
2. A cabin attendant is telling a passenger how to pick up his checked baggage after landing.
3. A cabin attendant is explaining to a passenger how to get to downtown from the airport after landing.

Translate the following sentences into English.

1. 预计抵达时间是下午6:25。
2. 由于机械故障造成的延误,我们的飞机将在7点左右到达虹桥机场。
3. 您可以乘坐机场大巴、出租车或地铁。
4. 为了遵循规定,所有的电子设备应该关掉。
5. 我一直在想我今天能不能赶上中转航班。
6. 在国际到达大厅您要花大约两个小时办理入境手续。
7. 然后,您需要去国内出发大厅乘坐中转航班。
8. 在通过海关检查时您需要海关申报单和其他表格。
9. 请您把桌板收起来好吗?
10. 请您把座椅背调直好吗?

Part C
Public Announcements

Customs Form

Ladies and gentlemen,

We will be landing at _____ airport shortly. Before you go through Customs and Immigration, it is necessary for you to fill out all the forms required by the _____ Government. In order to speed your passage through Customs and Immigration, we will be giving out the forms to you, and you can complete them before we land. If you have any questions about completing the forms, please ask a cabin attendant for help. They will be very happy to assist you.

Thank you!

Quarantine Regulations at Destinations

Ladies and gentlemen,

We will be landing at _____ airport shortly. According to the regulations of _____ Government, passengers may not bring in such items as fresh fruits, flowers, plants and meat products. Passengers who are in procession of such items, please dispose of them or give them to your cabin attendant before landing.

Thank you.

Spraying of Cabin

Ladies and gentlemen,

The local authorities require the cabin of this aircraft to be disinfected with a non-toxic spray recommended by the World Health Organization. If you think the spray may affect you, please cover your nose and mouth. For passengers wearing contact lenses, your are advised to close your eyes during the spraying.

Thank you for your cooperation.

Unit 17　Before Landing

Colleting the Headsets

Ladies and gentlemen,

　　We will soon be landing at _____ airport. The in-flight entertainment will be switched off for landing. The cabin attendants will be coming through the cabin to collect the headsets from you. Please have yours ready to give them and stow your personal video monitors.

　　Thank you.

Imminent Landing

Ladies and gentlemen,

　　We will be landing at _____ airport in about _____ minutes. Please stow your table, fasten your seat-belt and return your seatback to the upright position.

　　All electronic devices must be switched off for landing.

　　Thank you.

New Words and Expressions

Customs Form	[ˈkʌstəmz][fɔːm]	海关申报表
speed	[spiːd]	v. 加快……的速度
give out	[gɪv][aʊt]	分发
authority	[ɔːˈθɒrəti]	n. 当局, 权威
disinfect	[ˌdɪsɪnˈfekt]	v. 将…消毒
spray	[spreɪ]	v. 喷; 喷洒 n. 喷雾
World Health Organization	[wɜːld] [helθ][ˌɔːgənaɪˈzeɪʃən]	n. 世界卫生组织
toxic	[ˈtɒksɪk]	adj. 有毒的
affect	[əˈfekt]	v. 影响, 感染
contact lenses	[ˈkɒntækt] [ˈlensɪz]	n. 隐形眼镜
collect	[kəˈlekt]	v. 收; 收集
headset	[ˈhedset]	n. 耳机
video monitor	[ˈvɪdiəʊ][ˈmɒnɪtə]	视频显示屏

Speaking Practice

⦿ **Practice making public announcements about Customs Form with these alternatives.**
- Tianjin Binhai International Airport/Chinese
- Heathrow Airport/British

235

- Seoul Incheon International Airport/Korean
- Chicago O'Hare International Airport/American

◉ **Please read following sentences in the right tone(′ for stress, ↗ for rising tone, ↘ for falling tone).**

1. Before you go through Customs and Immigration ↘ ,it is ′ necessary for you to fill out ′ all the forms. ↘
2. In order to ′ speed your passage through Customs and Immigration ↘ ,we will be ′ giving out the forms to you ↗, and you can complete them before we land. ↘
3. If you have any questions about ′ completing the forms↘, please ask a cabin attendant for help.↘
4. We will be ′ landing at Tianjin Binhai Internationak Airport ↗ shortly.↘
5. According to the ′ regulations of Chinese Government ↘,passengers may ′ not bring in such items ↘ such as fresh fruits ↗,flowers ↗, plants ↗ and meat products. ↘

◉ **Translate the following expressions into English and practice making public announcement about *Customs Form*.**
- 填写海关申请表
- 分发海关申请表
- 过海关
- 小桌板
- 赶上航班
- 计划到达时间
- 机场大巴
- 客舱消杀
- 行李提取处
- 公共交通

Part D
Work-task

📋 **Try to discuss:**
1. Do you know why passengers have to fill out Customs Forms when entering a foreign country?
2. Do you know how to fill out a Customs Form?

How to Fill Out a Customs Form

One of the responsibilities the cabin crew take in international flights is to give assistance to passengers when they complete all the forms, e.g. Customs Form and entry card they need to enter the country of destination.❶ The following picture is a sample of U.S. Customs Declaration Form and the way to fill out it will also be introduced.

1. Print your last (family) name. Print your first (given) name. Print the first letter of your middle name.

2. Print your date of birth in the appropriate day/month/year boxes.

3. Print the number of family members traveling with you (do not include yourself).❷

4. Print your current street address in the United States. If you are staying at a hotel, include the hotel's name and street address. Print the city and the state in the appropriate boxes.

5. Print the name of the country that issued your passport.❸

6. Print your passport number.

7. Print the name of the country where you currently live.

8. Print the name of the country or countries that you visited on your trip prior to arriving to the United States.❹

9. If traveling by airplane, print the airline's name and flight number. If traveling by vessel (ship), print the vessel's name.

10. Mark an X in the Yes or No box. Are you traveling on a business (work-related) trip?

11. Mark an X in the Yes or No box. Are you bringing with you:

- fruits, plants, food, or insects?
- meats, animals, or animal/wildlife products?
- disease agents, cell cultures, or snails?
- soil or have you visited a farm/ranch/pasture outside the United States?

12. Mark an X in the Yes or No box. Have you or any family members traveling with you been in close proximity of (such as touching or handling) livestock outside the United States?❺

13. Mark an X in the Yes or No box. Are you or any family members traveling with you bringing $10,000 or more in U.S. dollars or foreign equivalent in any form into the United States?❻

14. Mark an X in the Yes or No box. Are you or any family members traveling with you bringing commercial merchandise into the United States? Examples: all articles intended to be sold or left in the United States, samples used for soliciting orders, or goods that are not considered personal effects.❼

15. If you are a U.S. resident, print the total value of all goods (including commercial merchandise) you or any family members traveling with you have purchased or acquired abroad (including gifts for someone else, but not items mailed to the United States) and are bringing into the United States.❽

If you are a visitor (non-U.S. Resident), print the total value of all goods (including commercial merchandise) you or any family members traveling with you are bringing into the United States and will remain in the United States.❾

(资料来源：http://www.cbp.gov/travel/us-citizens/sample-declaration-form)

Unit 17　Before Landing

📔 Notes

❶ One of the major responsibilities the cabin crew take in international flights is to give assistance to passengers when they complete all the documents, e.g. Customs Form and entry card they need to enter the country of destination.

句子大意：帮助旅客填写进入目的国所需的各类文件,如海关表格和入境卡,是国际航班乘务员肩负的一个重要职责。

其中，the cabin crew take 为定语从句,修饰主语one of the major responsibilities；when they complete all the documents为时间状语从句；they need to enter the country of destination为定语从句,修饰all the documents。

❷ Print the number of family members traveling with you (do not include yourself).

句子大意：请用印刷体填写与您一起旅行的家庭成员数量(不包括您自己)。

其中，traveling with you是现在分词结构,做family members的后置定语。

❸ Print the name of the country that issued your passport.

句子大意：请用印刷体填写您的护照签发国名称。

其中，that issued your passport为定语从句,修饰name of the country。

❹ Print the name of the country or countries that you visited on your trip prior to arriving to the United States.

句子大意：请用印刷体填写在到达美国之前您旅途访问的国家名称。

其中，that you visited on your trip为定语从句,修饰the country or countries；prior to为介词结构,意为"在……之前",后跟名词或动名词。

❺ Have you or any family members traveling with you been in close proximity of (such as touching or handling) livestock outside the United States?

句子大意：您或一起旅行的任意家庭成员是否在美国境外近距离接触(例如触摸或处理)过家畜？

❻ Are you or any family members traveling with you bringing $10,000 or more in U.S. dollars or foreign equivalent in any form into the United States?

句子大意：您或一起旅行的任意家庭成员是否携带超过(含)10000美元或任何形式的等值外币进入美国？

❼ Are you or any family members traveling with you bringing commercial merchandise into the United States? Examples: all articles intended to be sold or left in the United States, samples used for soliciting orders, or goods that are not considered personal effects.

句子大意：您或一起旅行的任意家庭成员是否携带商品进入美国？例如：打算在美国出售或留在美国的所有物品、用于获得订单的样品或非个人使用的物品。

❽ If you are a U.S. resident, print the total value of all goods (including commercial merchandise) you or any family members traveling with you have purchased or acquired abroad (including gifts for someone else, but not items mailed to the United States) and are bringing into the United States.

句子大意：如果您为美国居民,请用印刷体填写您或一起旅行的任意家庭成员在境外购买或获得,并将带入美国境内的所有物品(包括商品)的总价值,这些物品包括送给他人的礼

239

物，但不包括邮寄到美国的物品。

其中，you or any family members traveling with you have purchased or acquired abroad and are bringing into the United States 为定语从句，修饰 all goods。

❾ If you are a visitor (non-U.S. Resident), print the total value of all goods (including commercial merchandise) you or any family members traveling with you are bringing into the United States and will remain in the United States.

句子大意：如果您为访客（非美国居民），请用印刷体填写您或一起旅行的任意家庭成员带入或未来将留在美国境内的所有物品（包括商品）的总价值。

其中，you or any family members traveling with you are bringing into the United States and will remain in the United States 为定语从句，修饰 all goods。

New Words and Expressions

country of destination	[ˈkʌntrɪ][əv][ˌdestɪˈneɪʃən]		目的国
Customs Declaration Form	[ˈkʌstəmz][dekləˈreɪʃən][fɔːm]		海关申报表
print	[prɪnt]	v.	用印刷体填写
issue	[ˈɪʃuː; ˈɪsjuː]	v.	签发
currently	[ˈkʌrəntlɪ]	adv.	当前；目前
vessel	[ˈvesəl]	n.	船；舰
disease agent	[dɪˈziːz][ˈeɪdʒənt]		病原体
cell culture	[sel][ˈkʌltʃə]		细胞培养物
snail	[snel]	n.	蜗牛
ranch	[rɑːntʃ]	n.	农场；牧场
pasture	[ˈpɑːstʃə]	n.	草地；牧场
in proximity of	[ɪn][prɒkˈsɪmɪtɪ][əv]		靠近……；在……附近
livestock	[ˈlaɪvstɒk]	n.	家畜
commercial	[kəˈmɜːʃəl]	adj.	商业的
merchandise	[ˈmɜːtʃəndaɪs; -z]	n.	商品；货物
sample	[ˈsɑːmpəl]	n.	样品；样本
solicit	[səˈlɪsɪt]	v.	征求；招揽
resident	[ˈrezɪdənt]	n.	居民
acquire	[əˈkwaɪə]	v.	获得；取得

Part E
Supplementary Reading

> **Try to discuss:**
> 1. What kinds of Beijing food have you ever tasted?
> 2. What is your favorite Beijing local snack?

Beijing Local Snacks

Beijing snacks have a glorious history. Everyone who has been to Beijing must be crazy about Beijing snacks after tasting them, especially the roast duck in Quanjude.

Beijing snacks can be divided into three types: Han flavor, Hui flavor and Palace flavor. In terms of cooking methods, there are various ways such as steaming, frying, brazing, blasting, roasting, rinsing, simmering, and boiling, about a hundred kinds in total. Some people compare Beijing snacks to a "living fossil" of the history of the thousand-year-old capital.

Roast duck is a special Beijing delicacy. It is famous at home and abroad for its red color, tender meat, mellow taste, and fat but not greasy flavor. The color is slightly yellow, soft and fragrant. It is eaten with other meat and vegetarian foods. It is a common dish for banquets. Aiwowo, with the steamed glutinous rice used for the outer skin, the filling is also fried in advance with peach kernels, melon kernels, sesame kernels and white sugar, so one can eat them immediately after they are done. Bee cake is a kind of snack made by steaming flour or rice noodles with sugar and fruit. This type of cake has more honeycomb-shaped holes after it is broken, so it is called bee cake. Steamed sheep's head is one of the finest Beijing snacks. It is a kind of food made by boiled and sliced sheep's head in white water and sprinkled with salt and pepper. The Ginkgo rice cake has two colors of yellow and white, which symbolizes gold and silver, and has the auspicious meaning of "progress and prosperity". Spring cakes are eaten at the beginning of spring. They are also called lotus leaf cakes. Use two small pieces of water to grease the middle and roll them into thin cakes. They are eaten with rolled vegetables, including cooked and stir-fried vegetables. Soy juice, drinking must be accompanied by extremely finely chopped homemade pickles. Generally, it is eaten with brown and crispy fried coke rings.

The well-known writer Mr. Shu Yi summarized the connotation of Beijing snacks in a concise manner——"Snack Art". There is a song in the lyrics that says "There are enormous types of Beijing snacks which really hit the spot."

(资料来源: https://baike.baidu.com/item/%E5%8C%97%E4%BA%AC%E7%BB%8F%E5%85%B8%E5%B0%8F%E5%90%83/19277303?fr=aladdin)

参考译文

北京特色小吃

北京风味小吃有辉煌的历史,凡到过北京的人,都会对北京小吃颇感兴趣,尤其是全聚德烤鸭。

北京小吃可分为汉民风味、回民风味和宫廷风味三种。在烹制方式上又有蒸、炸、煎、烙、爆、烤、涮、冲、煨、熬等各种做法,共计百余种。有人将北京小吃比作千年都城史的"活化石"。

烤鸭是特色北京美食,它以色泽红艳、肉质细嫩、味道醇厚、肥而不腻的特色,被誉为"天下美味"而驰名中外。色泽略黄,柔软淡香,夹卷其他荤素食物食用,为宴席常用菜点,更是家常风味美食。艾窝窝,外皮用的糯米是已经蒸熟的,馅也用桃仁、瓜仁、芝麻仁和白糖事先炒好,所以做好后就能食用。蜂糕是用面粉或米面加糖、果料等蒸制而成的一种糕食小吃。因为这类糕食掰开后,内中有较多蜂窝状的小孔,故名蜂糕。白水羊头是北京小吃中的精品,它是羊头用白水煮熟切片,撒上椒盐的一种吃食。白果年糕有黄、白两色,象征金银,并有"年年高"的吉祥寓意。春饼在立春时食用,又叫荷叶饼,用两小块水面中间抹油后擀成薄饼烙熟,可揭成两张。春饼是用来卷菜吃的,菜包括熟菜和炒菜。豆汁,喝豆汁必须配切得极细的自制的酱菜,还要配套吃炸得焦黄酥透的焦圈,风味独到。

著名作家舒乙先生以"小吃大艺"四个字,言简意赅地概括了北京小吃的内涵。有段歌词中唱到"北京小吃九十九,样样叫你吃不够"。

Cabin Service English

Unit 18

Disembarkation

- Part A Useful Words and Expressions
- Part C Public Announcements
- Part E Supplementary Reading
- Part B Dialogues
- Part D Work-task

Students will be able to:
memorize the words and expressions about talking with passengers when they disembark;
make up the dialogues with passengers when they disembark;
obtain and improve public announcements skills about disembarkation;
know about debriefing;
introduce French food.
Suggested Hours: *4 class hours*

Part A
Useful Words and Expressions

⊙ **Please list as many expressions about talking with passengers when they disembark as they can.**

_____
_____

- taxi
- standstill
- disembarkation
- Baggage Claim Area
- arrival hall
- ferry bus
- souvenir
- Thank you for your advice, Madam.
- It takes about one hour to reach downtown.
- Thank you, Sir. It's so kind of you to make way for this senior gentleman.
- For the sake of safety, please remain seated with your seat-belt fastened and luggage stowed until the seat-belt sign is switched off.
- We have transportation near the aircraft to the terminal building.
- Please take the ferry bus when you get to the ground and it will carry you to the arrival hall.
- Mind/watch your step, please. / Be careful of the slippery floor.
- Please make sure to take all your hand luggage and personal items.
- Good bye, Sir. Enjoy your stay in Shanghai.
- We are looking forward to meeting you onboard again.
- Thank you for flying with us. Hope to see you again soon.
- We hope to have the pleasure of serving you again.

Culture Tips

➤ In China, traditionally there is no tipping for service (except Hong Kong and Macau). However, hotels that routinely serve foreign tourists allow tipping. An example would be tour guides and associated drivers.

➤ In France, tips are not expected since service charges are included in the bill. However, French people occasionally leave the small change after paying the bill or one or two Euros if they were satisfied with the service in some contexts, such as restaurants, hairdressers, deliveries.

> In United Kingdom, tips of 10% are common in restaurants, but not compulsory. It is a legal requirement to include all taxes and other obligatory charges in the prices displayed.
> In the United States, tipping is a widely practiced social custom. Tips are considered income. In restaurants, a gratuity of 15% to 20% of the amount of a customer's check is customary when good service is provided.
> In some circumstances, such as government workers or more widely with policemen, receiving gratuities (or even offering them) are illegal, as they may be regarded as bribery. For example, US law prohibits federal employees from receiving tips. Asking for, accepting or agreeing to take anything of value that influences the performance of an official act is generally not allowed.

Cabin Term

Complete standstill/Complete stop   完全停稳

在飞行过程中,起飞和下降的过程最危险。如果遇到强气流,飞行员飞行经验不足,就容易造成飞机侧翻,甚至出现严重的意外事故。因此,在起飞和降落的过程中,机舱都会发出信号,要求全体人员系好安全带。在飞行过程中,随时可能遭遇气流,导致机体颠簸,即便机舱内的信号灯指示可以解下安全带,但为了安全起见,建议旅客在飞机起飞到完全停稳(Complete standstill/Complete stop)的全过程中系好安全带。

● Match phrases or sentences in column B to the situations in column A.

Column A	Column B
1. Unfasten seat-belt when it's taxiing	a. We have provided transportation near the aircraft to the terminal building.
2. Inquiry about terminal building	b. You can go there by taking a taxi outside the terminal.
3. Inquiry about checked baggage	c. We would like you to accept this little gift as a souvenir.
4. Inquiry about the way to hotel	d. Thank you for flying with us.
5. About souvenir	e. You can get your checked baggage in the Baggage Claim Area.
6. Passenger disembarking	f. Please don't unfasten your seat belt until the plane stops.

● Make up a dialogue between cabin attendant and passenger when they disembark.

Part B
Dialogues

(CA=Cabin Attendant, PAX=Passenger)

(*When the plane is taxiing on the runway, a passenger unfastens his seat-belt to collect his baggage.*)

CA: Excuse me, Sir. Please don't unfasten your seat-belt until the plane comes to a complete standstill.

PAX: But we have landed at the airport, haven't we?

CA: Yes, for the sake of safety, please remain seated with your seat-belt fastened and luggage stowed until the seat-belt sign is switched off.

PAX: I know. But I'm afraid I don't have enough time to gather my bags before disembarkation.

CA: Don't worry about that. You'll have enough time to collect your belongings. Please remain in your seat with your seat-belt fastened until you gain permission to disembark.

PAX: Miss, where is the terminal building? Is it far away from here?

CA: Yes, Sir. Our plane lands far away from the terminal building.

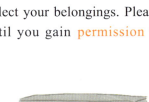

PAX: Oh. It's terrible. Do I have to walk over there?

CA: No, you don't. We have transportation near the aircraft to the terminal building.

PAX: That's wonderful. By the way, could you tell me where the Baggage Claim Area is?

CA: The Baggage Claim Area is in the arrival hall. When you arrive, you will see signs to the Baggage Claim Area and Exit. Follow them and you will find your baggage.

PAX: Thank you.

PAX: Excuse me. Could you tell me the way to my hotel from the airport? I have made a reservation at the Great Wall Hotel.

CA: I'll write down the name of your hotel in Chinese and you can give it to the taxi driver. You can easily take a taxi outside the terminal and go anywhere you like.

PAX: That's a good idea. How much is the taxi fare?

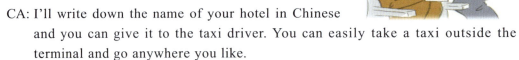

CA: About 100 RMB.
PAX: Is there an additional charge for baggage?
CA: No, you don't have to pay for it.
PAX: What's the standard tip these days?
CA: No, you don't need to do that. No tipping here.
PAX: Thanks a lot. You have been very helpful.
CA: You are welcome. Now the ramp has just been put in position. You can get your belongings ready for disembarkation. Please take the ferry bus when you get to the ground and it will carry you to the arrival hall.
PAX: It's really nice of you.

4

CA: Excuse me, Madam. We are going to land at our destination airport. May I ask you a few questions about our service?
PAX: OK, sure.
CA: Is it the first time for you to take a CA flight?
PAX: Yes, it is.
CA: And how do you think about our cabin attendants' services?
PAX: On the whole, they are all working hard and helpful during the flight. But I think they can still improve. As far as the meal service is concerned, the congee is not hot enough, and the selection of main dishes is limited.
CA: Thank you for your advice, Madam. Hope to meet you again and enjoy our better service.

5

CA: May I assist you with your wheelchair?
PAX: No, thank you. I can manage it.
CA: Please mind the step. Let me take these 2 bags for you.

PAX: OK, then. When I am at home, I try to do everything by myself. I don't want to leave an impression on anyone that I am useless.
CA: Not at all, from what you did and said just now, I can tell you have a strong sense of self-confidence, and self-reliance.
PAX: You are so nice, thank you for your encouragement.

6

CA: Now we'd like you to accept this little gift as a souvenir.
PAX: Well, what a lovely gift!
CA: I'm glad you like it. Are you sure nothing is left behind?
PAX: Yeah. I have everything with me. I'm very impressed by your service. It's been a wonderful journey.
CA: Thank you for flying with us. We hope to have the pleasure of serving you again. Goodbye, Sir.
PAX: I hope so, too. Goodbye.

CA: Hope you have a nice stay in China.

New Words and Expressions

taxi	['tæksɪ]	v. 滑行
standstill	['stæn(d)stɪl]	n. 静止
disembarkation	[dɪsˌembɑːˈkeɪʃən]	n. 下飞机
permission	[pəˈmɪʃən]	n. 允许
charge	[tʃɑːdʒ]	n. 收费
tip	[tɪp]	n. 小费
ramp	[ræmp]	n. 扶梯
ferry bus	[ˈferɪ][bʌs]	摆渡车
arrival hall	[əˈraɪvəl][hɔːl]	到港大厅
wheelchair	[ˈhwiːlˌtʃɛə]	n. 轮椅
self-confidence	[selfˈkɒnfɪdəns]	n. 自信
self-reliance	[ˌselfrɪˈlaɪəns]	n. 自立,自力更生

● Role play the cabin attendant's responses.

PAX: Could you help with my baggage when I get off the plane?
CA: _____.
PAX: Thank you. The plane has come to a stop, why is everyone still waiting in the cabin?
CA: _____.
PAX: Thanks. Can you tell me where I can deal with my transit procedures?
CA: _____.
PAX: OK. Thanks for your help.

PAX: Miss, how far is it to the terminal building?
CA: _____.
PAX: By the way, where can I get my checked baggage?
CA: _____.
PAX: But I don't know where the Baggage Claim Area is.
CA: _____.
PAX: Thank you.

● Discuss the following questions.

1. When the plane has just landed, a passenger unfastens his seat-belt. What would you say to stop him?

2. When the plane is taxiing on the runway, a passenger stands up to collect her baggage. How would you stop her?
3. The plane lands far away from the terminal building. Passengers ask: "Do we have to walk over there?" What would you say to them?
4. A passenger asks: "Where is the Baggage Claim Area?" What would you say?
5. What would you say to passengers when they disembark?

◉ **Make up dialogues based on the following situations.**
1. Before landing, the cabin attendant checks the cabin carefully and prevents any passenger from causing any trouble or danger while landing.
2. Before the plane has completely stopped, a passenger wants to get his luggage, and the cabin attendant tries to calm him down and tells him there is no need to hurry.
3. While landing, it is raining outside, the cabin attendant reminds the passengers to be careful and assists the disabled passenger get off the plane first.

◉ **Translate the following sentences into English.**
1. 请在飞机停稳后再解开安全带。
2. 到达市中心需要花费1h的时间。
3. 请确保带上所有手提行李和个人物品。
4. 为了安全起见，请在安全带提示灯关闭前系好安全带、放好行李。
5. 再见先生，在上海一切愉快，期待下次在航班上见到您！
6. 感谢您的建议，女士。
7. 您将有充足的时间整理您的私人物品。
8. 您可以乘坐交通工具直达航站楼。
9. 请注意脚下台阶。
10. 期待下次旅途再会。

Part C
Public Announcements

Shuttle Bus Not in Position

Ladies and gentlemen,

We regret to inform that you can't disembark at the moment since the bus, which was scheduled to take us to the terminal/the bridge, hasn't been put in position. Please remain seated and we will keep you informed.

Your understanding will be much appreciated.

Landing with Possible Transfer

Ladies and gentlemen,

We have landed at _____ airport. The local time is _____. The ground temperature is _____ degrees Centigrade or _____ degrees Fahrenheit.

Please remain in your seat until the "Fasten Seat-belt" sign is turned off. Use caution when opening the overhead lockers.

If you have an onward flight, you should go to the transit desk in the airport.

Thank you!

Taxiing

Ladies and gentlemen,

Welcome to _____. The local time is _____. Please remain seated with your seat-belt fastened and luggage stowed until the aircraft comes to a complete stop, the engines shut down and the "Fasten Seat-belt" sign is switched off. May we remind you to use caution when opening the overhead lockers.

Thank you for your cooperation.

Landing at a Final Destination

Good morning (afternoon/evening), ladies and gentlemen,

We have landed at _____ international airport. The local time is _____. The ground temperature is _____ degrees Centigrade or _____ degrees Fahrenheit.

Please remain in your seat until the "Fasten Seat-belt" sign is turned off. Use caution when opening the overhead lockers. Please take all your personal belongings with you when you disembark. Your checked baggage may be claimed at the Baggage Claim Area.

Thank you!

Disembarkation

Ladies and gentlemen,

Thank you for waiting. Our plane has come to a complete stop. Please take all your belongings and disembark from the front (back) exit.

We hope to see you again soon and thank you for flying with _____ (Airlines).

Unit 18 Disembarkation

New Words and Expressions

shuttle bus	['ʃʌtl][bʌs]	摆渡车
terminal	['tə:minəl]	n. 航站楼；末端
bridge	[brɪdʒ]	n. 廊桥；桥
caution	['kɔ:ʃən]	n. 小心，谨慎
onward flight	['ɒnwəd][flaɪt]	联程航班
transit desk	['trænsɪt][desk]	中转柜台
claim	[kleɪm]	v. 认领；要求；声称

Speaking Practice

◉ **Practice making public announcement about Landing at a Final Destination with these alternatives.**
- Beijing Capital International Airport/ 8:10 / 23 / 74
- Shanghai Pudong International Airport/ 2:40 / 28 / 82
- Charles De Gaulle International Airport / 11:00 / 24 / 75
- Heathrow Airport / 12:20 / 21 / 70
- John F.Kennedy International Airport / 16:30 / 18 / 64

◉ **Please read following sentences in the right tone(′ for stress, ↗ for rising tone, ↘ for falling tone).**
1. We have ′ landed at Tianjin Binhai International Airport.↘
2. Please ′ remain in your seat ↘ until the "Fastenbeat-belt" ′ sign ↗ is turned off. ↘
3. Use ′ caution when opening the ′ overhead lockers. ↘
4. Please take ′ all your personal ′ belongings with you ↘ when you disembark. ↘
5. Your ′ checked baggage may be claimed ↘ at the Baggage Claim Area. ↘

◉ **Translate the following expressions into English and practice making public announcement about landing at a final destination.**
- 飞机落地
- 地面温度
- 中转柜台
- 摆渡车
- 滑行
- 飞机停稳
- 打开行李舱
- 携带随身行李
- "系紧安全带"信号牌
- 前舱门
- 后舱门
- 托运行李
- 行李提取处

Part D Work-task

Try to discuss:
1. Do you know what is debriefing for?
2. Do you know, as a cabin attendant, what's your role in a debriefing?

Debriefing

The term "debriefing" refers to conversational meetings that centers on the sharing and examining of information after a specific event has taken place. Debriefing is a safe environment to explore feelings and learning from the experience.

There are several purposes of a debriefing, such as to promote improvement through self-evaluation, to evaluate own/team performance in depth, to identify where things went well/not so well, to determine remedial action etc.❶

During the debriefing, the role and responsibility of each crew is to analyze their performance, to evaluate how things turned out and why, to determine what they would continue to do/do differently in future, and how this might be achieved.❷

There are some basic elements of debriefing. Analysis of strengths greatly increases the learning of a particular skill, and psychologically rewards the crew for doing a good job. Analysis of weaknesses must show what he is doing wrong and explain why he made the error. Specific areas for improvement are probably the most important elements of debriefing. Each crew must profit from the debriefing and, therefore, the debriefing give specific guidance for correcting any weakness. Any negative criticism that does not point toward improvement should be ignored.❸

The debriefing must respect each crew and should avoid attacking each one's need for self-esteem. Ridicule, sarcasm, anger, or fears have no place in the critique.❹ A debriefing need not be all smiles and happiness, but must be straight forward and honest and must contain at least the following two features:

- Objectivity—The effective debriefing is focused on each crew and his performance, and should not reflect personal opinions and biases. An objective critique will be based on the performance and not influenced by general impressions of each other.
- Constructiveness—The debriefing should offer a solution to each one's problems, if the problem does exit.❺

(资料来源：http://www.raes-hfg.com/wp-content/uploads/2013/02/CCSG_HF_Bulletin_EffectiveDebriefingSkillsTechniques-20mar12.pdf; http://www.iaftp.org/2012/11/effective-briefing-and-debriefing-techniques/)

Notes

❶There are several purposes of a debriefing, such as to promote improvement through self-evaluation, to evaluate own/team performance in depth, to identify where things went well/not so well, to determine remedial action etc.

句子大意：讲评会目的有如下几个：通过自我评价提升自我，全面评估自己/团队的表现，挖掘表现良好的地方/表现不如意的地方，以及确定相应的补救方案等。

❷During the debriefing, the role and responsibility of each crew is to analyze their performance, to evaluate how things turned out and why, to determine what they would continue to do/do differently in future, and how this might be achieved.

句子大意：在讲评会上，乘务员的职责与责任是评价每位机组成员的表现，总结客舱服务的成效及其原因，确定应发扬的优点/需改进的地方，以及确定如何做到相应的改进。

❸Any negative criticism that does not point toward improvement should be ignored.

句子大意：任何不利于提高服务水平的负面评价都不应出现在讲评会中。

❹Ridicule, sarcasm, anger, or fears have no place in the critique.

句子大意：嘲笑、讽刺、愤怒以及惧怕等负面情绪都不应出现在讲评会的良性评价中。

❺The debriefing should offer a solution to each one's problems, if the problem does exit.

句子大意：如果每人身上确实都存在某些问题，讲评会应为其提供相应的解决办法。

其中，"if the problem does exit"为条件状语从句，助动词"does"修饰动词"exit"，在这里表示强调，意为"确实"，如：

If he does decide to quit, he would become the only victim of the accident.

如果他确实打算退出，那么他将成为这次事故的唯一受害者。

New Words and Expressions

debriefing	[dɪˈbriːfɪŋ]	n.	讲评会
conversational	[ˌkɒnvəˈseɪʃənəl]	adj.	对话的
explore	[ɪkˈsplɔː]	v.	探索；探测
promote	[prəʊˈməʊt]	v.	促进；提升
evaluate	[ɪˈvæljʊeɪt]	v.	评价；评估
performance	[pəˈfɔːməns]	n.	表现；性能
remedial	[rɪˈmiːdɪəl]	adj.	治疗的；补救的
analysis	[əˈnæləsɪs]	n.	分析；分解
strength	[streŋθ]	n.	长处；力量
psychologically	[ˌsaɪkəˈlɒdʒɪkəli]	adv.	心理上地
error	[ˈerə]	n.	错误；误差
guidance	[ˈgaɪdəns]	n.	指导；引导
negative	[ˈnegətɪv]	adj.	负的；消极的
criticism	[ˈkrɪtɪsɪzəm]	n.	批评
ignore	[ɪgˈnɔː]	v.	忽视
attack	[əˈtæk]	v.	攻击；抨击
self-esteem	[ˌselfɪˈstiːm]	n.	自尊
ridicule	[ˈrɪdɪkjuːl]	n.	嘲笑；愚弄

sarcasm	['sɑ:kæzəm]	n. 讽刺；挖苦
critique	[krɪ'ti:k]	n. 批判；批评
objectivity	[ˌɒbdʒek'tɪvəti]	n. 客观；客观性
effective	[ɪ'fektɪv]	adj. 有效的，起作用的
reflect	[rɪ'flekt]	v. 反射，映现
bias	['baɪə]	n. 偏见；偏爱
impression	[ɪm'preʃən]	n. 印象；效果
constructiveness	[kən'strʌktɪvnɪs]	n. 建设性
solution	[sə'lju:ʃən]	n. 解决方案

Part E
Supplementary Reading

Try to discuss:
1. What kinds of French food have you ever tasted?
2. Why is French afternoon tea so popular among office clarks?

French Gourmet

The three famous cuisines in the world are Chinese cuisine, French cuisine and Turkish cuisine, which have a very large influence in the gastronomy industry. French cuisine includes those from many countries such as Europe, America, Oceania, etc., with western food as the main course.

France's food culture is extensive and profound. The traditional French cuisine still ranks first in the world due to its delicate taste, delicious sauces, rich variety, and gorgeous tableware. French cuisine prefers beef, veal, lamb, poultry, seafood, vegetables, snails, truffles for materials. Foie gras and caviar, and a large amount of wine, butter, fresh cream and various spices are used as the ingredients. In terms of cooking style, French cuisine can be divided into three mainstreams: Classic cuisine/ Haute cuisine, Bourgeoise cuisine, and Nouvelle cuisine.

Tasting a French meal, in addition to enjoying the happiness that the food brings to the soul, you can also experience the elegant dining culture of France. Different from the dining habits of other countries, the selection and serving of French meals will follow a certain order: appetizer, soup, fish, jelly, middle dish, barbecue, salad, and dessert.

French cuisine is represented by famous dishes such as foie gras and truffles. During the time of Louis XVI, the foie gras was tributed to the French court. The king loved it very much after tasting it, and it has since become a delicacy in the court. At that time, many well-known musicians, writers and celebrities all rushed to taste it, and since then established its status as a top gourmet. Together with the foie gras, the truffle is called a world-class gourmet. It is a mushroom that grows underground. The truffles with the reputation of "Black Diamond" in France are fragrant and delicious, rich in nutrition and crispy taste. The best season for tasting black truffles is from December to March every year. It tastes great with Bordeaux red wine.

(资料来源：https://baike. baidcl. com / item/% E6% B3% 95% E5% 9B% BD% E8% 8F% 9C/2386280？fr=aladdin)

参考译文

法 国 美 食

世界上著名的三大菜系分别是中国菜系、法国菜系和土耳其菜系，在美食界有非常大的影响力。法国菜系包括欧洲、美洲、大洋洲等许多国家的菜系，以西餐为主题。

法国的美食文化博大精深，传统的法式大餐凭借着口感细腻、酱料美味、品种丰富、餐具华美的特点至今仍位列世界西餐之首。法国菜在材料的选用上较偏好牛肉、小牛肉、羊肉、家禽、海鲜、蔬菜、蜗牛、松露、鹅肝及鱼子酱；而在配料方面采用大量的酒、牛油、鲜奶油及各式香料。按烹调风格而言，法国菜肴可分为三大主流派系：古典法国菜派系、家常法国菜派系、新派法国菜派系。

品尝法国大餐，除了享受美食带给心灵的幸福感，也可体验到法国这个国家优雅的用餐文化。与其他国家餐饮习惯不同，法国大餐选菜、上菜都会遵循一定的顺序，即开胃菜、汤、鱼、冻、间菜、烧烤、沙律、甜品的顺序。

法国大餐以鹅肝酱、松露等著名菜式为代表。路易十六时期，鹅肝被进贡到法国宫廷，国王在品尝之后非常喜爱，从此成为宫廷的佳肴。当时许多知名的音乐家、作家和社会名流都争相赞颂，自此奠定其顶级美食的地位。和鹅肝并称为世界级美食的松露，是一种长在地下的菌菇。在法国有"黑钻石"美名的松露，清香可口，营养丰富，口感脆嫩。品尝黑松露最好的季节是在每年的十二月到次年三月间，搭配波尔多红酒味道极佳。

Words and Expressions List

30-second review ['sekənd][rɪ'vjuː] 30s静默	Unit 4-Part D
a selection of [ə][sɪ'lekʃən][əv] 一系列的	Unit 7-Part C
a serving of [ə]['səːvɪŋ][əv] 一份	Unit 7-Part B
aboard [ə'bɔːd] v. 登机	Unit 1-Part B
Able-Bodied Passengers (ABPs) [ˌeɪbl'bɒdɪd] ['pæsɪndʒəs] 体格健壮的旅客	Unit 4-Part D
abnormal [æb'nɔːməl] adj. 反常的,不规则的	Unit 2-Part D
abundance [ə'bʌndəns] n. 充裕,丰富	Unit 9-Part D
access ['æk'ses] v. 使用	Unit 5-Part C
access ['ækses] n. 通道	Unit 15-Part D
accidentally [æksɪ'dentəli] adv. 意外地;偶然地	Unit 15-Part B
accommodation [əˌkɒmə'deɪʃən] n. 住处,住宿	Unit 11-Part B
accordance [ə'kɔːdəns] n. 一致	Unit 4-Part C
acquire [ə'kwaɪə] v. 获得;取得	Unit 17-Part D
adaptive [ə'dæptɪv] adj. 适应的	Unit 13-Part D
adjust [ə'dʒʌst] v. 调整,校准	Unit 2-Part C
adjust [ə'dʒʌst] v. 调整;调节	Unit 15-Part C
adjustable [ə'dʒʌstəbl] adj. 可调节的	Unit 5-Part B
adopt [ə'dɒpt] v. 采取;接受	Unit 2-Part D
adverse ['ædvəːs] adj. 相反的;不利的	Unit 13-Part C
affair [ə'fer] n. 事件,事情	Unit 13-Part C
affect [ə'fekt] v. 影响,感染	Unit 17-Part C
afford [ə'fɔːrd] v. 花费得起;承担得起(后果)	Unit 11-Part D
air conditioning system [eə(r)][kən'dɪʃənɪŋ] ['sɪstəm] 空调系统	Unit 5-Part C
air traffic control (ATC) [eə(r)]['træfɪk][kən'trəʊl] 空中交通管制	Unit 4-Part C
air vent [eə(r)][vent] 通风系统	Unit 5-Part C
air-conditioning [(r)əkən'dɪʃənɪŋ] n. 空调	Unit 4-Part C
aircraft ['eəkrɑːft] n. 飞机,航空器	Unit 5-Part B
aircrew ['eəkruː] n. 全体机组人员	Unit 1-Part D
airflow system ['eəfləʊ]['sɪstəm] 通风系统	Unit 5-Part B
airline ['eəlaɪn] n. 航空公司;航线	Unit 1-Part D
airsickness ['eəsɪknɪs] n. 晕机	Unit 12-Part B
airsickness bag ['eəsɪknɪs][bæg] 呕吐袋	Unit 14-Part B
aisle [aɪl] n. 通道	Unit 1-Part C
alcoholic ['ælkəhɒlɪk] n. 含酒精的	Unit 6-Part D
allergic [ə'ledʒɪk] adj. 过敏	Unit 7-Part B
allergic to [ə'ledʒɪk][tuː] 对……过敏	Unit 7-Part B
allowance [ə'laʊəns] n. 津贴,零用钱;允许;限额	Unit 10-Part D
alteration [ˌɔːltə'reɪʃən] n. 改变;变更	Unit 13-Part D

alternate ['ɔːltərnət] *adj.* 交替的；轮流的	Unit 11-Part B
alternative [ɔːl'tɜːnətɪv] *n./adj.* 取舍；选择余地/两者择一的	Unit 8-Part B
altitude ['æltɪˌtjuːd] *n.* 海拔；高度	Unit 15-Part C
ambassador [æm'bæsədə(r)] *n.* 代表，大使	Unit 2-Part C
amenity [ə'miːnəti] *n.* 便利设施	Unit 5-Part B
analysis [ə'næləsɪs] *n.* 分析；分解	Unit 18-Part D
anchor ['æŋkə] *n.* 锚	Unit 15-Part D
angle ['æŋɡl] *n.* 角	Unit 9-Part B
ankle ['æŋkl] *n.* 脚踝	Unit 14-Part B
announcement [ə'naʊnsmənt] *n.* 通知；通告	Unit 13-Part C
appetite ['æpɪtaɪt] *n.* 胃口	Unit 7-Part B
appreciate [ə'priːʃieɪt] *v.* 欣赏；感激	Unit 5-Part C
approach [ə'prəʊtʃ] *n.* 方法；途径	Unit 5-Part D
appropriate [ə'prəʊprieɪt] *adj.* 适当的	Unit 2-Part D
armrest ['ɑːmrest] *n.* 扶手	Unit 3-Part D
arrival hall [ə'raɪvəl][hɔːl] 到港大厅	Unit 18-Part B
asbestos [æz'bestɒs] *n.* 石棉	Unit 15-Part D
aspirin ['æspərɪn] *n.* 阿司匹林	Unit 14-Part B
assertive [ə'sɜːtɪv] *adj.* 肯定的；坚定而自信的	Unit 4-Part D
assess [ə'ses] *v.* 评定；估价	Unit 4-Part D
assessment [ə'sesmənt] *n.* 评定；估价	Unit 14-Part B
assigned [ə'saɪnd] *adj.* 指定的	Unit 2-Part B
assigned seats [ə'saɪnd][siːt] 指定座位	Unit 1-Part C
assist [ə'sɪst] *v.* 帮助	Unit 3-Part D
assistance [ə'sɪstəns] *n.* 援助，帮助	Unit 5-Part C
at risk [æt][rɪsk] 处于危险中	Unit 16-Part D
ATC (Air Traffic Control) 空中交通管制	Unit 1-Part B
athlete ['æθliːt] *n.* 运动员	Unit 2-Part C
attachment [ə'tætʃmənt] *n.* 附件；配件	Unit 16-Part C
attack [ə'tæk] *v.* 攻击；抨击	Unit 18-Part D
attend to [ə'tend][tuː] 处理	Unit 15-Part B
attention [ə'tenʃən] *n.* 注意	Unit 8-Part C
audio-on-demand ['ɔːdɪəʊɒndɪ'mɑːnd] *n.* 声音点播	Unit 9-Part D
authority [ɔː'θɒrəti] *n.* 当局，权威	Unit 17-Part C
automatically [ˌɔːtə'mætɪkli] *adv.* 自动地；机械地	Unit 15-Part C
available [ə'veɪləbl] *adj.* 可获得的；有空的	Unit 2-Part C
availability [əˌveɪlə'bɪləti] *n.* 可用性；有效性；实用性	Unit 9-Part D
aviator ['eɪvieɪtə] *n.* 飞行员	Unit 5-Part B
award [ə'wɔːd] *v.* 授予；判定	Unit 4-Part C
aware [ə'weə] *adj.* 意识到的	Unit 16-Part D
axe [æks] *n.* 斧子	Unit 15-Part D
Baggage Claim Area ['bæɡɪdʒ][kleɪm] 行李提取处	Unit 17-Part B
balance ['bæləns] *n.* 平衡	Unit 2-Part B
band [bænd] *n.* 带子	Unit 15-Part B
belongings [bɪ'lɒŋɪŋz] *n.* 行李；财产	Unit 2-Part B
benefit ['benɪfɪt] *v.* 有益于，对……有益	Unit 5-Part B

beverage ['bevərɪdʒ] n. 饮料	Unit 4-Part C
bias ['baɪə] n. 偏见；偏爱	Unit 18-Part D
black coffee [blæk]['kɒfɪ] 黑咖啡	Unit 6-Part B
Black Label [blæk]['leɪbəl] 酒水名称，黑方威士忌	Unit 6-Part B
blanket ['blæŋkɪt] n. 毯子	Unit 16-Part C
blindfold ['blaɪndfəʊld] n. 眼罩；障眼物	Unit 13-Part D
blizzard ['blɪzəd] n. 暴风雪，大风雪	Unit 11-Part D
block [blɒk] v. 阻碍	Unit 3-Part B
board [bɔːd] v. 上（飞机、车、船等）	Unit 16-Part C
book the flight [bʊk][flaɪt] 预订机票	Unit 7-Part C
book ticket [bʊk]['tɪkɪt] 预订机票	Unit 8-Part C
booked [buːkt] adj. 预订的；登记了的	Unit 2-Part C
boost [buːst] v. 促进；增加	Unit 9-Part D
bounce [baʊns] v. 弹起	Unit 16-Part B
brace for impact [breɪs][fɔː]['ɪmpækt] 防冲撞姿态	Unit 4-Part D
brace position [breɪs][pə'zɪʃən] 防冲撞姿势	Unit 16-Part B
bracelet ['breɪslɪt] n. 腕带；手镯	Unit 14-Part D
breakdown ['breɪkdaʊn] n. 崩溃；故障	Unit 9-Part C
breathe [briːð] v. 呼吸	Unit 15-Part B
breathtaking ['breθ,teɪkɪŋ] adj. 令人激动的	Unit 2-Part B
break out [breɪk][aʊt] 爆发	Unit 15-Part B
bridge [brɪdʒ] n. 廊桥；桥	Unit 18-Part C
brief [briːf] v. 向……说明	Unit 16-Part D
briefing ['briːfɪŋ] n. 航前准备会	Unit 2-Part D
broadcast ['brɔːdkɑːst] vt. 广播	Unit 9-Part C
brochure [brəʊ'ʃʊə] n. 手册，小册子	Unit 10-Part C
browse [braʊz] v. 随便看看；浏览	Unit 10-Part B
buckle ['bʌkəl] n. 安全带扣	Unit 3-Part C
Buddhist ['bʊdɪst] n. 佛教徒	Unit 8-Part D
built-in [,bɪlt'ɪn] adj. 嵌入的	Unit 9-Part D
bump [bʌmp] n. 肿块，隆起物	Unit 14-Part B
business class ['bɪznəs][klɑːs] 商务舱	Unit 2-Part C
business jet aircraft [dʒet]['eəkrɑːft] 商用喷气飞机	Unit 1-Part D
calorie ['kæləri] n. 卡路里（热量单位）	Unit 8-Part D
cabin crew ['kæbɪn][bruː] 乘务组；航班空服人员	Unit 1-Part D
call button [kɔːl]['bʌtən] 呼唤铃	Unit 5-Part B
cancel ['kænsəl] v. 取消	Unit 11-Part C
canopy ['kænəpɪ] n. 天棚	Unit 15-Part D
capable ['keɪpəbəl] Adj. 有能力的	Unit 15-Part D
captain ['kæptɪn] v. 机长	Unit 1-Part C
carbon dioxide ['kɑːbən][daɪ'ɒksaɪd] 二氧化碳	Unit 15-Part D
carbonated ['kɑːbəneɪtɪd] adj. 碳化的，含碳酸的	Unit 6-Part B
care for [keə][fɔː] 照顾；喜欢	Unit 9-Part B
carpet ['kɑːpɪt] n. 地毯	Unit 5-Part C
carry-ons ['kærɪɒnz] n. 手提行李，随身行李	Unit 3-Part D

Words and Expressions List

cash [kæʃ] *n.* 现款，现金	Unit 3-Part C
cater for ['keɪtə][fɔː] 满足……的需要，迎合	Unit 8-Part D
catering company ['keɪtərɪŋ]['kʌmp(ə)nɪ] 餐饮公司	Unit 6-Part D
catering services ['keɪtərɪŋ]['sɜːvɪsɪs] 餐饮服务	Unit 7-Part D
carrier ['kærɪə(r)] *n.* 承运人；载体	Unit 10-Part D
carousel [ˌkærə'sel] *n.* 行李传送带；传播	Unit 17-Part B
caution ['kɔːʃən] *n.* 小心，谨慎	Unit 18-Part C
cell culture [sel]['kʌltʃə] 细胞培养物	Unit 17-Part D
cellular phone ['seljʊlə][fəʊn] 手机	Unit 3-Part C
centigrade ['sentɪgreɪd] *n.* 摄氏度	Unit 13-Part B
champagne [ʃæm'peɪn] *n.* 香槟酒	Unit 6-Part D
charge [tʃɑːdʒ] *n.* 收费	Unit 18-Part B
charter flight ['tʃɑːtə(r)][flaɪt] 包机	Unit 1-Part C
channel ['tʃænl] *n.* 频道；途径；海峡	Unit 9-Part B
change [tʃeɪndʒ] *n.* 零钱，变化；换洗衣物	Unit 10-Part B
check [tʃek] *v.* 检查	Unit 2-Part B
chemical ['kemɪkəl] *n.* 化学制品	Unit 15-Part D
cherish ['tʃerɪʃ] *v.* 珍爱，珍惜	Unit 1-Part C
chewing gum ['tʃuːɪŋ][gʌm] 口香糖	Unit 4-Part B
chief purser [tʃiːf]['pɜːsə(r)] 主任乘务长	Unit 1-Part C
Chinese cuisine [ʃaɪ'niːz][kwɪ'ziːn] 中国风味	Unit 7-Part C
cholesterol [kə'lestərɒl] *n.* 胆固醇	Unit 8-Part D
choice [tʃɔɪs] *n.* 选择；精选品	Unit 4-Part C
cigarette [ˌsɪgə'ret] *n.* 香烟	Unit 4-Part B
circadian [sɜː'keɪdɪən] *adj.* 与生理节奏有关的	Unit 13-Part D
circulation [ˌsɜːkjʊ'leɪʃən] *n.* 血液流通；传播	Unit 13-Part D
circumstance ['sɜːkəmstəns] *n.* 环境，情况	Unit 4-Part D
Civil Aviation Administration of China ['sɪvɪl][eɪvɪ'eɪʃən][ədmɪnɪ'streɪʃən] [əv]['tʃaɪnə] 中国民用航空局	Unit 4-Part C
claim [kleɪm] *v.* 认领；要求；声称	Unit 18-Part C
clasp [klɑːsp] *v.* 紧握；抱紧	Unit 16-Part C
clearance ['klɪərəns] *n.* 许可	Unit 1-Part B
cloisonné [ˌklɒʊzə'ne] *n.* (法)景泰蓝瓷器	Unit 10-Part B
clot [klɒt] *n.* 血块；凝块	Unit 13-Part D
cockpit ['kɒkpɪt] *n.* 驾驶舱	Unit 1-Part D
cold drink [kəʊld][drɪŋk] 冷饮	Unit 6-Part C
colleague ['kɒliːg] *n.* 同事	Unit 1-Part B
collect [kə'lekt] *v.* 收；收集	Unit 17-Part C
collectively [kə'lektɪvlɪ] *adv.* 共同地，全体地	Unit 1-Part D
come to [kʌm][tuː] 想起；共计	Unit 10-Part B
comedy ['kɒmədɪ] *n.* 喜剧；有趣的事情	Unit 9-Part B
comfort ['kʌmfət] *n.* 舒适	Unit 5-Part B
command [kə'mɑːnd] *n.* 指挥，控制；命令	Unit 4-Part D
commercial [kə'mɜːʃəl] *adj.* 商业的	Unit 17-Part D
commercial airline [kə'mɜːʃəl]['eəlaɪn] 商业航空公司	Unit 9-Part D

commercial flight [kəˈməːʃəl][flaɪt] 商业航班	Unit 1-Part D
communication [kəˌmjuːnɪˈkeɪʃən] n. 通信，交流	Unit 2-Part D
communication system [kəˌmjuːnɪˈkeɪʃən] 通信系统	Unit 4-Part B
compensation [ˌkɒmpenˈseɪʃən] n. 补偿；赔偿金	Unit 11-Part D
competence [ˈkɒmpɪtəns] n. 资格；能力	Unit 16-Part B
competent [ˈkɒmpɪtənt] adj. 胜任的；有能力的	Unit 16-Part B
competitive price [kəmˈpetətɪv][praɪs] [物价] 竞争价格	Unit 10-Part B
complete [kəmˈpliːt] v. 完成	Unit 3-Part D
compliance [kəmˈplaɪəns] n. 顺从，服从；承诺	Unit 12-Part D
complicated [ˈkɒmplɪkeɪtɪd] adj. 复杂的	Unit 13-Part B
complimentary [ˌkɑmplɪˈmentri] adj. 免费的	Unit 6-Part B
comply with [kəmˈplaɪ][wɪð] 遵守，遵从	Unit 1-Part C
concise [kənˈsaɪs] adj. 简明的，简洁的	Unit 2-Part D
condiment [ˈkɒndɪmənt] n. 调味品，佐料	Unit 7-Part D
confined [kənˈfaɪnd] adj. 狭窄的；有限制的	Unit 1-Part D
confused [kənˈfjuːzd] adj. 困惑的	Unit 13-Part B
congee [ˈkɒndʒi] n. 粥；告别	Unit 8-Part B
congest [kənˈdʒest] v. 使充满；使拥塞	Unit 11-Part D
connecting flight [kəˈnektɪŋ][flaɪt] 转接航班	Unit 11-Part B
considerably [kənˈsɪdərəbli] adv. 显著地；十分	Unit 6-Part D
considerate [kənˈsɪdərɪt] adj. 体贴的；体谅的；考虑周到的	Unit 8-Part B
consist [kənˈsɪst] v. 由……组成	Unit 14-Part D
constraint [kənˈstreɪnt] n. 约束；限制	Unit 12-Part D
constructiveness [kənˈstrʌktɪvnɪs] n. 建设性	Unit 18-Part D
contact [kənˈtækt] v. 联系，接触	Unit 2-Part C
contact lenses [kənˈtækt] [ˈlensɪz] n. 隐形眼镜	Unit 17-Part C
contain [kənˈteɪn] v. 包含；控制	Unit 4-Part D
controversy [ˈkɒntrəvəːsi] n. 争议；(公开的)争论	Unit 9-Part D
convenience [kənˈviːnɪəns] n. 方便，合宜	Unit 6-Part C
convenient [kənˈviːnjənt] adj. 方便的	Unit 5-Part B
conventional design [kənˈvenʃnl][dɪˈzaɪn] 传统图案	Unit 10-Part B
conversational [ˌkɒnvəˈseɪʃənəl] adj. 对话的	Unit 18-Part D
cooperation [kəʊˌɒpəˈreɪʃən] n. 合作	Unit 1-Part C
cope with [kəʊp][wɪð] 处理；应付	Unit 16-Part B
co-pilot [kəʊˈpaɪlət] n. 副驾驶	Unit 16-Part B
copy [ˈkɒpi] n. 一册；一份	Unit 9-Part B
crash axe [kræʃ][æks] 应急斧子	Unit 15-Part D
crayon [ˈkreɪən] n. 蜡笔；有色粉笔	Unit 9-Part B
crew [kruː] n. 全体人员	Unit 14-Part C
cost-effective [kɒstɪˈfektɪv] adj. 成本效益好的；划算的	Unit 5-Part D
cot [kɒt] n. 简易床	Unit 5-Part B
counter [ˈkaʊntə] v. 反击；反对	Unit 13-Part D
country of destination [ˈkʌntri][əv][ˌdestɪˈneɪʃn] 目的国	Unit 17-Part D
covering [ˈkʌvərɪŋ] n. 遮盖物	Unit 15-Part D
criticism [ˈkrɪtɪsɪzəm] n. 批评	Unit 18-Part D
critique [krɪˈtiːk] n. 批判；批评	Unit 18-Part D

crowbar ['krəubɑ:] *n.* 铁锹	Unit 15-Part D
cruising altitude ['kru:zɪŋ]['æltɪtju:d] 巡航高度	Unit 4-Part B
cuisine [kwɪ'zɪn] *n.* 风味	Unit 7-Part C
cumulative ['kju:mjələtɪv] *adj.* 累积的；渐增的；累计的	Unit 11-Part D
cumulonimbus [ˌkju:mjʊləʊ'nɪmbəs] *n.* [气象] 积雨云	Unit 12-Part D
currency ['kʌrənsɪ] *n.* 货币；通货	Unit 10-Part B
currently ['kʌrəntlɪ] *adv.* 当前；目前	Unit 17-Part D
cushion ['kʊʃən] *n.* 垫子	Unit 16-Part C
customer satisfaction card ['kʌstəmɒ] [ˌsætɪs'fækʃən] [kɑ:d] 旅客意见卡	Unit 4-Part C
Customs ['kʌstəmz] *n.* 海关	Unit 10-Part C
Customs Declaration Form [deklə'reɪʃən] [fɔ:m] 海关申报表	Unit 17-Part D
Customs Form [fɔ:m] 海关申报表	Unit 17-Part D
cutlery ['kʌtlərɪ] *n.* 刀叉餐具	Unit 7-Part D
daily ['deɪlɪ] *n.* 日报	Unit 9-Part B
dangerous goods ['deɪndʒərəs] [gʊdz] 危险品	Unit 3-Part D
deactivate [di:'æktɪveɪt] *v.* 使无效；使不活动	Unit 5-Part D
debriefing [dɪ'bri:fɪŋ] *n.* 讲评会	Unit 18-Part D
defect ['di:fekt] *n.* 缺点；缺陷	Unit 11-Part D
definitive [dɪ'fɪnɪtɪv] *adj.* 决定性的；最后的	Unit 14-Part D
degree [dɪ'gri:] *n.* 度，等级	Unit 13-Part B
dehydration [ˌdi:haɪ'dreɪʃən] *n.* 脱水	Unit 13-Part B
deicing [ˌdi:'aɪsɪŋ] *n.* 除冰	Unit 11-Part C
delay [dɪ'leɪ] *n.* 耽搁	Unit 5-Part D
deliver [dɪ'lɪvə] *v.* 实现；传送；履行	Unit 5-Part D
demonstrator life jacket ['demənstreɪtə][laɪf]['dʒækɪt] 示范用救生衣	Unit 3-Part D
denture ['dentʃə] *n.* 假牙	Unit 16-Part C
depart [dɪ'pɑ:t] *v.* 离开；出发	Unit 17-Part B
departure [dɪ'pɑ:tʃə] *n.* 离开；出发	Unit 3-Part C
delicacy ['delɪkəsɪ] *n.* 美味；精美	Unit 7-Part B
deploy [dɪ'plɔɪ] *v.* 展开	Unit 16-Part C
depressurization [di:ˌpreʃəraɪ'zeɪʃən] *n.* 失压	Unit 15-Part C
derive [dɪ'raɪv] *v.* 源于；得自	Unit 1-Part D
descend [dɪ'send] *v.* 下降	Unit 5-Part B
descent [dɪ'sent] *n.* 下降	Unit 15-Part C
designated ['dezɪgˌneɪtɪd] *adj.* 指定的；特指的	Unit 2-Part D
destination [ˌdestɪ'neɪʃən] *n.* 目的地，终点	Unit 13-Part C
detailed ['di:teɪld] *adj.* 详细的，精细的	Unit 2-Part D
determine [dɪ'tə:mɪn] *v.* 确定；决定	Unit 14-Part D
device [dɪ'vaɪs] *n.* 装置	Unit 3-Part C
diabetes [ˌdaɪə'bɪtɪz] *n.* 糖尿病；多尿症	Unit 8-Part B
diabetic [daɪə'betɪk] *adj.* 糖尿病的，患糖尿病的	Unit 8-Part D
diet ['daɪət] *n.* 饮食	Unit 8-Part C
dietary ['daɪəˌterɪ] *adj.* 饮食的	Unit 8-Part D
digest [daɪ'dʒest] *v.* 消化	Unit 7-Part B
diligently ['dɪlɪdʒəntlɪ] *adv.* 勤勉地	Unit 11-Part C

dim [dɪm] v. 使暗淡；使变暗	Unit 5-Part C
direction [dɪ'rekʃən] n. 方向	Unit 5-Part B
disability [ˌdɪsə'bɪlətɪ] n. 残疾	Unit 14-Part D
discount ['dɪskaʊnt] n. 折扣；贴现率	Unit 10-Part B
disease agent [dɪ'ziːz]['eɪdʒənt] 病原体	Unit 17-Part D
disembarkation [dɪsˌembɑː'keɪʃən] n. 下飞机	Unit 18-Part B
disinfect [ˌdɪsɪn'fekt] v. 将……消毒	Unit 17-Part C
dispose [dɪs'pəʊz] v. 处理	Unit 3-Part B
distinguished [dɪ'stɪŋgwɪʃt] adj. 高贵的，著名的	Unit 2-Part C
distort [dɪ'stɔːt] v. 扭曲；使失真；曲解	Unit 9-Part D
disturb [dɪ'stɜːb] v. 扰乱；妨碍	Unit 9-Part B
ditching [dɪtʃɪŋ] n. 水面迫降	Unit 4-Part D
divert [daɪ'vɜːt] v. 转移；使……欢愉	Unit 11-Part C
dizzy ['dɪzɪ] adj. 使人头晕的	Unit 2-Part B
document ['dɒkjʊmənt] n. 文件；文档	Unit 3-Part D
documented ['dɒkjʊməntɪd] adj. 备有证明文件的	Unit 4-Part D
domestic [də'mestɪk] adj. 国内的	Unit 17-Part B
double-edged ['dʌbl'edʒd] adj. 双刃的	Unit 9-Part D
drain [dreɪn] v. 耗尽；使流出	Unit 13-Part B
drill [drɪl] n. 训练；操练	Unit 4-Part D
drop [drɒp] v. 落下；跌倒；下降	Unit 12-Part B
dutiable ['djuːtɪəbəl] adj. 应纳税的；应征税的	Unit 17-Part B
duty-paid ['djuːtɪ'peɪd] adj. 已完税的；已纳税的	Unit 9-Part D
ear ringing [ɪə]['rɪŋɪŋ] 耳鸣	Unit 14-Part B
earring ['ɪərɪŋ] n. 耳环	Unit 16-Part C
ease [iːz] v. 减轻，缓和	Unit 13-Part D
easily digested ['iːzɪlɪ][daɪ'dʒestɪd] 容易消化的	Unit 7-Part B
e-cigarette [ɪˌsɪgə'ret] n. 电子烟	Unit 13-Part C
economy class [i'kɒnəmɪ][klɑːs] 经济舱	Unit 2-Part B
edge [edʒ] n. 边缘	Unit 2-Part B
effective [ɪ'fektɪv] adj. 有效的，起作用的	Unit 18-Part D
eggplant ['egplænt] n. 茄子	Unit 8-Part B
elastic [ɪ'læstɪk] adj. 有弹性的	Unit 15-Part B
electronic [ˌɪlek'trɒnɪk] adj. 电子的	Unit 3-Part C
element ['elɪmənt] n. 元素；要素	Unit 4-Part D
emblem ['embləm] n. 象征；徽章	Unit 14-Part D
emergency exit [ɪ'mɜːdʒənsɪ]['eksɪt] 紧急出口	Unit 3-Part B
Emergency Locator Transmitter (ELT) [ɪ'mɜːdʒənsɪ][ləʊ'keɪtə][trænz'mɪtə] 应急定位发射器	Unit 15-Part D
emergency landing ['lændɪŋ] 紧急着陆	Unit 14-Part C
encounter [ɪn'kaʊntə(r)] v. 遭遇；邂逅；遇到	Unit 12-Part C
engine ['endʒɪn] n. 发动机	Unit 16-Part B
engross [ɪn'grəʊs] v. 使全神贯注	Unit 11-Part D
enhance [ɪn'hɑːns] v. 增强，加强	Unit 5-Part C
enjoy the leisure [ɪn'dʒɒɪ] 享受休闲时光	Unit6-Part B

Words and Expressions List

ensue [ɪn'sjuː] v. 接着发生	Unit 16-Part D
ensure [ɪn'ʃʊə] v. 保证,确保	Unit 2-Part D
entertainment [,entə'teɪnmənt] n. 娱乐;消遣;款待	Unit 9-Part B
entitle to [ɪn'taɪtl][tuː] 拥有……的权利	Unit 11-Part D
entry formality [fɔː'mælɪtɪ] 入境手续	Unit 17-Part B
envision [ɪn'vɪʃən] v. 想象;预想	Unit 1-Part D
equivalent [ɪ'kwɪvələnt] adj. 等价的,相等的	Unit 10-Part B
error ['erə] n. 错误;误差	Unit 18-Part D
escape slide [ɪ'skeɪp][slaɪd] 逃离滑梯	Unit 16-Part B
estimated ['estɪmetɪd] adj. 估计的;预计的	Unit 13-Part C
European Football Champ-ionship [jʊərə'piːən]['fʊtbɔːl]['tʃæmpɪənʃɪp] 欧洲足球锦标赛	Unit 2-Part B
evacuate [ɪ'vækjʊeɪt] v. 疏散;撤离	Unit 16-Part B
evacuation [ɪ,vækjʊ'eɪʃən] n. 疏散;撤离	Unit 3-Part D
evaluate [ɪ'væljʊeɪt] v. 评价;评估	Unit 18-Part D
exact [ɪg'zækt] adj. 精密严谨的;确切的	Unit 9-Part D
excellent ['eksələnt] adj. 优秀;美德	Unit 4-Part D
exchange rate [ɪks'tʃeɪndʒ][reɪt] 汇率;兑换率	Unit 10-Part B
exclusive [ɪk'skluːsɪv] adj. 高级的;新式的	Unit 10-Part C
Exception Request Form[ɪk'sepʃən][rɪ'kwest][fɔːm] 免责单	Unit 14-Part B
exit ['eksɪt] n. 出口	Unit 1-Part C
extra ['ekstrə] adj. 额外的	Unit 12-Part C
expect [ɪk'spekt] v. 期望;预料	Unit 12-Part B
expectation [,ekspek'teɪʃən] n. 期待;预期;指望	Unit 2-Part D
expert ['ekspɜːt] n. 专家	Unit 14-Part D
expired [ɪks'paɪəd] adj. 过期的;失效的	Unit 10-Part B
explore [ɪk'splɔː] v. 探索;探测	Unit 18-Part D
export [ek'spɔːt] n. 出口;出口商品	Unit 10-Part D
extend [ɪk'stend] v. 延伸;伸出;给予	Unit 2-Part C
extension [ɪk'stenʃən] n. 延长	Unit 12-Part B
extemal [ɪk'stɜːnəl] adj. 外部的;外面的	Unit 16-Part D
extinguish [ɪk'stɪŋgwɪʃ] v. 熄灭	Unit 15-Part B
extinguisher [ɪk'stɪŋgwɪʃə] n. 灭火器	Unit 15-Part D
eye shade [aɪ][ʃeɪd] 遮光眼罩	Unit 4-Part B
fahrenheit ['færəhaɪt] adj. 华氏的;华氏温度计的	Unit 13-Part C
failure ['feɪljə] n. 故障	Unit 16-Part B
fasten ['fɑːsən] v. 使固定,扣紧	Unit 3-Part C
fast-forward ['fɑːst'fɔːwəd] vi. 快进	Unit 9-Part D
fatigue [fə'tiːg] n. 疲劳	Unit 9-Part C
fault [fɔːlt] n. 错误	Unit 15-Part B
Federal Aviation Administration (FAA) ['fedərəl][eɪvɪeɪʃən][ədmɪnɪ'streɪʃən] 美国联邦航空管理局	Unit 11-Part D
feedback ['fiːdbæk] n. 反馈;成果	Unit 2-Part D
ferry bus ['ferɪ][bʌs] 摆渡车	Unit 18-Part B
fiber ['faɪbə] n. 纤维;光纤(等于fibre)	Unit 8-Part D

filter ['fɪltə] n. 过滤器	Unit 15-Part D
firefighting equipment ['faɪəfaɪtɪŋ][ɪ'kwɪpmənt] 灭火设施	Unit 3-Part D
firmly ['fɜ:mlɪ] adv. 坚定地；坚固地	Unit 15-Part C
first class [fɜ:st][klɑ:s] 头等舱	Unit 2-Part C
flashlight ['flæʃlaɪt] n. 手电筒；闪光灯	Unit 3-Part D
flavour ['fleɪvə(r)] n. 香味，滋味	Unit 7-Part B
fleet [fli:t] n. 舰队	Unit 5-Part B
flight crew [flaɪt][kru:] 飞行机组	Unit 2-Part D
flight deck [flaɪt][dek] 驾驶舱	Unit 15-Part D
Flight Mode [məʊd] 飞行模式	Unit 3-Part C
flight number ['nʌmbə] 航班号	Unit 2-Part C
float [fləʊt] v. 漂浮；浮动	Unit 16-Part C
flu [flu:] n. 流感	Unit 13-Part D
fluid ['flu(:)ɪd] n. 流体；饮料	Unit 13-Part D
flushed [flʌʃt] adj. 脸发红的	Unit 14-Part B
forecast ['fɔ:kɑ:st] n. 预测；预想	Unit 11-Part B
fold-up [fəʊldʌp] adj. 适于折叠的；可折拢的	Unit 9-Part D
follow suit ['fɒləʊ][sju:t] 跟着做；学样	Unit 1-Part D
for goodness sake [fə(r)]['gʊdnɪs][seɪk] 天哪；务请；看在老天爷分上	Unit 12-Part B
for the convenience of sb [fɔ:][ðə][kən'vɪnɪəns][əv] 为了某人的方便	Unit 6-Part C
forehead ['fɔ:hed] n. 前额	Unit 14-Part B
forward cabin ['fɔ:wəd]['kæbɪn] 前舱	Unit 2-Part B
fragile item ['fædʒaɪl]['aɪtəm] 易碎品	Unit 3-Part B
fragrance ['freɪgr(ə)ns] n. 香味，芬芳	Unit 10-Part B
fresh air [freʃ][ɛə] 新鲜空气	Unit 5-Part B
freshen ['freʃən] v. 使清新；使新鲜	Unit 13-Part D
fruit juice [fru:t][dʒu:s] n. 果汁	Unit 6-Part B
frustrated [frʌˈstreɪtɪd] adj. 沮丧的，不得志的	Unit 8-Part B
further ['fə:ðə] adv. 进一步地	Unit 10-Part C
gadget ['gædʒɪt] n. 小玩意；小器具；小配件	Unit 10-Part D
galley ['gælɪ] n. 厨房	Unit 3-Part B
galley equipment ['gælɪ][ɪ'kwɪpmənt] 厨房设施	Unit 3-Part D
garnish ['gɑrnɪʃ] n. 装饰	Unit 6-Part D
gas [gæs] n. 气体	Unit 15-Part D
gauze [gɔ:z] n. 纱布	Unit 14-Part B
generate ['dʒenəreɪt] 产生	Unit 15-Part D
generation [dʒenə'reɪʃən] n. 一代；产生	Unit 9-Part D
generator ['dʒenəreɪtə] n. 发生器	Unit 15-Part D
give birth [gɪv][bɜ:θ] v. 分娩	Unit 14-Part C
give sb a lift [gɪv][eɪ][lɪft] 提神	Unit 6-Part B
give out [gɪv][aʊt] 分发	Unit 17-Part C
glassware ['glɑ:sweə] 玻璃器皿 [玻璃]	Unit 7-Part D
global ['gləʊbəl] adj 全球的	Unit 9-Part B
gloves [glʌvz] n. 手套	Unit 14-Part D
gluten ['glu:tən] n. 面筋；麸质；谷蛋白	Unit 8-Part D

go through [gəʊ][θruː] 通过	Unit 17-Part B
goggle ['gɒgəl] *n.* 护目镜	Unit 15-Part D
gourmet ['gʊəmeɪ] *n.* 美食家	Unit 7-Part D
guidance ['gaɪdəns] *n.* 指导，引导	Unit 18-Part D
Halon extinguisher ['heɪlɑːn][ɪk'stɪŋgwɪʃə] 海伦灭火器	Unit 15-Part D
hand baggage [hænd]['bægɪdʒ] 手提行李	Unit 1-Part C
have a nap [hæv][ə][næp] 休息一下；小睡一会儿	Unit 9-Part B
headset ['hedset] *n.* 耳机	Unit 17-Part C
headwind ['hedwɪnd] *n.* 顶头风，逆风	Unit 12-Part B
heaving line [hiːvɪŋ][laɪn] 系留绳	Unit 15-Part D
heel [hiːl] *n.* 脚后跟；鞋后跟	Unit 16-Part C
hemisphere ['hemɪˌsfɪə] *n.* 半球	Unit 13-Part B
hesitate ['hezɪteɪt] *v.* 犹豫	Unit 1-Part B
highlight ['haɪlaɪt] *v.* 突出；强调	Unit 2-Part D
Hindu ['hɪnduː] *adj.* 印度的；印度教的	Unit 8-Part D
hold-up [həʊldʌp] *n.* 停顿；耽误	Unit 11-Part B
hood [hʊd] *n.* 头罩	Unit 15-Part D
hook [hʊk] *n.* 钩	Unit 15-Part D
horrible ['hɒrəbəl] *adj.* 令人恐惧的	Unit 16-Part B
hors d'oeuvres [ɔːr'dʒːvrəs] *n.* （法）开胃菜	Unit 7-Part B
host [həʊst] *n.* 乘务员（男）；主人（男）	Unit 1-Part D
hostess ['həʊstɪs] *n.* 乘务员（女）；主人（女）	Unit 1-Part D
hot drink [hɒt][drɪŋk] 热饮	Unit 6-Part C
hurricane ['hʌrɪkən] *n.* 飓风；暴风	Unit 11-Part D
identification [aɪˌdentɪfɪ'keɪʃən] *n.* 鉴定，识别	Unit 14-Part D
identified [aɪ'dentɪfaɪd] *v.* 鉴定（identify过去分词）	Unit 2-Part D
identify [aɪ'dentɪfaɪ] *v.* 确定；识别	Unit 14-Part C
ignore [ɪg'nɔː] *v.* 忽视	Unit 18-Part D
image ['ɪmɪdʒ] *n.* 印象；图像；影像	Unit 5-Part D
immediate [ɪ'miːdɪət] *adj.* 直接的；立即的	Unit 16-Part D
immediately [ɪ'miːdɪətlɪ] *adv.* 立即	Unit 4-Part B
immigration [ɪm'greɪʃn] *n.* 移民局	Unit 17-Part B
immobility [ˌɪməʊ'bɪlətɪ] *n.* 不动，固定	Unit 13-Part D
impression [ˌɪm'preʃən] *n.* 印象；效果	Unit 18-Part D
improve [ɪm'pruːv] *v.* 改善，增进	Unit 4-Part C
in a moment [ɪn][ə]['məʊm(ə)nt] 立刻，马上	Unit 6-Part C
in accordance with [ɪn][ə'kɔːdəns][wɪð] 依照；与……一致	Unit 1-Part C
in charge of [ɪn][tʃɑːdʒ][əv] 主管，掌管	Unit 1-Part B
in compliance with [ɪn][kəm'plaɪəns][wɪð] 遵守	Unit 15-Part D
in detail [ɪn]['diːteɪl] 详细地	Unit 15-Part B
in practice [ɪn]['præktɪs] 实际上；事实上	Unit 16-Part D
in proximity of [ɪn][prɒk'sɪmɪtɪ][əv] 靠近……；在……附近	Unit 17-Part D
inaugural flight [ɪ'nɔːgjʊrəl][flaɪt] 首航	Unit 5-Part C
incentive [ɪn'sentɪv] *n.* 动机；刺激	Unit 10-Part D
incompatible [ɪnkəm'pætɪbəl] *adj.* 不相容的	Unit 16-Part D

inconvenience [ˌɪnkən'viːnjəns] *n.* 不便；麻烦	Unit 5-Part C
incorporate [ɪn'kɔːpəreɪt] *v.* 包含	Unit 15-Part D
individual [ˌɪndɪ'vɪdjʊəl] *n.* 个人，个体	Unit 14-Part D
individually [ɪndɪ'vɪdjʊəlɪ] *adv.* 个别地；单独地	Unit 16-Part D
inevitably [ɪn'evɪtəblɪ] *adv.* 不可避免地	Unit 11-Part D
infant seat-belt ['ɪnfənt][siːtbelt] 婴儿座椅安全带	Unit 4-Part B
infection [ɪn'fekʃən] *n.* 传染病；传染，传播，感染	Unit 7-Part D
inflate [ɪn'fleɪt] *v.* 充气	Unit 15-Part B
in-flight ['ɪn'flaɪt] *adj.* 在飞行中的	Unit 16-Part D
ingredient [ɪn'griːdɪənt] *n.* 原料；要素；组成部分	Unit 2-Part D
in loop with [ɪn][luːp][wɪð] 循环	Unit 9-Part C
initial [ɪ'nɪʃəl] *adj.* 最初的	Unit 14-Part D
initiate [ɪ'nɪʃɪeɪt] *v.* 开始，创始；发起	Unit 4-Part D
injury ['ɪndʒərɪ] *n.* 伤害，损害	Unit 14-Part D
innovation [ˌɪnəʊ'veɪʃən] *n.* 创新，革新	Unit 5-Part D
innovative ['ɪnəvətɪv] *adj.* 革新的，创新的	Unit 9-Part D
insert [ɪn'səːt] *v.* 插入	Unit 4-Part B
inspection [ɪn'spekʃən] *n.* 视察，检查	Unit 5-Part D
installation [ˌɪnstə'leɪʃən] *n.* 设施；安装	Unit 5-Part C
instruction [ɪn'strʌkʃən] *n.* 指令，命令	Unit 4-Part D
insulated ['ɪnsəˌleɪtəd] *adj.* 绝缘的	Unit 15-Part D
interactive [ˌɪntər'æktɪv] *adj.* 交互式的；相互作用的	Unit 2-Part D
interest ['ɪntrɪst] *v.* 使感兴趣；使参与	Unit 10-Part B
interfere [ˌɪntə'fɪə] *v.* 干扰	Unit 4-Part B
international [ɪntə'næʃənəl] *adj.* 国际的	Unit 17-Part B
International Date Line [ˌɪntə'næʃənəl][deɪt][laɪn] 国际日期变更线	Unit 13-Part B
International Long Route [ˌɪntə'næʃənəl][lɒŋ][ruːt] 国际长途航线	Unit 13-Part C
interrupt [ˌɪntəˈrʌpt] *v.* 打扰，妨碍	Unit 3-Part B
invisible [ɪn'vɪzəb(ə)l] *adj.* 无形的，看不见的	Unit 12-Part D
involvement [ɪn'vɒlvmənt] *n.* 牵连；包含	Unit 1-Part D
irritating ['ɪrɪteɪtɪŋ] *adj.* 令人不愉快的	Unit 11-Part B
irritating ['ɪrɪteɪtɪŋ] *adj.* 气人的，使愤怒的	Unit 13-Part B
issue ['ɪʃjuː] *v.* 签发	Unit 17-Part D
item ['aɪtəm] *n.* 物品	Unit 16-Part D
jack [dʒæk] *n.* [信]插孔，插座；	Unit 9-Part B
jet lag [dʒet][læg] 飞行时差反应	Unit 13-Part B
Jew [dʒuː] *n.* 犹太人；犹太教徒；守财奴	Unit 8-Part B
jolt [dʒəʊlt] *n.* 颠簸，摇晃	Unit 14-Part B
juicy ['dʒuːsɪ] *adj.* 多汁的	Unit 7-Part B
keep clear of [kiːp][klɪə(r)][əv] 避开，不接触	Unit 1-Part C
kilometer ['kɪləʊmiːtə] *n.* 公里	Unit 2-Part C
kit [kɪt] *n.* 工具箱；成套工具	Unit 5-Part B
knee [niː] *n.* 膝盖	Unit 16-Part C
knob [nɒb] *n.* 把手；球形突出物	Unit 5-Part B
knob [nɒb] *n.* 旋钮	Unit 17-Part B

kosher [ˈkəʊʃə] adj. (食物,尤指肉类)卫生合格的,经正式处理的, 清净的(依照犹太人的规矩而烹调的)	Unit 8-Part D
lactose [ˈlæktəʊz] n. [有化] 乳糖	Unit 8-Part D
laptop computer [ˈlæptɒp] 笔记本电脑	Unit 3-Part C
latex [ˈleɪteks] n. 乳胶	Unit 14-Part D
lavatory [ˈlævətərɪ] n. 洗手间	Unit 4-Part B
LCD video screen [ˈvɪdɪəʊ][skriːn] 液晶显示屏	Unit 9-Part D
leading-edge [ˈliːdɪŋedʒ] adj. 尖端的,前沿的;领先优势的	Unit 9-Part D
legroom [ˈlegruːm] n. (飞机的)伸腿空间	Unit 2-Part B
leisure [ˈleʒə] n. 休闲时光	Unit 6-Part B
lettuce [ˈletɪs] n. 生菜,莴苣	Unit 8-Part B
lie flat seat [laɪ][flæt][siːt] 平躺座位	Unit 5-Part B
life raft [laɪf][rɑːft] 救生筏	Unit 15-Part D
light meal[laɪt][miːl] 便餐	Unit 6-Part C
limited [ˈlɪmɪtɪd] adj. 有限制的;少的;见识不广的	Unit 10-Part B
limousine [ˈlɪmuziːn] n. 机场巴士	Unit 17-Part B
link [lɪŋk] n. 链环,连接片	Unit 4-Part B
lip-stick [ˈlɪpstɪk] n. 口红;唇膏	Unit 10-Part B
litter [ˈlɪtə] n. 垃圾	Unit 3-Part B
live [lɪv] adj. 活的;直播的;现场的	Unit 9-Part D
livestock [ˈlaɪvstɒk] n. 家畜	Unit 17-Part D
locate [ləʊˈkeɪt] v. 定位	Unit 5-Part C
locator [ləʊˈkeɪtə] n. 定位器	Unit 15-Part D
logistics [ləʊˈdʒɪstɪks] n. 后勤	Unit 5-Part D
long-haul [ˈlɒŋˈhɔːl] adj. 长途的	Unit 13-Part D
lovely [ˈlʌvlɪ] adj. 美丽的,极好的,可爱的	Unit 10-Part B
lunar [ˈljuːnə] adj. 阴历的;月亮的	Unit 2-Part C
main course [kɔːs] 主食	Unit 6-Part C
maintain [meɪnˈteɪn] v. 维持;继续;维修	Unit 5-Part D
maintenance [ˈmeɪntɪnəns] n. 维持,保持;维修	Unit 11-Part C
major [ˈmeɪdʒə] adj. 主要的	Unit 10-Part B
majority [məˈdʒɒrətɪ] n. 多数,大多数	Unit 6-Part C
make your choice [meɪk][jʊr][tʃɔɪs] 做出选择	Unit 6-Part C
make-up set [meɪkʌp][set] 化妆品套装	Unit 10-Part B
malfunction [mælˈfʌŋkʃən] n. 故障	Unit 16-Part D
mandate [ˈmændeɪt] n. 授权;命令;委托管理	Unit 1-Part D
maneuver [məˈnʊvə] v. 演习;调遣	Unit 12-Part D
manually [ˈmænjʊəlɪ] adv. 手动地	Unit 15-Part C
measure [ˈmeʒə] n. 措施;测量	Unit 14-Part D
mechanical [məˈkænɪkl] adj. 机械的;呆板的	Unit 11-Part C
mechanical fault [mɪˈkænɪkəl][fɔːlt] 机械故障	Unit 15-Part B
media [ˈmiːdɪə] n. 传播媒介;(medium的复数)媒体;新闻媒介	Unit 9-Part D
meet with [miːt][wɪð] 经历;遭受	Unit 16-Part B
memorabilia [memərəˈbɪlɪə] n. 大事记;值得纪念的事物	Unit 10-Part B
menu [ˈmenju] n. 菜单	Unit 7-Part B
merchandise [ˈmɜːtʃəndaɪz] n. 商品;货物	Unit 9-Part D
metal [ˈmetəl] v. 金属的	Unit 16-Part C

microburst [maɪkrəʊ'bə:st] *n.* 小型爆发(射电),瞬间阵风	Unit 11-Part D
military aircraft ['mɪlətrɪ]['eəkrɑ:ft] 军用飞机	Unit 1-Part D
milliliter ['mɪlɪli:tə] *n.* 毫升	Unit 10-Part C
mineral water ['mɪnərəl]['wɔ:tə] 矿泉水	Unit 6-Part B
minister ['mɪnɪstə(r)] *n.* 部长,太医	Unit 2-Part C
minor ['maɪnə] *adj.* 较小的	Unit 11-Part C
minus ['maɪnəs] *adj.* 负的	Unit 13-Part B
Model Flight ['mɒdəl] 模范航班	Unit 4-Part C
moderate ['mɒdərət] *adj.* 中等的	Unit 12-Part B
moist [mɔɪst] *adj.* 潮湿的,湿润的	Unit 7-Part D
monitor ['mɒnɪtə] *v.* 监控	Unit 3-Part D
Moslem ['mɒzləm] *adj.* 穆斯林的,伊斯兰的,伊斯兰教的	Unit 8-Part D
motivate ['məʊtɪveɪt] *v.* 激发	Unit 16-Part D
mouth is watering [maʊθ][ɪz]['wɔ:tərɪŋ] 流口水	Unit 7-Part B
mouthpiece ['maʊθpi:s] *v.* 吹口	Unit 15-Part B
mushroom ['mʌʃrʊm] *n.* 蘑菇,伞菌;蘑菇形物体;暴发户	Unit 8-Part B
Muslim ['mʊzlɪm] *adj.* 穆斯林;穆罕默德信徒	Unit 8-Part B
Muslim meal ['mʊzlɪm;'mʌz-][mi:l] 穆斯林餐	Unit 8-Part B
nap [næp] *n.* 打盹儿	Unit 14-Part B
napkin ['næpkɪn] *n.* 装饰	Unit 6-Part D
nauseous ['nɔ:zɪəs] *adj.* 令人作呕的,厌恶的	Unit 14-Part B
navigation system [ˌnævɪ'geɪʃən]['sɪstəm] 导航系统	Unit 4-Part B
necklace ['neklɪs] *n.* 项链	Unit 14-Part D
necktie ['nektaɪ] *n.* 领带	Unit 16-Part C
negative ['negətɪv] *adj.* 负的;消极的	Unit 18-Part D
newly ['nju:li:] *adv.* 新近,最近	Unit 9-Part B
normally ['nɔ:məlɪ] *adv.* 正常地	Unit 15-Part B
nose-drop ['nəʊz'drɒp] *n.* 滴鼻液	Unit 14-Part B
obey [ə'beɪ] *v.* 服从;按照……行动	Unit 16-Part B
object ['ɒbdʒɪkt] *n.* 物体	Unit 15-Part D
objective [əb'dʒektɪv] *n.* 目的;目标	Unit 2-Part D
objectivity [ˌɒbdʒek'tɪvətɪ] *n.* 客观;客观性	Unit 18-Part D
occasional [ə'keɪʒənəl] *adj.* 偶尔的	Unit 13-Part B
occupant ['ɒkju:pənt] *n.* 乘客	Unit 12-Part D
occupation [ˌɒkjʊ'peɪʃən] *n.* 占有;职业	Unit 2-Part C
occupied ['ɒkjʊpaɪd] *adj.* 已占用的,无空闲的	Unit 2-Part B
oceanic [ˌəʊʃɪ'ænɪk] *adj.* 海洋的;广阔无垠的	Unit 13-Part B
offence [ə'fens] *n.* 违反;攻击	Unit 4-Part C
off-load ['ɒfləʊd] *vt.* 卸货	Unit 11-Part D
on behalf of [ɒn][bɪ'hɑ:f][əv] 代表	Unit 1-Part C
Oneworld [wʌnwɜ:ld] 寰宇一家	Unit 1-Part C
onward flight ['ɒnwəd][flaɪt] 联程航班	Unit 18-Part C
operate ['ɒpəreɪt] *v.* 操作;运转	Unit 9-Part B
operator ['ɒpəreɪtə(r)] *n.* 操作员;管理者	Unit 11-Part D
opportunity [ˌɒpə'tju:nɪtɪ] *n.* 机会	Unit 2-Part C
option ['ɒpʃən] *n.* 选择权;可选物	Unit 9-Part D

out of order [aʊt][əv][ˈɔːdə] 故障	Unit 6-Part C
overall [ˈəʊvərɔːl] *adj.* 全部的；全体的	Unit 5-Part D
overhead compartment [ˈəʊvəhed][kəmˈpɑːtmənt] 头顶上方的行李柜	Unit 2-Part B
overhead locker [ˈlɒkə(r)] 头顶行李箱	Unit 1-Part C
overnight [ˌəʊvəˈnaɪt] *adj.* 一整夜的	Unit 11-Part C
overwing [ˌəʊvəˈwɪŋ] *adj.* 机翼上的	Unit 16-Part D
oxygen mask [ˈɒksɪdʒən][mɑːsk] 氧气面罩	Unit 3-Part D
panic [ˈpænɪk] *v.* 惊慌	Unit 16-Part B
parcel [ˈpɑːs(ə)l] *n.* [气象]气块	Unit 12-Part D
particle [ˈpɑːtɪkəl] *n.* 颗粒物	Unit 15-Part D
passenger service Unit (PSU) [ˈpæsɪndʒə(r)] [ˈsɜːvɪs] [ˈjuːnɪt] 旅客服务组件	Unit 5-Part B
passenger ship [ˈpæsɪndʒə(r)][ʃɪp] 客船，客轮	Unit 1-Part D
passenger train [ˈpæsɪndʒə(r)][treɪn] 客运列车；客车	Unit 1-Part D
pasture [ˈpɑːstʃə] *n.* 草地；牧场	Unit 17-Part D
patience [ˈpeɪʃns] *n.* 耐心	Unit 5-Part D
pay-per-view [ˈpeɪpəvjuː] *adj.* 按次计费的	Unit 9-Part D
peanut [ˈpɪnʌt] *n.* 花生	Unit 8-Part D
peanut free [ˈpiːnʌt][friː] 不含坚果的	Unit 8-Part D
perform [pəˈfɔːm] *v.* 执行；完成	Unit 4-Part D
performance [pəˈfɔːməns] *n.* 表现；性能	Unit 18-Part D
perfume [ˈpɜːfjuːm] *n.* 香水；香味	Unit 10-Part D
periodically [ˌpɪəriˈɒdɪkəli] *adv.* 定期地；周期性地	Unit 5-Part D
permanent [ˈpɜːmənənt] *adj.* 永久的，永恒的	Unit 14-Part D
permit [pəˈmɪt] *v.* 许可；允许	Unit 16-Part C
permission [pəˈmɪʃən] *n.* 允许	Unit 18-Part B
personnel [ˌpɜːsəˈnel] *n.* 人员；人事部门	Unit 14-Part C
pertinent [ˈpɜːtɪnənt] *adj.* 相关的；中肯的	Unit 4-Part D
phase [feɪz] *n.* 阶段	Unit 4-Part D
physical [ˈfɪzɪkəl] *adj.* 身体的	Unit 16-Part D
physiological [ˌfɪziəˈlɒdʒɪkəl] *adj.* 生理学	Unit 13-Part D
pillow [ˈpɪləʊ] *n.* 枕头	Unit 16-Part C
pin [pɪn] *n.* 别针	Unit 16-Part C
plastic [ˈplæstɪk] *adj.* 塑料的	Unit 10-Part C
plug [plʌg] *n.* 塞子；插头	Unit 9-Part B
pole [pəʊl] *n.* 杆	Unit 15-Part D
popular [ˈpɒpjʊlə] *adj.* 流行的；受欢迎的	Unit 10-Part B
position [pəˈzɪʃən] *n.* 位置，方位；职位	Unit 3-Part D
possession [pəˈzeʃən] *n.* 财产；所有物	Unit 16-Part D
potential [pəˈtenʃl] *adj.* 潜在的；可能的	Unit 7-Part D
pouch [paʊtʃ] *n.* 袋子	Unit 15-Part B
precaution [prɪˈkɔːʃən] *n.* 预防措施	Unit 12-Part B
pre-departure [priːˈdɪpɑːtʃə] *adj.* 行前的；出发前的	Unit 16-Part D
predict [prɪˈdɪkt] *v.* 预计	Unit 2-Part D
premier [ˈpremɪə(r)] *n.* 首相	Unit 2-Part C
preparation [ˌprepəˈreɪʃən] *n.* 预备；准备	Unit 3-Part C

presentation [ˌprezənˈteɪʃən] n. 呈现；陈述；介绍	Unit 5-Part D
pressure [ˈpreʃə] n. 压力	Unit 14-Part B
primarily [ˈpraɪmərəlɪ] adv. 首先；主要地，根本上	Unit 1-Part D
primary [ˈpraɪmərɪ] adj. 主要的；基本的	Unit 5-Part C
print [prɪnt] v. 用印刷体填写	Unit 17-Part D
prior to [ˈpraɪə(r)][tuː] 在……之前	Unit 11-Part C
problematic [ˌprɒbləˈmætɪk] adj. 问题的；有疑问的	Unit 11-Part D
proceed to [prəˈsiːd] 继续	Unit 16-Part D
prohibit [prəʊˈhɪbɪt] v. 阻止，禁止	Unit 3-Part C
prolonged [prəˈlɒŋd] adj. 延长的；拖延的	Unit 13-Part D
promote [prəʊˈməʊt] v. 促进；提升	Unit 18-Part D
proper [ˈprɒpə] adj. 适当的	Unit 16-Part D
properly [ˈprɒpəlɪ] adv. 适当地	Unit 4-Part C
prosperous [ˈprɒspərəs] adj. 繁荣的；兴旺的	Unit 2-Part C
protective [prəˈtektɪv] adj. 防护的	Unit 15-Part D
protein [ˈprəʊtiːn] n. 蛋白质	Unit 8-Part D
provision [prəʊˈvɪʒən] n. 提供，准备；条款	Unit 14-Part D
psychologically [ˌsaɪkəˈlɒdʒɪkəlɪ] adv. 心理上地	Unit 18-Part D
pump [pʌmp] n. 泵	Unit 15-Part D
purchase [ˈpɜːtʃɪs] n. 购买；紧握 v. 购买	Unit 10-Part B
purchase [ˈpɜːtʃɪs] n. 购买；紧握	Unit 10-Part B
purine [ˈpjʊəriːn] n. [有化] 嘌呤	Unit 8-Part D
purser [ˈpɜːsə(r)] n. 乘务长	Unit 1-Part B
quality [ˈkwɒlətɪ] n. 质量，品质	Unit 4-Part C
qualified [ˈkwɒlɪfaɪd] adj. 合格的；有资格的	Unit 15-Part D
quarantine [ˈkwɒrəntiːn] n. 检疫	Unit 3-Part B
quarantine [ˈkwɒrəntiːn] n. 检疫	Unit 17-Part B
quarters [ˈkwɔːtəz] n. 住处；四分之一（quarter的复数）	Unit 1-Part D
radio-frequency [ˈreɪdɪəʊˈfriːkwənsɪ] n. 射频	Unit 15-Part D
ramp [ræmp] n. 扶梯	Unit 18-Part B
ranch [rɑːntʃ] n. 农场；牧场	Unit 17-Part D
range [reɪndʒ] n. 范围，幅度	Unit 5-Part C
rapid [ˈræpɪd] adj. 快速的	Unit 15-Part C
reading light [ˈriːdɪŋ][ˈlaɪt] 阅读灯	Unit 5-Part B
rear [rɪə] adj. 后面的	Unit 4-Part B
receipt [rɪˈsiːt] n. 收据；发票	Unit 10-Part B
reclaim [rɪˈkleɪm] vt. 开拓；回收再利用	Unit 10-Part D
recline [rɪˈklaɪn] v. 使斜倚，使躺下	Unit 4-Part B
recommend [ˌrekəˈmend] vt. 推荐；建议；劝告	Unit 5-Part C
recoup [rɪˈkuːp] v. 收回，恢复；偿还；扣除	Unit 9-Part D
rectify [ˈrektɪfaɪ] v. 调整；矫正	Unit 3-Part D
reduction [rɪˈdʌkʃən] n. 减少；下降	Unit 5-Part D
reflect [rɪˈflekt] v. 反射，映现	Unit 18-Part D
refill [riːˈfɪl] v. 再装满	Unit 6-Part B
refrain [rɪˈfreɪn] v. 节制，克制	Unit 4-Part C

refrain from [rɪ'freɪn][frəm] 限制，抑制	Unit 1-Part C
refresh [rɪ'freʃ] v. 更新；使……恢复	Unit 5-Part B
refreshment [rɪ'freʃmənt] n. 点心	Unit 6-Part B
registered nurse ['redʒɪstəd][nɜːs] 注册护士	Unit 1-Part D
regret [rɪ'gret] v. 后悔，遗憾	Unit 13-Part C
regulations [regjʊ'leɪʃ(ə)nz] n. 条例；章则	Unit 2-Part B
reimbursement [ˌriːɪm'bɜːsmənt] n. 偿还；赔偿；偿付	Unit 11-Part D
relay ['riːleɪ] v. 转达	Unit 16-Part D
release [rɪ'liːs] vt. 发布；发行	Unit 9-Part B
relevant ['reləvənt] adj. 有关的；中肯的	Unit 2-Part D
reliability [rɪˌlaɪə'bɪlətɪ] n. 可靠性	Unit 5-Part D
rely on [rɪ'laɪ][ɒn] 依靠；依赖	Unit 16-Part B
remarkable [rɪ'mɑːkəbl] adj. 卓越的；非凡的	Unit 5-Part B
remedial [rɪ'miːdɪəl] adj. 治疗的；补救的	Unit 18-Part D
remind [rɪ'maɪnd] v. 提醒；使想起	Unit 4-Part C
remote [rɪ'məʊt] adj. 远程的；遥远的	Unit 3-Part C
remove [rɪ'muːv] v. 摘下；脱下	Unit 15-Part C
replace [rɪ'pleɪs] v. 取代，代替	Unit 1-Part D
Report of Irregularity [rɪ'pɔːt][əv][ɪˌregjʊ'lærətɪ] 事故报告书	Unit 14-Part D
request [rɪ'kwest] v. 请求；需要	Unit 4-Part C
rerouting [ˌrɪə'ruːtɪŋ] n. 重编路由	Unit 11-Part D
rescuer ['reskjʊə] n. 救助者	Unit 15-Part D
reservation [ˌrezə'veɪʃən] n.（火车，旅馆，机票的）的预约和预订	Unit 8-Part D
reserve [rɪ'zɜv] vi. 预订	Unit 8-Part B
resident ['rezɪdənt] n. 居民	Unit 17-Part D
respective [rɪ'spektɪv] adj. 各自的，各个的	Unit 7-Part D
response [rɪ'spɒns] n. 响应；反应	Unit 14-Part D
responsibility [rɪˌspɒnsə'bɪlɪtɪ] n. 责任，职责	Unit 4-Part D
responsible [rɪ'spɒnsɪbəl] adj. 负责的	Unit 16-Part D
restless ['restləs] adj. 焦躁不安的	Unit 12-Part B
restock [ˌriː'stɒk] v. 补充货源；补足	Unit 5-Part D
restriction [rɪ'strɪkʃən] n. 限制	Unit 3-Part C
restrict [rɪ'strɪkt] v. 节流（的）[科技] 限制	Unit 7-Part D
retail price ['riːteɪl][praɪs] 零售价	Unit 10-Part B
revenue ['revənjuː] n. 收益；税收	Unit 5-Part D
revolve [rɪ'vɒlv] v. 使……旋转；使……循环	Unit 1-Part D
rhythm ['rɪðəm] n. 节奏	Unit 13-Part D
ridicule ['rɪdɪkjuːl] n. 嘲笑；愚弄	Unit 18-Part D
rough [rʌf] adj. 粗糙的，崎岖不平的	Unit 12-Part B
sachet ['sæʃeɪ] n. 小袋，小香袋	Unit 7-Part D
safety briefing ['seɪftɪ]['briːfɪŋ] 安全说明	Unit 16-Part D
safety check ['seɪftɪ][tʃek] 安全检查	Unit 3-Part D
safety demonstration [ˌdemən'streɪʃən] 安全演示	Unit 3-Part C
safety instruction [ɪn'strʌkʃən] 安全须知	Unit 16-Part B
sample ['sɑːmpəl] n. 样品；样本	Unit 17-Part D

sarcasm ['sɑ:kæzəm] n. 讽刺；挖苦	Unit 18-Part D
satellite ['sætəlaɪt] n. 卫星	Unit 9-Part D
say [seɪ] v. 比如说	Unit 9-Part B
scan [skæn] v. 扫描；浏览	Unit 9-Part D
scarves [skɑ:vz] n. 围巾；领带（scarf的复数）	Unit 10-Part B
scattered ['skætəd] adj. 分散的，散乱的	Unit 13-Part B
schedule ['ʃedju:əl] n. 时刻表	Unit 13-Part B
scheduled ['ʃedju:ld] ['skedʒəld] adj. 预定的；预先安排的	Unit 11-Part B
scream the place down [skri:m][ðə][pleɪs][daʊn] 拼命叫喊	Unit 12-Part B
seatback [si:tbæk] 座椅靠背	Unit 4-Part B
seat-belt [si:tbelt] 安全带	Unit 1-Part C
safety belt ['seɪftɪ] [belt] 安全带	Unit 3-Part C
seat number ['nʌmbə] 座位号	Unit 1-Part C
secondary ['sekəndərɪ] adj. 第二的；中等的；次要的	Unit 1-Part D
selection [sɪ'lekʃən] n. 选择，挑选	Unit 10-Part C
self-confidence [self'kɒnfɪdəns] n. 自信	Unit 18-Part B
self-esteem [ˌselfɪ'sti:m] n. 自尊	Unit 18-Part D
self-preservation [self,prezə'veɪʃn] n. 自卫本能，自我保护	Unit 12-Part D
self-reliance [ˌselfrɪ'laɪəns] n. 自立，自力更生	Unit 18-Part B
senior ['si:nɪə] adj. 资深的；高级的	Unit 16-Part D
Seoul [səʊl] n. 首尔	Unit 13-Part B
serve [sɜ:v] v. 服务	Unit 1-Part B
service ['sɜ:vɪs] n. 服务	Unit 1-Part B
severe [sɪ'vɪə] adj. 严重的	Unit 12-Part B
severity [sɪ'verɪtɪ] n. 严重；严格；猛烈	Unit 12-Part D
sharp [ʃɑ:p] adj. 锋利的	Unit 16-Part B
short flights [ʃɔ:t][flaɪt] 短途航班	Unit 7-Part B
short-haul [ˈʃɔ:t'hɔ:l] n. 短途	Unit 6-Part D
shower ['ʃaʊə] n. 阵雨；淋浴	Unit 13-Part B
shuttle bus ['ʃʌtl][bʌs] 摆渡车	Unit 18-Part C
signal ['sɪgnəl] n. 信号	Unit 15-Part D
Sky Team [skaɪ][ti:m] 天合联盟	Unit 1-Part C
slippers ['slɪpəz] n. 拖鞋	Unit 13-Part D
smoke detector [sməʊk][dɪ'tektə] 烟雾探测器	Unit 5-Part D
smoking section ['sekʃən] 吸烟区	Unit 4-Part B
snack [snæk] n. 小吃，点心	Unit 6-Part C
snail [sneɪl] n. 蜗牛	Unit 17-Part D
sodium ['səʊdɪəm] n. [化学] 钠（11号元素，符号Na）	Unit 8-Part D
soft drinks [sɒft][drɪŋks] 软饮料（不含酒精）	Unit 6-Part C
solicit [sə'lɪsɪt] v. 征求；招揽	Unit 17-Part D
solution [sə'lju:ʃən] n. 解决方案	Unit 18-Part D
solve [sɒlv] v. 解决	Unit 11-Part C
sophisticated [sə'fɪstɪkeɪtɪd] adj. 复杂的；精致的	Unit 9-Part D
sore [sɔ:] adj. 疼痛的	Unit 14-Part B
souvenir [ˌsu:və'nɪə] n. 纪念品	Unit 6-Part C

spare [speə] *adj.* 备用的；多余的；闲置的	Unit 11-Part D
spares [speəz] *n.* 备件	Unit 5-Part D
specialty ['speʃəltɪ] *n.* 招牌菜	Unit 7-Part B
special diet ['speʃ(ə)l]['daɪət] 特殊餐饮	Unit 7-Part C
special meal ['speʃ(ə)l][mi:l] 特殊餐饮	Unit 8-Part C
specific [spɪ'sɪfɪk] *adj.* 特殊的，特定的	Unit 2-Part D
specify ['spesɪfaɪ] *v.* 详细说明；指定；阐述	Unit 11-Part D
speed [spi:d] *v.* 加快……的速度	Unit 17-Part C
speedily ['spi:dɪlɪ] *adv.* 迅速地	Unit 16-Part C
splash [splæʃ] *v.* 泼洒；刊登	Unit 12-Part D
sprite [spraɪt] *n.* 雪碧；妖精	Unit 6-Part B
spoil [spɒɪl] *vt.* 溺爱	Unit 10-Part B
sprain [spreɪn] *n.* 扭伤	Unit 14-Part B
spray [spreɪ] *v.* 喷；喷洒　*n.* 喷雾	Unit 17-Part C
staff [stɑ:f] *n.* 职员	Unit 11-Part C
Star Alliance [stɑ:(r)][ə'laɪəns] 星空联盟	Unit 1-Part C
standstill ['stæn(d)stɪl] *n.* 静止	Unit 18-Part B
stew [stju:] *v.* 炖；忧虑	Unit 8-Part B
sterilize ['sterɪlaɪz] *v.* 使不育，杀菌	Unit 7-Part D
steward ['stju:əd] *n.* 乘务员(男)；管家(男)	Unit 1-Part D
stewardess ['stju:ədɪs] *n.* 乘务员(女)；管家(女)	Unit 1-Part D
stipulated time ['stɪpjʊletɪd] [法] 约定期限	Unit 11-Part D
stock [stɒk] *n.* 股票，股份；库存	Unit 10-Part B
stopover ['stɒp,əʊvə] *n.* 中途停留	Unit 4-Part C
storage ['stɔ:rɪdʒ] *n.* 存储；仓库；储藏所	Unit 9-Part D
stow [stəʊ] *v.* 收起，收藏	Unit 1-Part C
straight or on the rocks [streɪt][ɔ:][ɒn][ðə][rɒks] 直喝还是加冰喝(酒水)	Unit 6-Part B
strain [streɪn] *n.* 拉紧；负担	Unit 12-Part D
strap [stræp] *v.* 用带子系	Unit 12-Part B
strength [streŋθ] *n.* 长处；力量	Unit 18-Part D
stressed [strest] *adj.* 紧张的，感到有压力的	Unit 13-Part D
stretch [stretʃ] *v.* 伸展	Unit 2-Part B
stuff [stʌf] *v.* 堵塞	Unit 14-Part B
subdivide [sʌbdɪ'vaɪd] *v.* 把……再分	Unit 12-Part D
subject to ['sʌbdʒekt] 使服从；受……管制	Unit 11-Part D
subway ['sʌbweɪ] *n.* 地铁	Unit 17-Part B
sufferer ['sʌfərə] *n.* 患者；受害者	Unit 13-Part D
sunshade ['sʌnʃeɪd] *n.* 遮阳板	Unit 4-Part C
superior [sju:'pɪrɪə] *adj.* 优秀的，出众的	Unit 5-Part D
supervise ['su:pəvaɪz] *v.* 监督；管理	Unit 16-Part D
survival kit [sə'vaɪvəl][kɪt] 救生包	Unit 15-Part D
survivor [sə'vaɪvə] *n.* 幸存者；生还者	Unit 15-Part D
suspend [sə'spend] *v.* 暂停	Unit 4-Part B
swallow ['swɒləʊ] *v.* 吞咽	Unit 14-Part B
swelling ['swelɪŋ] *n.* 肿胀；膨胀	Unit 13-Part D

swing-out [s'wɪŋ'aʊt] 摇动式	Unit 9-Part D
swipe [swaɪp] *vt.* 刷……卡	Unit 9-Part D
switch [swɪtʃ] *v.* 转变,转换	Unit 7-Part D
switch on/off [swɪtʃ][ɒn]/[ɒf] 打开/关闭	Unit 3-Part C
symptom ['sɪmptəm] *n.* 症状	Unit 13-Part B
tab [tæb] *n.* 悬重物	Unit 15-Part B
tablecloth ['teɪb(ə)lklɒθ] *n.* 台布,桌布	Unit 7-Part D
tablet ['tæblɪt] *n.* 药片	Unit 13-Part D
take-off ['teɪkɒf] *n.* 起飞	Unit 2-Part B
take order [teɪk]['ɔːdə] 点餐	Unit 7-Part C
take your choice [teɪk][jʊr][tʃɔɪs] 做出选择	Unit 6-Part C
tamper ['tæmpə] *v.* 做手脚;违反	Unit 4-Part C
taxi ['tæksɪ] *v.* 滑行	Unit 18-Part B
technical ['teknɪkl] *adj.* 技术的;专业的	Unit 11-Part D
technique [tek'niːk] *n.* 技巧,技术	Unit 14-Part D
temperature ['tempərɪtʃə] *n.* 温度	Unit 5-Part C
temporarily ['tempərərɪlɪ] *adv.* 临时地	Unit 2-Part C
temporary ['tempərərɪ] *adj.* 暂时的,临时的	Unit 14-Part D
terminal ['təːmɪnəl] *n.* 航站楼;末端	Unit 18-Part C
terrified ['terɪfaɪd] *adj.* 非常害怕的	Unit 16-Part B
terrific [təˈrɪfɪk] *adj.* 极好的;非常的;可怕的	Unit 11-Part B
terrorism ['terərɪzəm] *n.* 恐怖主义	Unit 15-Part D
throughout [θrʊ'aʊt] *prep.* 遍及;贯穿	Unit 6-Part D
thunder cloud ['θʌndə][klaʊd] *n.* 雷暴云	Unit 12-Part D
tie [taɪ] *v.* 系;打结;连接	Unit 15-Part B
tightly ['taɪtlɪ] *adv.* 紧紧地;坚固地	Unit 5-Part B
time difference [taɪm] ['dɪfrəns] *n.* 时差	Unit 13-Part C
time zone [taɪm][zəʊn] *n.* 时区	Unit 13-Part B
tip [tɪp] *n.* 小费	Unit 18-Part B
torch [tɔːtʃ] *n.* 火炬;手电筒	Unit 3-Part D
tornado [tɔːˈneɪdəʊ] *n.* 龙卷风;旋风	Unit 11-Part D
touch screen [tʌtʃ][skriːn] *n.* 触摸屏	Unit 9-Part B
thoughtful ['θɔːtfl] *adj.* 深思的;体贴的	Unit 7-Part B
toxic ['tɒksɪk] *adj.* 有毒的	Unit 17-Part C
towelette [ˌtaʊəˈlet] *n.* 湿餐巾纸 [纸]	Unit 7-Part D
transaction [trænˈzækʃən] *n.* 交易;事务;办理	Unit 10-Part D
transform [trænsˈfɔːm] *v.* 变换,改变	Unit 5-Part B
transit desk ['trænsɪt][desk] 中转柜台	Unit 18-Part C
transparent [trænsˈpærənt] *adj.* 透明的	Unit 10-Part C
trash [træʃ] *n.* 垃圾;废物	Unit 6-Part D
tray [treɪ] *n.* 盘,托盘,碟	Unit 6-Part D
tray table [treɪ]['teɪbl] (座椅)小桌板	Unit 3-Part C
trolley ['trɒlɪ] *n.* 手推车,台车;无轨电车;有轨电车	Unit 6-Part D
traditional design [trəˈdɪʃənl][dɪˈzaɪn] 传统图案	Unit 10-Part B
turbulence ['təːbjʊləns] *n.* 颠簸;紊流	Unit 3-Part B

twisting ['twɪstɪŋ] n. 扭转；缠绕	Unit 13-Part D
unfasten [ˌʌn'fɑːsən] v. 解开	Unit 14-Part B
unfavorable ['ʌn'feɪvərəbl] adj. 不宜的	Unit 11-Part B
unforeseen [ˌʌnfɔːr'siːn] adj. 无法预料的	Unit 11-Part B
United Airlines [juˈnaɪtɪd]['erlaɪns] 美国联合航空公司	Unit 1-Part D
unserviceable [ʌn'sɜːvɪsəb(ə)l] adj. 无用的	Unit 3-Part D
updated [ʌp'deɪtɪd] adj. 更新的	Unit 13-Part C
upgrade ['ʌpgreɪd] v. 升舱	Unit 2-Part B
upper ['ʌpə] v. 上部的	Unit 16-Part C
upright ['ʌpraɪt] adj. 正直的，垂直的	Unit 1-Part C
urgently ['ɜːdʒəntlɪ] adv. 迫切地，紧急地	Unit 14-Part C
utensil [juːˈtensəl] n. 器皿，器具	Unit 7-Part D
valuable ['væljʊəbl] n. 贵重物品	Unit 16-Part B
valuable item ['væljʊəbl]['aɪtəm] 贵重物品	Unit 3-Part C
vary ['veərɪ] v. 改变；使多样化	Unit 2-Part D
vegan ['viːgən] n. 严格的素食主义者	Unit 8-Part D
vegetarian [ˌvedʒɪ'teərɪən] n. 素食主义者，素食餐	Unit 7-Part C
vegetarian diet [ˌvedʒɪ'teərɪən]['daɪət] 素食餐	Unit 7-Part C
vegetarian meal [ˌvedʒɪ'teərɪən][miːl] 素食餐	Unit 8-Part B
version ['vɜːʃən] n. 版本	Unit 9-Part B
vessel ['vesəl] n. 船；舰	Unit 17-Part D
via ['vaɪə] prep. 通过；经由	Unit 16-Part D
video monitor ['vɪdɪəʊ]['mɒnɪtə] 视频显示屏	Unit 17-Part C
video-on-demand [ˌvɪdɪəʊɒndɪ'mɑːnd] n. 影视点播	Unit 9-Part D
visibility [ˌvɪzɪ'bɪlətɪ] n. 能见度	Unit 13-Part B
volume ['vɒljuːm] n. 音量	Unit 5-Part B
vomit ['vɒmɪt] v. 呕吐	Unit 12-Part B
waist [weɪst] n. 腰，腰部	Unit 15-Part B
wallet ['wɒlɪt] n. 钱包	Unit 3-Part B
wardrobe compartment ['wɔːdrəʊb] [kəm'pɑːtmənt] n. 衣橱，衣物存储行李箱	Unit 3-Part B
weight [weɪt] n. 重量	Unit 2-Part B
well-run ['wel'rʌn] adj. 经营良好的	Unit 11-Part D
Western cuisine ['westən] [kwɪ'ziːn] 西方风味	Unit 7-Part C
wheelchair ['hwiːltʃeə] n. 轮椅	Unit 18-Part B
whichever [hwɪtʃ'evə] adj. 无论哪个	Unit 5-Part B
window seat ['wɪndəʊ][siːt] 临窗座位	Unit 4-Part C
window shade [ʃeɪd] 遮阳板	Unit 5-Part B
withstand [wɪð'stænd] v. 抵挡；禁得起	Unit 11-Part D
witness ['wɪtnɪs] v. 目击，见证	Unit 13-Part B
World Health Organization [wɜːld] [helθ] [ˌɔːgənaɪ'zeɪʃən] n. 世界卫生组织	Unit 17-Part C
wound [waʊnd] n. 创伤，伤口	Unit 14-Part D
wrap [ræp] v. 包扎	Unit 14-Part B
wrist [rɪst] n. 手腕；腕关节	Unit 16-Part C
zip-lock ['zɪpl'ɒk] n. 封锁	Unit 10-Part C